*The*

# REALLY USEFUL PRIMARY LANGUAGES BOOK

*The Really Useful Primary Languages Book* is an easily accessible guide, full of handy resources and activities that are perfect to dip into for enjoyable, engaging and ultimately effective language lessons.

Providing principles, approaches and ideas to help bring the teaching of languages to life in your classroom, this highly practical book will be essential reading for the development of children's language skills across key stage 2. With examples of practice included throughout, the book covers key topics such as:

- principles of good planning
- mixed age classes
- developing skills such as literacy and oracy
- phonics
- grammar
- storytelling, poems and songs
- using language games and activities
- activities for developing reading skills
- supporting children's writing
- integrating learning a language with daily routines
- cross-curricular language learning
- peer and self-assessment
- involving parents in language work at school.

The experienced author team draws upon their own personal teaching experience, coupled with knowledge of primary best practice and government guidance, to ensure that *The Really Useful Primary Languages Book* is a stimulating resource to help busy teachers, trainee teachers and teaching assistants to develop their own effective teaching style.

**Jayne Wright** is a practising primary school teacher, with responsibility for languages across the school. Her work has involved supporting other schools as an Advanced Skills Teacher. Jayne has also worked with primary trainee teachers at the University of the West of England, UK.

**Alison Taylor** is a freelance language specialist, with a range of teaching experience at secondary level. Alison previously worked in Teacher Education (secondary and primary) at the University of the West of England, UK.

# The Really Useful Series

*The*

# REALLY USEFUL PRIMARY LANGUAGES BOOK

## Practical strategies and ideas for enjoyable lessons

Jayne Wright

and

Alison Taylor

Routledge
Taylor & Francis Group

LONDON AND NEW YORK

First published 2017
by Routledge
2 Park Square, Milton Park, Abingdon, Oxon OX14 4RN

and by Routledge
711 Third Avenue, New York, NY 10017

*Routledge is an imprint of the Taylor & Francis Group, an informa business*

*British Library Cataloguing in Publication Data*
A catalogue record for this book is available from the British Library

*Library of Congress Cataloging in Publication Data*
Names: Wright, Jayne, author.
Title: The really useful primary languages book : practical strategies and
ideas for enjoyable lessons / Jayne Wright and Alison Taylor.
Description: Milton Park, Abingdon, Oxon; New York,
NY: Routledge, 2017.
Identifiers: LCCN 2015047113 | ISBN 9781138900806 (hardback) |
ISBN 9781138900813 (pbk.) | ISBN 9781315707044 (ebook)
Subjects: LCSH: Languages, Modern – Study and teaching (Primary)
Classification: LCC LB1578 .W75 2016 | DDC 372.65 – dc23LC record
available at http://lccn.loc.gov/2015047113

ISBN: 978-1-138-90080-6 (hbk)
ISBN: 978-1-138-90081-3 (pbk)
ISBN: 978-1-315-70704-4 (ebk)

Typeset in Palatino and Gill Sans
by Florence Production Ltd, Stoodleigh, Devon, UK

MIX
Paper from
responsible sources
FSC® C013604

Printed and bound by CPI Group (UK) Ltd, Croydon, CR0 4YY

# Contents

# Photocopiable masters

# Tables

# Acknowledgements

The authors wish to acknowledge and thank the many people they have worked with who have inspired their thinking and thereby contributed to the book.

Particular thanks are due to:

- the children, staff and parent helpers involved in 'Mission Impossible' at St. Anne's Primary School, South Gloucestershire;
- the children and staff at Christ Church Juniors CE VC school, South Gloucestershire;
- Katie D'Alton Goode and the pupils of Alveston Primary School, South Gloucestershire, for the account of their Costa Rican link;
- Marie-France Perkins, for her advice and help in checking the French;
- Uxía Iglesias Fuertes, for her help and advice in checking the Spanish and recording the Spanish eResource;
- Jean-Yves Faou, for his help in recording the French eResource; and
- Molly Sage and João Pedro Fonseca Castella, for their attractive illustrations.

# Introduction

This book is written for anyone with an interest in the teaching of primary languages. The audience will include primary class teachers, subject leaders and teaching assistants, head teachers and school governors. It is a practical guide to developing children's language skills across key stage 2, where the teaching of a new language is part of the national curriculum for England and Wales.

We also intend the book for secondary modern languages (ML) colleagues who liaise with their primary feeder schools or who have a teaching role there. They would be the first to recognise the skills of primary colleagues as regards methodology.

We hope, too, that the book will be used by primary teacher educators, in that it is also written for primary teachers in training (following the PGCE or another training route) and not merely for those trainees who have a qualification in a language. It has become increasingly important for all primary teachers to understand how to teach a language effectively.

Secondary teachers in training (following the PGCE or another route) and their teacher educators should also find this book useful since, increasingly, they will be involved in teaching/liaising with feeder primary schools; they will also be teaching pupils who already have some knowledge of language, and designing schemes of work which take into account what is being taught at primary level.

The authors have been involved with the development of primary languages for the last ten years, during which time they have worked with both teachers and trainees in many schools and settings. This has given them first-hand experience of how children learn and opportunities both to observe and try different approaches to teaching a new language.

The thinking in the book has been developed as a result of this personal teaching experience, together with knowledge of primary best practice and of the government guidance and schemes of work used by many teachers over the last decade; a number of these are now archived. They include the key stage 2 schemes of work for languages (QCA, 2000), The key stage 2 Framework for Languages (DfES, 2005) and *Making and Marking Progress on the DCSF Languages Ladder* (OCR, 2010).

With primary languages becoming statutory in the primary national curriculum (DfE, 2013), it is hoped that this will be a useful reference book, which draws together ideas on a variety of aspects of teaching and learning. The book should be helpful at different levels and stages of teaching, in that it provides basic ideas for the teacher in training or the less experienced/less linguistically confident primary teacher; this is seen particularly in the chapters on planning, how to introduce the use of target language and ways to monitor and assess progression.

Furthermore, it outlines different approaches to the teaching of a new language (for example, through the use of story and song) as well as suggesting different levels of integrating language teaching into the primary curriculum. These range from the basic level of incorporating phrases from the new language within daily classroom routines to suggestions for teaching in and through the target language for those teachers whose language skills are more advanced.

It is beyond the scope of the book to include examples in all the languages currently being taught at primary level. The authors have decided to exemplify most ideas through French, since this is the language most commonly taught at primary level; additionally, the phonics chapter concentrates heavily on French since this is far more problematic for children than Spanish or German. We have, however, been able to include some examples in Spanish in the book. It is important to note that most of the ideas and activities can be converted to any language, or are generic.

# 1 Setting the scene

## RECENT HISTORY

The teaching of primary languages has been statutory since September 2014, following the publication of the key stage 2 programmes of study (DfE, 2013). To set this in context, we will refer briefly to official documentation since 2002.

The National Languages Strategy (DfES, 2002) had three objectives: to improve the teaching and learning of languages, including delivering an entitlement to language learning for pupils at key stage 2; to introduce a recognition scheme to give learners credit for their language skills; and to increase the number of people studying languages.

In 2005, the KS2 Framework for Languages (DfES) stated: 'Every child should have the opportunity through key stage 2 to study a foreign language and develop their interest in the culture of other nations.'

Many primary schools introduced or extended their teaching of a language over the following years. In 2010, learning a new language at key stage 2 became an entitlement, and it was anticipated that in 2011, this would become a statutory requirement. However, a change in government brought delay and uncertainty while the whole primary curriculum was under review. It took until 2014 for the statutory teaching of a language to become a reality.

The focus of this book is on primary language teaching at key stage 2. However, there is much good practice at key stage 1, despite the fact that learning another language before key stage 2 has never been an entitlement, or statutory. Some helpful guidance for early language learning is provided in part 3 of the key stage 2 Framework for Languages (2005: 86). It suggests that 'one of two main approaches' can be taken: 'either apprenticeship and experience of more than one language or an early start in the chosen language that will be taught in key stage 2'.

In the next section we will consider the benefits of all children learning a language from an early age.

## EARLY LANGUAGE LEARNING: THE BENEFITS

The many advantages for children starting to learn a new language by the age of seven, or earlier, have been well documented by a number of researchers and authors, including Satchwell and de Silva (1995: 2), who stressed the fact that young children are more receptive to, and naturally curious about, new language, absorbing it easily and imitating and performing it with fewer inhibitions. Furthermore, confidence gained in the language classroom can be transferable to other areas.

It is generally recognised that early language learning educates the ear and the tongue, enhancing a child's sensitivity to new sounds and intonation patterns. At a time when the brain is more flexible and the muscles in the ear and speech mechanisms are not fully formed, this is highly advantageous. As a result of using the skills required to learn a new language, the ability to listen to important points and to concentrate are both likely to improve. Malcolm Gladwell, following the psychologist James Flynn, describes the mind as being similar to a muscle and needing cognitive exercise.

Research into the effects of bilingualism indicates that children who speak another language develop better problem-solving skills, greater creativity, more flexible thinking and communication skills (Dinçay, 2011). This author also mentions their having a clearer focus on tasks, better memory, and an ability to plan and to multi-task.

Links with other classes and cultural connections in countries where the language is spoken give children a more realistic world view and help them develop an ability to see things from other perspectives.

There are also advantages for learning in the first language and ultimately for future learning. As Golinkoff states: 'Learning another language actually enhances a child's overall verbal development' (Golinkoff and Hirsh-Pasek, 2000). By comparing structures in the new language with English, they understand better the way in which their own language operates, become more confident and proficient in reading and later in critical thinking and writing, according to American research (Dinçay, 2011).

## MODELS OF DELIVERY

Primary schools adopt different models to help them teach primary languages. Some use specialist language teachers, including secondary colleagues. The advantage of this is that it provides the children with a good linguistic role model; many of these secondary teachers are aware, however, that they are not conversant with primary methodology. Total reliance on this model may also mean that the new language is not embedded at other times in the week. Therefore, many schools try to combine a partner approach, which relies on the specialist language teacher providing the main teaching input and the class teacher engaging the children in some follow-up learning activities. While this can be effective, it does require more time for discussion and often additional expense.

The other popular model is that of the class teacher taking responsibility for teaching his/her own class the new language. This has many advantages, including the teacher's knowledge of primary methodology, classroom management skills, the relationship of trust and knowledge of individual children that class teachers develop within their class, as well as opportunities to integrate language teaching into the curriculum during the week.

While some primary class teachers may feel lacking in confidence to teach another language, they are already well equipped to do so in that they understand much of the process of teaching and learning a language through their teaching of literacy. The new language can be viewed as teaching a new type of literacy and the primary teacher already has a good understanding of how children develop their linguistic skills. The parallels between literacy and the new language should not be underestimated. Comparing and contrasting the two is beneficial to all learners. It is the experience of the authors, and already mentioned earlier, that children often gain a better understanding of English grammar through exposure to the new language.

Children with English as an additional language (EAL) benefit from being on a level playing field with their peers, particularly if the target language is actively used during the lesson. In some schools EAL learners are removed from the language lesson to develop their English. While it is important for such learners to improve their English, it nevertheless deprives them of the opportunity to do well in another language. They are often very good language learners and the success they have in a language builds self-esteem and hopefully transfers to other learning. EAL learners who are literate in their first language tend to make excellent progress in reading and writing in another language. The National Association for Language Development in the Curriculum

(NALDIC) has a rich website (www.naldic.org.uk), with advice and links to many helpful publications, for example 'Access and engagement in modern foreign languages' (KS3 National Strategies: DfES, 2002), which gives guidance that is also useful in the KS2 classroom.

Learning a new language can benefit all children. Comparing and contrasting grammatical points extends the higher attainers but, very importantly, it often clarifies understanding for lower-attaining children. The use of terminology reinforces the aspects of grammar that are relevant and tested in literacy in the Spelling, Punctuation and Grammar (SPAG) test, which currently forms part of the year 6 national tests.

In the authors' experience, there are many advantages for children with Special Educational Needs learning a new language. They, too, are sometimes removed from the languages class to do extra work in English, whereas they could be benefiting greatly from participation in the languages lesson. Many children with Special Educational Needs derive great enjoyment from the activities and particularly relate to oral work and role-play. We have observed that the confidence they gain through language learning is often transferred to other areas of the curriculum.

# 2 Mapping the way

## RATIONALE

Good planning is essential. Subject leaders, head teachers, governors and external parties might all need to see evidence of well-planned lessons. However, the most important reason for careful planning is to support teachers in delivering high-quality lessons. Planning provides opportunities to align learning objectives, methodology, appropriate learning activities and assessment, all of which will enhance children's learning and progress. The term 'constructive alignment', to express this, is described by Biggs and Tang (2011: 11). The particular format for planning will depend on each school but there are several basic principles and guidelines that might be helpful when planning primary language lessons.

## PRINCIPLES OF GOOD PLANNING

It is helpful to start with a clear idea of the desired learning outcome(s) and the necessary learning objectives to reach it/them. The teacher can then break the learning into small steps and plan a logical teaching sequence. Every lesson will have its own learning outcome(s); however, an individual lesson might be a stepping stone on the way to achieving a bigger outcome, for example a fashion show, role-play, cartoon story poem or poster. It is therefore helpful to decide on the timescale needed to reach the planned learning outcome. How much time is available? How many lessons are needed?

Over any period of time or series of lessons, it is important to plan for the development of all four skills, usually progressing from listening and understanding to speaking, reading and writing. Maximising the use of a small amount of language is key, and all skills can be developed through the same core language, although not necessarily all of them in every lesson!

Giving children opportunities to show their initial understanding through a non-verbal response is really valuable. Chorusing new language as part of a large group helps to develop individual confidence to remember and say words independently. Practising words, just as children would be encouraged to do in their first language, is the next step. Reading and writing are higher level skills, which children subsequently develop.

## SCHEMES OF WORK

Many helpful schemes of work are available to support primary language teaching. There are advantages in using commercial schemes since they often provide user-friendly resources, support the non-specialist and provide thought-out progression. It is helpful if the commercial scheme allows an electronic copy to be made which can then be overwritten and adapted as necessary. In this way, the school can personalise the materials and create its own scheme of work. Often schools use several sources, including their own planning. This approach often has the advantage of providing more variety in methodology.

**Content**

At the time of writing, schools can teach a modern language, ancient Greek or Latin. There is no specific content required for primary languages. Instead, the curriculum is skills-based. The school will choose which language to teach and the topics and language content they wish to cover. The knowledge and skills that the children need to learn are then addressed through the chosen language. If ancient Greek or Latin is taught, the focus will be on reading and writing.

**Shaping the learning**

Building on previously learnt language and providing opportunities for children to revisit the language in a new context is a way of developing linguistic progression; it has a 'snowball' effect. For example, if children in year 3 learn the names for family members and make simple sentences to introduce their own or a fictitious family: *Voici mon père* (Here is my father), they could revisit this topic in upper key stage 2, by learning how to further describe family members. This could be using the third person to give information about their names and jobs: by year 6 this could include a description of their character or physical appearance. As a final outcome, the children could do a presentation for an audience. Another example of building on the key nouns for family learned in lower key stage 2 is to learn to ask and answer questions about who is in the family – numbers of brothers, sisters and cousins.

**MIXED AGE CLASSES**

When dealing with mixed age classes, as in other curriculum areas, rolling programmes avoid repetition of topic areas. The advantage of such programmes is that they can provide the opportunity for children to revisit language and skills in new contexts.

Joan Dickie (www.joandickielanguages.co.uk), who is well recognised for the work she has done in this field, helpfully advises that there are three basic principles that can help with the creation of a mixed age language scheme of work. They are as follows:

- create an appropriate rolling programme in which key language structures (e.g. vocabulary phrases) and skills (e.g. phonics) can be revisited in different contexts;
- identify appropriate learning outcomes for new pupils and returning pupils, where returning pupils are expected to show progression when returning to previously learned structures or skills; and
- when structures or skills are revisited, plan for differentiated activities for returning pupils to demonstrate higher level/progressive language skills.

It is important to allow the returning children in the class to respond at an appropriate level for their prior learning and ability, by including a structure or question from a previous unit of work. To show progression, the teacher could expect them to: increase the amount of language they use, show improved pronunciation and intonation, take the lead in asking questions and cope more independently with differentiated tasks.

One way to differentiate the learning, not just for those in mixed age classes, is to plan questioning or tasks at different levels. The authors' adapted version of Bloom's taxonomy for primary languages (Bloom, 1956), in the form of a table at the end of this chapter, provides some suggestions.

### Phonics

It is also essential to build in phonics teaching and to make the children aware of the pronunciation rules in the language being taught; this will avoid the temptation to use known English phonics and will help them read aloud with increasingly accurate pronunciation. Where the new language is taught through a series of lessons around a topic, story or song, key sounds can be identified through the topic vocabulary, and activities to practise them can be planned into the lessons. Short phonic activities are often a good lesson starter and can provide opportunities to revisit both new and previously learned sounds (refer to the 'Sounds different' chapter for further ideas).

### Authentic resources

A scheme of work will also include the use of different types of texts, some of which should be authentic.

### STAGES IN PLANNING

Planning can be broken down into three stages.

### Long term

First, a general outline or overview of what will be taught is needed. This represents the big picture of the school's planning cycle. Essentially very brief, it may just be a topic, unit title or heading. However, when a scheme of work for single or mixed age classes is initially being created, it is helpful to have considered the following: which topics or areas of study will be taught; when and where they might link to other curriculum areas in order to provide opportunities for integrating language learning. Careful consideration of the topics will also maximise the opportunity to choose those that will naturally provide the context for revisiting language in a new context.

### Medium term

Once the topics are identified, a fuller medium term plan of what learning will take place each term is needed. This will have more detail of learning objectives, outcomes, core language and structures to be taught/revisited, coverage of the national curriculum, together with cross-curricular and assessment opportunities. It should be a helpful document that will enable a clear and logical progression of lessons to be planned.

### New topic

At the start of a new topic, a 'wow' opener is an effective way of capturing children's attention and imagination; it also motivates them to learn. This might be a treasure hunt for hidden clues that reveal the topic of the learning. Giving them an overview of what they will be doing and learning can also help them engage with the process.

### Short term

Each lesson should be flexible and may need to change according to the children's learning needs and progress. It is good practice to use assessment from one lesson to inform the next. For this purpose, highlighting and annotating the original plan is often considered the most efficient way of doing this. It can be helpful to add specific questions on the lesson plan as a prompt for any differentiated questions that the teacher intends to use and for assessing children's learning. More information on this is provided in the chapter on 'Assessment and progression'.

The starting point for an individual lesson will be to consider the next step in children's learning, the expected progress they will make and how it can be measured. It is helpful to consider these questions:

- What will be taught?
- How will it be taught?
- What will the children learn?
- How will children know if they are successful?

## Planning a variety of activities

Primary language teaching, by its very nature, meets the needs of different types of learners in that there is generally a balance of activities involving opportunities to listen, look and do. See the following chapter for further discussion on learning styles. It is also important to plan for whole class, group or pair work, as well as independent learning activities. An initial lesson on a topic is likely to be more 'teacher-led' but there are opportunities for pair work at this stage, too.

## INDIVIDUAL LESSONS

### Lesson opener

The lesson should have an engaging opening activity; this could be a song (to fit with a topic, revise past learning, attune the learner's ear, or simply become part of a routine to signal the start of a language lesson). It might be a rhyme (finger rhymes are appropriate for lower key stage 2) or a game/activity to review previous learning. A lesson opener that is unusual and takes the children by surprise has the benefit of drawing them in and gaining their attention in order to start the learning. A surprise element at the start of a lesson can help gain even the most reluctant learners' attention – almost catching them before they have time to think or be off-task!

### Lesson objectives and success criteria

Schools often have their own preferred method for explaining the lesson objective and success criteria. Some schools use the acronyms LO or LI ('learning objective' or 'learning intention'); others use WALT or WALA ('we are learning to . . .' or 'we are learning about . . .'). For learning outcomes or success criteria, some schools use the acronym WILF ('what I'm looking for'), others, a must/should/could approach or a traffic light system. The important thing is that the children understand what is expected of them. This should be clearly communicated, usually at the start of a lesson. However, if the point of the lesson is developing children's language detective skills, it might not be appropriate to give the learning objective in detail at the start.

### Progression within a lesson

The amount of language to cover in a lesson depends on many factors, including the ability of the children and learning outcomes that are realistically achievable in the time available. It is important to maintain an appropriate pace and to make an informed judgement as to the children's learning (see the chapter on 'Assessment and progression'). If too much time is spent at word level, while some children might continue to enjoy the lesson because they feel happy to be in their comfort zone, other children may become bored and demotivated. The language needs to progress step by step. In any one lesson, the teacher is constantly assessing children's understanding and readiness to move on in their learning.

## Differentiation

The teacher will need to consider how different children can be challenged and meet the lesson's objective(s). According to Convery and Coyle (1999), differentiation may be achieved by:

- outcome (all children have the same task);
- task (in the context of reading, the same text for all children but easier/harder tasks available);
- text (different reading texts to suit different abilities);
- support (different support materials, including dictionaries and adult or peer support);
- ability (grouping strategically: mixed ability to support lower attainers; higher attainers working together, with extension activities; lower attainers working together with support); and
- interest (children self-select resources for interest and level of challenge).

A good language lesson will usually incorporate:

- a song, rhyme or familiar game (at the start/in later teaching activity);
- learning objectives and outcomes clearly stated (written in child-friendly language);
- revision of known language in a familiar or new context;
- a small amount of new language;
- opportunities for choral and individual repetition;
- differentiation where appropriate;
- some use of target language by the teacher;
- a variety of whole class/small group/pair/individual work;
- different resources – with a strong visual element (e.g. flashcards, pictures on the interactive whiteboard, big books, puppets);
- action and enjoyment;
- praise for children's effort and achievement;
- review of the learning during/at the end of a lesson, in the form of (mini-)plenaries; and
- use of informal assessment strategies.

In conclusion, we have discussed principles for good planning, planning for progression, mixed age classes and features of a good lesson. Each primary school will devise an individual scheme of work to suit its needs.

**Table 2.1** Questions and activities for primary languages, based on Bloom's taxonomy

| Levels | Types of question | Activities |
|---|---|---|
| **1 Remembering** | *Repeat/copy/show/recall*<br>• Can you repeat/copy?<br>• Can you label this?<br>• Show me the word that says . . . ?<br>• Can you spell . . . ?<br>• What words can you remember?<br>• How do we write the sound . . . ? | • Tell you/write words they know<br>• Do a list on a mind map or on mini-whiteboard<br>• Recite a poem<br>• Lotto games |
| **2 Understanding** | *Understanding/translate/discuss*<br>• What does this word mean . . . ? Translate<br>• What do you think this means? | • Draw a picture/cartoon suggested by a story<br>• Discuss meaning/how they know<br>• Answer some questions (in English) on a short text |
| **3 Applying** | *Using knowledge/skills*<br>• Can you think of a question/ sentence or phrase to use here?<br>• Can you change a word in this sentence?<br>• Can you put the text in order?<br>• What would help you be successful?<br>• Can you perform . . . / write . . . using the new vocabulary? | • Reuse familiar vocabulary<br>• Know when to use *Bonjour/Salut*<br>• Role-play with new language<br>• Spell words containing known graphemes<br>• Design a board game<br>• Design a stop motion animation |
| **4 Analysing** | *Explaining*<br>• Why do you think that might be a verb?<br>• Have you noticed . . . ?<br>• What conclusions can you draw from what you see?<br>• What evidence is there . . . ?<br>• What is the relationship between . . . and . . . ?<br>• Investigate . . . | • Make up your own grammar rule (with a partner)<br>• Sorting words into groups |
| **5 Evaluating** | *Drawing conclusions/justifying*<br>• What can you work out from the tone of the person speaking about how they are feeling?<br>• Justify your opinion about X (creating extended sentences) | • Listen and judge the emotion<br>• Group work task: justify your opinion about this famous person |
| **6 Creating** | *Inventing/making something new*<br>• How would you test a rule?<br>• Can you adapt a dialogue for a different situation? | • Create an e-book<br>• Give a performance<br>• Run a puppet show<br>• Find other examples of the language |

# 3 Developing skills

## RATIONALE

The aim of introducing languages at key stage 2 has long been considered one of developing an enthusiasm for language learning and providing an opportunity for children to develop language learning skills. If they can experience what it is like to hear new words, play with language and begin to compare and contrast their knowledge of one language with another, they will be better prepared and motivated to learn languages in the future.

The key stage 2 languages programmes of study (DfE, 2013) set out an expectation that children will have made significant progress in a language by the end of the key stage. Given the demands of the primary curriculum, and the amount of time that can be allocated to primary language teaching, it is likely that schools will choose to study one main language in order for children to achieve the expected progress.

In teaching any modern language, there are two distinct areas – oracy and literacy. Within oracy we are thinking about children's ability to listen well and understand what they hear, then how clearly they speak in order to present information and engage in conversations with others. In literacy we want the children to understand the written word, read aloud with increasing confidence and accurate pronunciation, and tackle the reading of unfamiliar texts. Finally, children need to develop the ability to write from memory, using familiar language.

## ORACY

### Listening and looking

It is a prerequisite for all learning that children listen carefully and are engaged. This is particularly important when they are learning a new language.

Getting children ready for learning in terms of listening and looking carefully is paramount, particularly when the teacher is beginning a different topic or introducing some new vocabulary. Children live in an age of digital technology. They are surrounded by colour and action; however, concentration shown by children when playing computer games does not necessarily mean that they are able to focus and listen carefully in the classroom. As teachers, we may need to adopt strategies for training them to concentrate. It is noticeable that children who are trained to listen carefully early in lower key stage 2 find this easier in upper key stage 2.

Teachers have many strategies for getting children to focus, listen and look at a particular moment; all these tried and tested methods are helpful. It is generally considered good methodology to introduce new vocabulary with images or flashcards (digitally on the whiteboard, physically with cards, or a mixture of both) or through the use of real objects (realia). Mime and gesture are effective at this stage. Meaning will be linked to the words through association with the objects, pictures and actions.

At the same time children need to hear a good model for pronunciation (the teacher saying the words or using sound on the whiteboard or other digital recordings).

For these reasons, it is important that every child can see the teacher and the materials. They need to link the meaning of the words and hear the sound correctly so that they can repeat them accurately after the teacher. Watching the teacher's mouth will aid their understanding. Where sounds are similar, it is very easy for children to copy what they think they have heard. A common example in English is the 'th' being mistaken for 'f'. Consequently, children mispronounce words such as 'think', both saying and then writing the word as 'fink'. Watching the position of the teacher's mouth (lips and tongue) helps them avoid this problem. A quick activity to help children learn this strategy is for the teacher or a child to silently 'mouth' a word/phrase and for the others to chorus it aloud; this can also be done in pairs by the children.

The layout of the room is therefore extremely important in enabling children to see clearly. In lower key stage 2, children might learn better on the carpet in front of the teacher or whiteboard. Circles do not work well when initially introducing new vocabulary since it is difficult for the children immediately to the left or right of the teacher to see properly. There are, however, many engaging circle games for practising and reinforcing vocabulary (please refer to 'The magic of games' chapter for suggestions). Equally, at upper key stage 2, where the carpet is used more sparingly, it is important to think about how the children are positioned. They must be able to focus and be close enough to the action; this may entail asking children to move their chairs to be at a different angle, or bringing them closer. The term 'cinema seats' is useful to get all children facing the board. Below are some suggestions for helping children to focus on the learning:

### Top tips for improving concentration

- Children follow instructions to draw something simple on a sheet of paper before beginning the lesson.
- Use 'brain breaks'. There are a number of ideas suggested by Smith and Call (2001). Brain break/brain gym activities, such as saying letters of the alphabet and following pictorial instructions below each letter (right, left, duck and jump) and 'Pass the beanbag' (Wakely and Morrison, 2004) are effective. For further details, refer to the chapter on 'Integrating language learning'.
- Present words that are colours in the new language but written in a different colour – children have to say the colour, not read the name of the colour. This works well if the words are animated in PowerPoint.
- When asked, children repeat the last word the teacher just said/predict the next word.

### Presenting new vocabulary

The most important step for the children is to be able to recognise the new words and show their understanding. Recognition of meaning and repeated practice of the sound comes before independent production.

Here are some suggestions for introducing nouns. It is helpful to:

- teach a few nouns at a time – probably six to eight words. This might depend on the children's age and the complexity of the words;
- mark noun flashcards in some way to show the gender; this helps visual learners. A colour scheme or using symbols would work well. This idea is expanded in the 'Fun with grammar' chapter;
- teach one gender group at a time, presenting masculine, then feminine words;
- teach any cognates first – words that have the same meaning and spelling, or similar spelling, in English;

- teach every noun with an article (definite or indefinite – the/a). So, for example, *le marché* (the market) or *la poste* (the post office), *un parc* (a park) or *une banque* (a bank). The choice of whether to use the definite or indefinite article (a/the) will depend on the types of sentences the teacher wishes the children to construct later. The definite (*le/la/l'*) and indefinite (*un/une*) article should generally not be mixed when introducing new words;
- engage the children by introducing an element of surprise – for example, hiding the cards in a surprise bag and drawing them out one by one, or asking individual children to draw the next card. This works well for younger children;
- get children to listen and repeat the new language as many times as possible when each flashcard/image is displayed. In order to make this enjoyable, any of the following techniques can be used for *varied repetition*:
  - voices – children repeat showing different emotions in their voice (angry, sad, happy, surprised); these are either determined by the teacher or the children's choice – or the random throw of a dice (see the chapter 'A helping hand');
  - speed (the children repeat faster and slower);
  - pitch (the children repeat higher or lower);
  - volume (the children repeat loudly or softly);
  - table groups and other forms of grouping (the teacher asks children to repeat as a whole table, or groups of boys and girls);
  - repeating a phrase or sentence in segments from the end, rather than the beginning, can be very helpful (example: *Je vais à la poste* is practised by saying *poste – la poste – à la poste – vais à la poste – je vais à la poste*).

Using picture flashcards or realia is one way of presenting the new language; picture flashcards will be useful later for a variety of flashcard games to further practise and embed it. However, some teachers might prefer to present the new language using the interactive whiteboard, which offers different advantages. Animated pictures are engaging, and boys in particular are motivated by the 'moving image', as shown in the research article by King and Gurian (2006: 60); they describe how the male visual system 'relies more heavily on type M ganglion cells, which detect movement'. Teachers can easily hide and reveal the images for repetition and response. Images can also be made to fly across the screen so fast that pupils have to concentrate fully. Alternatively, repetition of each new word can be made fun by the children repeating it over and over again until a new picture is shown.

Some teachers also have a class puppet, which takes on the identity of a character from the country where the new language is spoken. The puppet can also be a useful resource for introducing new vocabulary to the children and acting short role-plays with the teacher.

## Miming sequence

After the initial presentation of vocabulary, it is helpful if the children add a mime, gesture or action for the word. The teacher – or the children, who love to invent their own individual mimes/gestures/actions – could choose these. Some teachers also use Makaton signs if they know them.

Once a mime, gesture or action is agreed, the following sequence can be used:

- children show the mimes corresponding to the new vocabulary said by the teacher (this can be done at varying speeds, first going through a set order of new items of vocabulary and then in a random order);
- the roles are then reversed – the teacher performs the mime and the children chorus the language;
- finally, confident children can ask the teacher to mime. It is often fun for the class to correct the teacher, who has deliberately made a mistake.

This sequence provides immediate feedback on the level of children's understanding (Who is able to perform the correct actions and mimes quickly?) and their level of confidence in recalling the new language.

Gestures and mimes also aid the memorisation of new language, as mentioned in the key stage 2 languages programmes of study (DfE, 2013). A boy making an Easter card with a chicken on asked to be reminded of the word for 'chicken' in French. Following a quick flapping of arms by the teacher, the small boy happily said *'la poule'* and went back to creating his card.

## Practising and reinforcing

Children are quick to learn and equally quick to forget! The amount of practice needed can never be overestimated in order to really embed the language and give children the confidence to produce and use the language for themselves. When learning their mother tongue, children begin to develop their communication skills by listening to sounds and speech around them. They can often understand and follow complex instructions before they speak. Some children may require longer at this stage than others and it is important to bear this in mind when teaching young children another language. Therefore, while it is good to encourage children to join in, the teacher should be aware that some children may speak later than others.

Regular practice (little and often) is ideal and puts the class teacher in the best position for developing the children's oracy skills, because they have a special relationship of trust and can seize different opportunities to practise at times during the day, in addition to the timetabled language lesson.

Chorusing activities are crucial for embedding the new language. The teacher can also build in opportunities for confident children to speak individually. It is helpful to bear in mind some techniques for asking open and closed questions; this provides an opportunity for the teacher to assess progress. The following sequence shows the progression from closed to open questions:

- *C'est la bouche? Oui/non.* (Is it a mouth? Yes/no.)
- *C'est la bouche ou le nez? La bouche.* (Is it a mouth or a nose? A mouth.)
- *Qu'est-ce que c'est? C'est le nez.* (What is it? It's a nose.)

This form of questioning can be used to provide differentiation when the teacher is adopting a 'hands down' approach; this is discussed later in the chapter on 'Assessment and progression'.

## Activities to rehearse new vocabulary

### *Show me – Montrez-moi*

Flashcards are displayed round the classroom and numbered. The teacher calls out an object on one of the flashcards and the children say the number. Alternatively, the teacher calls out the number and the class say the matching word/phrase.

### *Find the picture – Trouvez l'image*

In turn, children volunteer to say a word or sentence represented by a flashcard that the teacher is holding up. If correct, the child is given the card, which s/he hides behind her/his back. Once all the cards are distributed, other children try to remember where they are by naming the child and the item behind her/his back.

### *Stepping stones – Traversez la rivière*

Flashcards representing the new vocabulary are laid across the floor and represent stepping stones across the river. The aim is for a volunteer to cross the river as quickly as possible but in order to do so, s/he must recall the words for each stepping stone. Any hesitation means that they have fallen into the river. If it is taking too long, the teacher can give a signal and the class call out *plouf* (splash).

### *Pass it quickly – Passez-le vite!*

Children pass an object or card, representing vocabulary, from one person to the next, saying the word/phrase in both the new language and English, as fast as they can.

Young children often view primary languages as fun and they often quote playing games as the reason. While it is important for the children to have fun, it is also necessary for them to appreciate that the games are there for the purpose of learning and helping linguistic progress. They are a natural and enjoyable way to rehearse language and are therefore an important part of the language learning 'toolkit'. 'The magic of games' chapter provides detailed instructions for playing a wide variety of games, including the following well-loved examples, which are excellent for developing listening comprehension and speaking skills:

- stations
- touch the board
- fruit salad
- sound orchestra
- Kim's game
- prediction.

## Correcting children's mistakes

Correcting mistakes sensitively is important in order to encourage children to participate in the language lesson. If a child makes a mistake, the teacher can subtly model the correct pronunciation. If some words in a sentence are in the wrong order, the teacher can gesture with his/her hands to show that parts of the sentence need to be reversed. If an error is at the start of a sentence, s/he can say the first word in the sentence and gesture to the child to continue.

## Role-play and drama

In addition to games, role-play is another important feature of language teaching and can be developed for any topic; it provides opportunities for children both to ask and answer questions.

A model role-play could be presented and initially the children should be taught how to perform it. The dialogue could be reproduced with pictures/symbols, either instead of, or to support, a written text. This is similar to the use of story mapping to help oral storytelling, where the children are encouraged to retell a story from a picture. In a similar way, children can recall a role-play dialogue from symbols that have been linked to specific vocabulary.

It is important to provide sufficient practice before children are able to work in pairs to reproduce, and ultimately change, the dialogue. The sequence below is helpful in providing the necessary practice:

- the teacher reads the dialogue and the class listen and follow;
- the teacher reads each line and the children repeat ;
- two halves of the class read it/act it out with the teacher;
- the teacher asks if a volunteer could act it out with him/her;
- children then act it out from memory in pairs (with a mixed ability talk partner);
- differentiation can be through higher attainers changing an element in the dialogue.

Children enjoy acting out a role-play using different voices, such as that of an elderly person or a younger child. The technique of choosing a character voice is one way of providing varied repetition.

## Disappearing dialogue

Repetition increases children's familiarity and confidence in using new language before they are able to adapt it. A further way to provide repetition and aid memorisation is to make parts of the dialogue disappear.

The dialogue can either be removed one line at a time, or by removing words/symbols gradually until only a skeleton dialogue remains – or the first letters of some words are left. It is best to remove nouns or adjectives first. The interactive whiteboard is ideal for this activity and techniques for masking dialogue are explained in the 'Technology tools' chapter.

## Drama and performing

Giving children the opportunity to participate in choral speaking, reciting poetry or stories for an audience, or performing short plays in the target language are all valuable ways to develop confidence, memory and fluency within a 'real' context. There are performance ideas mentioned in some of the later chapters.

In conclusion, listening and speaking in the new language can be supported through:

- developing good listening skills;
- using mime and gesture to respond;
- fun and varied repetition of new vocabulary;
- opportunities to consolidate new vocabulary through games and other activities;
- learning how to use words within sentences;
- asking and answering questions through dialogues and role-play; and
- presenting spoken language with clarity and confidence.

## LITERACY

### Reading

When is the right time to introduce the written word? It is an age-old argument and teachers often subscribe to a specific view. Some think that showing the written word should be delayed until the learner is really confident with the spoken word; others feel that seeing the written word early on or even alongside the spoken word has advantages.

The reason for delaying the written word is for fear that introducing it too soon will be confusing and lead to mispronunciation. It is natural that children will apply their existing knowledge of English phonics and so the written word can easily become problematic, in some languages more than others. While it is crucial that children listen and copy the correct sounds, it is also important both to meet and develop children's different learning styles. The idea of visual, auditory and kinaesthetic (VAK) learners was described by Barbe *et al.* (1979) but became more widely known when modified by Fleming and Mills (1992). Introducing the written word gives visual learners an advantage in helping them to develop good oracy and memory skills. Therefore, introducing the written word early on can be beneficial (arguably, as soon as children have heard it/within the same lesson), with the proviso that any misconceptions about pronunciation are addressed and phoneme–grapheme representations highlighted where these differ from English. Furthermore, many children, including those who favour kinaesthetic learning, will often choose to write words to aid memory.

When learning to read in the new language, children can start by learning to identify the written graphemes for the new sounds they have learnt to recognise. Using sounds from the core topic vocabulary will also help with any misconceptions of the early introduction of the written word to support good oracy, as mentioned above. For example, if the children are learning the following food vocabulary *gâteau* (cake) and *biscuit* (biscuit), the teacher can work with the sounds *eau, i* and *ui*.

The need to reinforce and practise key sounds can never be overestimated; it is always good to keep revising previously learned sounds in order to elicit accurate pronunciation of both familiar and subsequently unfamiliar words. Phonology is the key to children being able to read aloud with increasingly accurate pronunciation and also to spell and write from memory. For further teaching ideas linked to phonics, please refer to the 'Sounds different' chapter.

Instructions can be found in 'The magic of games' chapter for the following games, which help children to read aloud with increasingly accurate pronunciation:

- secret signaller
- noughts and crosses
- beat the clock
- start again.

Another effective strategy is to introduce the words for reading practice in a PowerPoint, making the vocabulary items fly in from different directions, in different orientations and at various speeds. Covering up a word/phrase/sentence and slowly revealing it for the children to read aloud can also provide a degree of intrigue and interest.

A further way to improve both oracy and reading aloud is to give the children microphones and allow them to record themselves, with the aim of sounding as French/Spanish/German as they can. The recording can be played back, discussed and can subsequently become a 'benchmark' for improvement.

Developing good intonation in French can be helped through reading aloud a long sentence that has several commas. Children need to make their voices rise at each comma, then fall at the end of the sentence – unless it is a question!

> *Il y a une chaise dans la cuisine, une télé dans le salon, un lit dans la chambre et un chien dans le jardin!*

> (There is a chair in the kitchen, a television in the lounge, a bed in the bedroom and a dog in the garden!)

Reading aloud confidently and with good pronunciation and intonation is one aspect of reading. Other reading skills involve being able to identify written words when heard and understanding what they mean. Good strategies for developing these skills are asking children to:

- point to/hold up a word card when they hear the language spoken;
- select the correct phrase or sentence by giving its number or colour when they hear it. The children can be asked to say or write the answer. Number fans or coloured cubes, if used, have the added advantage of being visual, allowing the teacher to check children's understanding;
- 'jigsaw' pieces of text together (sentences from a short story or song) as they listen;
- 'jigsaw' words in a sentence together, as mentioned in the 'Fun with grammar' chapter;
- match pictures with text. This could be by drawing lines or selecting the correct numbers/letters for picture and text. Younger children enjoy physically cutting and sticking, whereas older children will probably benefit from multiple choice options;
- mime the meaning; this provides a kinaesthetic approach to learning. The children can use the same actions chosen when they initially learned the vocabulary; they mime words and shorter sentences, such as: *Bonjour* (Hello), *Il fait beau* (It is fine weather). When actions are also attached to connectives, it becomes possible for children to read longer sentences, for example: *Je porte mon petit pull bleu parce qu'il fait froid aujourd'hui* (I'm wearing my small blue sweater because it's cold today).

'The magic of games' chapter provides detailed instructions for playing the following games, which help to develop children's ability to match text to meaning. They can be played either as a whole class or in small groups or pairs:

- Pelmanism card games
- dominoes.

### Foreign language texts

Children will benefit from exposure to a wide variety of texts, including non-fiction: story, poem, rhyme, song, information text, instructions, email. The key stage 2 languages programmes of study (DfE, 2013) highlight the need to use some authentic texts. In the eResource, there are websites that can be used to find free authentic resources, including authentic story texts. Further activities to develop reading skills and exploit a story text can be found in the 'What's the story?' chapter.

### Gist comprehension

It is helpful to reassure children that they are not expected to understand every word in a text. Strategies for decoding need to be explored: looking for language they already know, or meaning they can derive from other clues (diagrams, pictures, punctuation, cognates or sentence structure). Most cognates are helpful; however, some are misleading but are, nonetheless, interesting for children. For example, *chips* in French means crisps and not, as children might guess, chips.

Asking the children to annotate the text – writing words they know or think they know – helps them begin to unpick the meaning. They might find it useful to colour-code the text, using different colours for known, guessable and new words. They could even record them in three separate columns.

The example below, a spy song at the start of the 'Mission Impossible' unit of work (more on the context is given in the 'Mission Impossible' chapter), demonstrates the level of comprehension from a year 5 child. The authors were impressed at the way children approached the task with confidence and enjoyment.

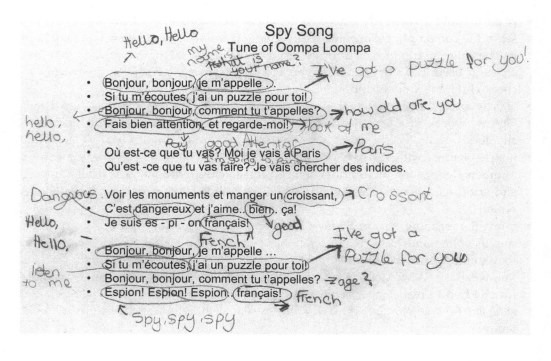

## Writing

In order to develop their writing skills, children need to practise copying words accurately, paying attention to any accents. They need to know that the accents are there to help with pronunciation and meaning. Below are some suggestions for helping children learn to copy and spell words in the new language.

### *Without paper!*

Ask children to pretend that they are writing with a magic finger or a beautiful pen (they can imagine whatever colour they like) and copy a familiar word in the air. This can be extended to writing with the same imaginary pen/finger on their arm or hand. They can also play a guessing game where partners are asked to guess a word written on their hand, arm or back. An alternative version is a team game where children work in groups of five or six, standing one behind the other in a line. The child at the back starts by writing a word on the back of the person standing in front of him/her. This continues along the line until the person at the front attempts to guess the word. That child might be asked either to say or show the correct word.

For this activity the children need to have the words they are practising clearly displayed for them to copy. Adding the English word or a picture further helps to reinforce meaning.

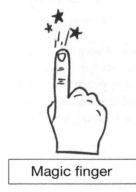

Magic finger

| ojos | eyes |
|------|------|
| nariz | nose |
| boca | mouth |
| oreja | ear |
| cabeza | head |
| hombros | shoulders |

### *Guess the secret word*

Introducing an element of competition can be motivational and provide the opportunity for plenty of writing/spelling practice. The teacher or a chosen child chooses one word from a list to write down in secret. The other children try to guess the 'secret' word, writing their choice on individual whiteboards. Once everyone has written a word, they stand up. The person who chose the 'secret' word

gradually eliminates each word on the list by reading them aloud. Children who have written those words sit down until eventually the winning word is left and all those still standing earn a point.

## Spelling

### *Rehearsing words silently*

In pairs, children can also be asked to challenge themselves to remember spellings within a set time limit. They practise looking at the words and saying them under their breath, before being tested by a partner.

### *Look, cover, write, check*

#### *Using PowerPoint*

Primary children are familiar with this method for practising English spelling. It proves popular as a whole class activity, especially if the children are writing on mini-whiteboards! The teacher uses the interactive whiteboard to display and hide the words being practised.

A motivating strategy is to award a time limit and point system corresponding to the number of letters and accents in each word or phrase being practised. PowerPoint works very well for this activity, with each word appearing on a separate slide. The children are given a number of seconds to study the word (this can be the equivalent of the number of letters and accents in it) and the slide is then hidden (pressing the letter 'B' on the keyboard quickly obscures the slide). The children have the same number of seconds to write the word before it is once again revealed for them to check and correct (pressing the letter 'B' key again to reveal the slide). Children award themselves the appropriate number of points. In this example of a Power Point slide, the picture and dot (which is red) provide a pictorial representation of the phrase, which also helps to reinforce the correct word order.

#### *Traditional method*

Alternatively, the more traditional 'look, cover, write and check' method used for practising English spellings can be used, where children have a list of words to practise, writing at their own pace. In order to make this more rewarding, the words can be given to them in a grid; children highlight words when they have copied them accurately. The words to practise could also be decided by throwing a dice.

### Look, cover, write and check

Roll a dice, cover the word for the number rolled.
Write that word in the empty box next to it.
If correct, colour in the box on the left.

| 1. un | |
| --- | --- |
| 2. deux | |
| 3. trois | |
| 4. quatre | |
| 5. cinq | |
| 6. six | |

### *Look, remember, write*

This technique has been suggested by a colleague, Marie-France Perkins, as an effective method for teaching spellings. A rolling PowerPoint displaying the words the teacher wants the children to use and spell is watched for a period of time, before they are asked to write as many words as they can from memory.

### ***Other spelling activities***

Further spelling practice activities are: jumbled words to unscramble, matching the beginnings and endings of words, and word searches. These help the children recognise words and their correct spellings.

## SENTENCE LEVEL WRITING

In order to move beyond word level, children will need to be shown how to use words within a sentence and compare word order with English. Before being expected to write sentences, it is good practice to allow children time to rehearse orally with a partner. A sentence switchboard can help to support both speaking and writing. The one below shows how children can be supported to speak and write sentences describing clothes by selecting their choice of vocabulary from each column.

A child might say or write: *Je mets mon pantalon rouge* (I am putting on my red trousers).

Pictures can be added, either in the right order or round the edges, to support less confident learners. They can be made more or less challenging by adjusting the amount of language in each column; the number of columns will determine the length/complexity of sentences. Below are some further examples of switchboards created to help children describe monsters. A year 3 child might use the first to label his/her picture of a monster. A year 4 child might use the second as support for writing some sentences to describe the face of his/her monster, using colours as adjectives.

Describing clothes

| Je mets | mon | pantalon<br>T-shirt<br>manteau<br>pull | rouge<br>bleu<br>jaune<br>vert |
|---|---|---|---|
| | ma | chemise<br>jupe<br>robe | rouge<br>bleue<br>jaune<br>verte |

| un | petit<br>grand | nez |
|---|---|---|
| une | petite<br>grande | tête<br>bouche |
| les | petits<br>grands | yeux<br>cheveux<br>pieds |
| les | petites<br>grandes | oreilles |

| J'ai...<br>Il a...<br>Elle a... | le nez | vert<br>rose<br>violet | noir<br>blanc<br>bleu | rouge<br>jaune |
|---|---|---|---|---|
| | le tête<br>le bouche | verte<br>rose<br>violette | noire<br>blanche<br>bleue | rouge<br>jaune |
| | les yeux<br>les cheveux | verts<br>roses<br>violets | noirs<br>blancs<br>bleus | rouges<br>jaunes |
| | les oreilles<br>les dents | vertes<br>roses<br>violettes | noires<br>blanches<br>bleues | rouges<br>jaunes |

Walt: write a description in French

Elle a un nez ~~violet~~ rose. ✓
Elle a une tête violette. ✓
Elle a une bouche rose~~s~~. ✓
Elle a les yeux jaunes. ✓
Elle a les cheveux verts. ✓
Elle a les dent blancs. blanches
Elle a les pieds noirs. ✓
Elle a ~~les~~ genoux violets. ✓
Elle a les oreilles rouges. ✓

The first switchboard shown here is more advanced and helps to build longer sentences. It supports children writing about the subjects they like or dislike at school and the reason why. A further task can be added at the bottom of the switchboard as an extension task. Here the children can add the teacher's name and their preferred subject.

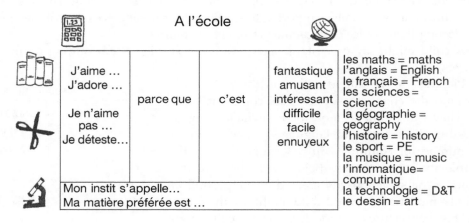

### A l'école

| J'aime …<br>J'adore …<br><br>Je n'aime pas …<br>Je déteste… | parce que | c'est | fantastique<br>amusant<br>intéressant<br>difficile<br>facile<br>ennuyeux | les maths = maths<br>l'anglais = English<br>le français = French<br>les sciences = science<br>la géographie = geography<br>l'histoire = history<br>le sport = PE<br>la musique = music<br>l'informatique= computing<br>la technologie = D&T<br>le dessin = art |

| Mon instit s'appelle…<br>Ma matière préférée est … |

Switchboards can also be created to enable the children to make sensible or silly sentences. They can be used with dice to play a game in which the roll of the dice indicates the way in which the sentence starts. For example, if a three is rolled, the sentence would begin with *Demain . . .*

| 1. Lundi | | | au parc |
| 2. Samedi | je vais | aller | un sandwich |
| 3. Demain | tu vas | danser | au cinéma |
| 4. Ce soir | on va | manger | la télévision |
| 5. Ce week-end | | acheter | les magasins |
| 6. Aujourd'hui | | visiter | des bonbons |
| | | regarder | au restaurant |
| | | | un film |

A further use for the switchboard shown above is the game of 'consequences'. Children are given pieces of paper and, in turn, add part of a sentence before folding the paper over and passing it to the child on their right. The first child begins by adding the time phrase, the second chooses the verb, and so on. After writing two complete sentences, the children take turns to read them out and the class vote (thumbs up/down) to indicate whether the sentence is sensible or silly.

## Snakes

This activity helps children to practise writing at sentence level. It is excellent for embedding a new sentence structure that the children have been learning and will help them learn to write from memory. This type of activity makes a good lesson opener to revise previous learning.

**Snake sentences**

BonjourMadame
J'aimeleschausettesmaisjepréfèrelesbottes.
Jepréfèrelesbottesparcequ'ellessontconfortables.

## EXTENDED WRITING

In order to help children write short or longer pieces of text accurately, they can be given writing frames, models, word mats or lists for support. The texts they write can be linked to any genre and ideally children should be exposed to writing for as many different purposes and audiences as possible. For example, they should have opportunities to write:

- poems
- simple stories
- cartoon captions
- menus

- invitations
- letters
- postcards

- emails
- fact files
- labels on diagrams.

## Gap fill activities

The text is copied and completed by filling the gaps with the correct words. Dashes representing the number of letters, an initial first letter and pictures may all be used to provide additional support. The children have a list of words to refer to in order to help them write accurately.

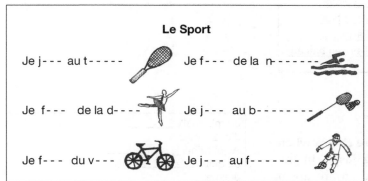

The example below is a picture gap fill task designed for year 6 children, who are learning to construct sentences using a simple future tense in the first person. This task enables them to write a letter about their holiday. Once completed, it could become a model for them to create their own letter.

## Visiting French-speaking Countries

### Days of the Week

lundi – Monday
mardi – Tuesday
mercredi – Wednesday
jeudi – Thursday
vendredi – Friday
samedi – Saturday
dimanche – Sunday

### Transport

à pied – by foot
en voiture – by car
en vélo – by bike
en bus – by bus
en bateau – by boat
en train – by train
en avion – by plane

Où vas-tu? –
Where are you going?
je vais – I am going
c'est loin – it is far away
c'est près – it is near
et – and

### Countries

en France – to France
en Belgique – to Belgium
en Guyane –to Guyana
au Luxembourg – to Luxembourg
au Sénégal –to Senegal
au Canada – to Canada
aux Seychelles – to the Seychelles

Lundi, je vais <u>en France</u>   <u>en vélo.</u>
Mardi, je vais <u>en Espagne</u>   <u>en voiture.</u>
Mercredi, je vais <u>en Belgique</u>   <u>en bus.</u>
Jeudi, je vais <u>au Canada</u>   <u>en avion.</u>
Vendredi, je vais <u>aux Seychelles</u>   <u>en bateau.</u>

## Writing models

These provide children with a sample of writing which they copy, substituting some words. In the examples below, children change the underlined words with appropriate choices of their own. A word list/mat can be provided for further support.

| Lundi, je vais en Belgique en train. | |
| --- | --- |
| Mardi, je vais en France en bateau. | ⛵ |
| Mercredi, je vais en Côte d'Ivoire en vélo. | 🚲 |
| Jeudi, je vais au Canada en vélo. | 🚲 |
| Vendredi, je vais en Haïti en avion. | ✈ |
| Samedi, je vais en Luxembourg en voiture. | 🚗 |
| Dimanche, je vais en Seychelles à pied. | 👞 |

## Writing frames

These allow children more choice when completing their writing tasks. In the example below, the children are given the sentence structure but have the freedom to create individual sentences with the support of a word mat.

Je m'appelle _____.
J'ai ____ ans.
Aujourd'hui je suis _____
Je quitte _____
J'aime _____
Je n'aime pas _____
Je suis _____ parce que je quitte _____
Je suis _____ parce que je quitte _____
Je suis _____ parce que je quitte _____

j'aime = I like
je n'aime pas = I don't like
j'adore = I adore
je déteste = I hate
je quitte = I am leaving
il y a = there is/are

la guerre = war
les soldats = soldiers
les bombes = bombs
les fusils = guns
le bruit = noise

ma maison = my house
ma famille = my family
mes amis = my friends
mes animaux = my pets
mon école = my school
ma ville = my town

### La Guerre

**Masculine**

content = happy
fâché = angry
triste = sad
nerveux = nervous
terrifié = terrified
surpris = surprised
choqué = shocked

**Feminine**

contente = happy
fâchée = angry
triste = sad
nerveuse = nervous
terrifiée = terrified
surprise = surprised
choquée = shocked

et = and
mais = but
parce que = because
aussi = also
donc = therefore
quand = when

Je m'appelle Lucas.
J'ai 11 ans.
Aujourd'hui je suis triste parce que je quitte ma famille.
Je suis triste parce que j'adore mes amis.
J'aime ma ville.
Je suis terrifié parce que je déteste les soldats.
Je suis triste parce que je mon chien
Je suis excité parce que je quitte les bombes

Je m'appelle Evie.
J'ai 10 ans.
Aujourd'hui je suis terrifiée.
Je quitte ma famille.

J'aime ma ville.
Je n'aime pas la guerre.

## PROGRESSION IN WRITING

Below are some examples of how writing might progress across key stage 2.

The year 3 example demonstrates a child copywriting familiar words and phrases in the context of writing a toy advertisement for Christmas.

In the year 4 example, the child had a simple writing frame to complete choosing an animal and a colour from a list and using the simple connective *et* (and). A second sentence to further describe the animal was added, using a familiar sentence structure from year 3. This writing was in the context of a topic on tropical rainforests.

The year 5 example, linked to an international football event, required children to find key facts about their favourite footballer and use the technical vocabulary they had learnt in French to complete a profile of the player, using a writing frame. An extension task was to write about a different person.

The context for the year 6 writing was to write about a trip abroad using familiar language from previous topics (travel and weather) and knowledge about adjectival position. The phrases about animals and their movements were taught as discrete items of vocabulary, using flashcards.

Year 3

Year 4

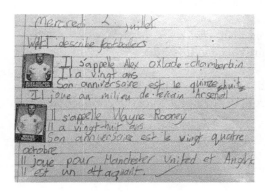

Year 5

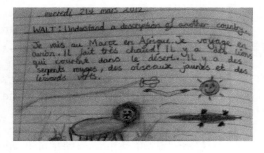

Year 6

### Recycling previously learnt language

As previously stated, progression can be achieved when children are given the opportunity to recycle and reuse language in a new context. For example, with relatively limited vocabulary and the ability to create simple sentences about wearing clothes and weather, the children could then learn to create a variety of longer sentences with the use of some connectives, for example: 'and', 'because' and 'therefore'. Using a vocabulary prompt sheet, the children could be challenged to create as many sentences as they can. This activity allows for natural differentiation by outcome. Lower-attaining children can continue to create and practise writing simple sentences while higher attainers will enjoy the challenge of creating extended and complex sentences in the new language. Early finishers could design a different chart or add two extra words to the existing chart to see how many more sentences could be made.

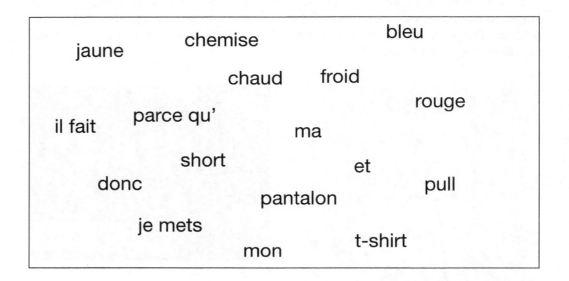

Some possible sentences are below:

> *Je mets mon pantalon parce qu'il fait froid*
> (I am putting on my trousers because it is cold).

> *Il fait chaud donc je mets mon T-shirt rouge*
> (It is hot therefore I am putting on my red T-shirt).

> *Je mets mon short et mon T-shirt parce qu'il fait chaud*
> (I am putting on my shorts and T-shirt because it is hot).

The task could be varied further by adding an even wider choice of nouns and adjectives. Greater challenge could come from a further choice of connectives (for example, 'when') and verb forms.

> *Quand il fait chaud, je porte mon short rouge*
> (When it is hot, I wear my red shorts).

## DICTIONARY SKILLS

Training children to use a bilingual dictionary when they are ready sets up good habits for the future. John Burdett, a Bristol teacher, taught this carefully and then created colourful tasks for children to do in pairs. Most involved a puzzle to be solved by looking up and matching words to pictures. For example, the task might be to find out, using a dictionary, what someone has in a shopping trolley. The children can then separate healthy or unhealthy foods.

The most basic thing for children to know is that there are two halves of a bilingual dictionary and that the new language comes at the front, with the English at the back. Children actually find this knowledge quite exciting! One little boy came into school, eagerly announcing that he had been given a dictionary for Christmas, adding, 'And do you know, it's got two halves!' Some dictionaries have blue lines along central pages to separate the two halves but, with others, it can help to demonstrate this by putting a ruler in the dictionary to separate the two sections.

Children also find it interesting that on a double page the word at the top of the left-hand page is the first word on the page, while the word at the top of the right-hand page is the last word on the page.

The following are some ideas to try once the children are ready:

- Sort a short list of words in the new language in alphabetical order.
- Put words beginning with the same letter in alphabetical order.
- From a mixture of English and French or Spanish words, get them to separate the two languages into columns, with the meaning in English alongside.
- Give children an unknown word, accompanied by three possible meanings. They can use the dictionary to find out the meaning.
- Talk about words with more than one meaning and teach children to select a suitable meaning when they look up a word.
- Give a situation (for example, packing a suitcase for going on holiday) and ask children to tick / circle five objects from a selection of words to put in the suitcase, using the dictionary, if necessary.
- Children are given a list of words – each with one letter missing – to check in the dictionary. The missing letters spell a new word.
- In order to do a word search in the new language, children are given a list of English words to look up the French / Spanish equivalents in the dictionary.
- Children match a list of grammatical abbreviations with the full words (for example, adj – adjective).

## IDEAS FOR EARLY FINISHERS

Dictionary activities are ideal for those children who complete their work early. Below are some further extension activities for early finishers:

- Select a card from a reading box containing short factual articles from magazines. This should include topics that tend to interest boys (football, fishing, cars). Some cards could have questions to answer, but it is important that some are just for enjoyment.
- Choose a 'spot the difference' puzzle, where two pictures have slight differences. Children can be encouraged to look up some of the vocabulary in a dictionary as they write a list of the differences they can see.

- Take a card with a long word written in the new language. Children have to copy it and see how many shorter words they can find hidden within the word. Dictionaries are allowed.
- Make up a word search for the class on the current topic.
- Create a warm-up activity for the class by using a dictionary to choose words out of order; the class sequences them correctly.
- Look at story books in the new language.
- Create a poem for the current topic area.
- Look at books or information cards about the culture of the country whose language they are learning.

In conclusion, reading and writing in the new language can be supported in much the same way as children are supported in learning to read and write in their first language. Teaching includes:

- practising decoding skills (using picture clues and prior learning to help gist comprehension);
- making physical responses, mimes and actions;
- focusing on phonics and spelling practice;
- making human sentences;
- looking at sentence structures – word order, grammar and word classes; and
- using models and writing frames to support writing.

# 4 Sounds different: phonics

## RATIONALE

It is not enough just to know the meaning of a word and understand how to put it into a sentence. It is also important to be able to recognise the sounds within a word so that it can be understood when heard, reproduced by the speaker by being read and spoken aloud accurately, and written correctly from memory. It is therefore essential to develop children's knowledge and understanding of phonology in the new language that they are learning. The key stage 2 languages programmes of study (DfE, 2013) expect children to

> explore the patterns and sounds of the new language . . . make links between the spelling, sound and meaning of words . . . develop accurate pronunciation when they are speaking and reading aloud . . . [and] write phrases from memory.

Therefore, a systematic approach to the teaching of phonics should be carefully planned so that children learn to recognise the new sounds and make the necessary phoneme–grapheme link to be able to read aloud with increasingly accurate pronunciation and begin to use their phonetic knowledge to help them spell.

## THE ALPHABET

Children enjoy being able to spell their own names in another language and they enjoy guessing the name of the person whose name is being spelt aloud. Knowing the alphabet is also very useful if the teacher spells a word for them to write.

The alphabet can easily be taught through chanting the letter names. Songs work well, too, for learning the order and names of the letters. In particular, the familiar army marching call and response song works very well for practising the French alphabet. There are also various children's songs, readily available on YouTube in several languages, which are helpful in teaching the letter names.

The 'Touch the board' activity, in 'The magic of games' chapter, is a good way to practise the more difficult letters in the French alphabet, which are: e, g, h, i, j, q, r, u, x, y.

Comparing and contrasting letter sounds with the English alphabet will help children to identify those that require different pronunciation. For example, the 'g' and 'j' are pronounced g (zhay) and j (zhee) in French. They will also come across additional or different letters in Spanish, such as *ñ*, *ch* and *ll*.

## THE FRENCH ALPHABET

| Letter | Pronunciation | Letter | Pronunciation |
|--------|---------------|--------|---------------|
| A | ah | N | en |
| B | bay | O | oh |
| C | say | P | pay |
| D | day | Q | koo |
| E | euh | R | air |
| F | eff | S | ess |
| G | zhay | T | tay |
| H | ahsh | U | oo |
| I | ee | V | vay |
| J | zhee | W | doo-bluh-vay |
| K | kah | X | eex |
| L | el | Y | ee-grek |
| M | em | Z | zed |

When the children are studying a new language where the alphabet is similar to the English alphabet, it is helpful to show them that the letters can be sorted into vowels and consonants. They also need to be aware that an accent can change the pronunciation of the letter.

A fun exercise in French is to practise each vowel by chanting each letter and phrase in turn. The teacher can model and then the children copy line by line.

> a e é i o u
> aaaa – Un pain au chocolat,
> eéeé – Je l'ai mangé,
> iiii – Je l'ai fini,
> oooo – Je suis si gros,
> uuuu – Je n'en veux plus!

### The vowel train

This is an activity to further practise the pronunciation of vowels. It is essentially a speaking and listening activity, although text cards are involved. Children are given a card with one of the vowels written on it. They must walk round the room saying their vowel while keeping the cards hidden. The aim is for all the vowels to group together and form a train going round the room. Ideally, the children need to put the carriages of the train in order, too. The activity can then progress to word cards containing the different sounds, for example: *chat, je, mangé, fini, gros, plus*. For additional practice, this could progress to other words containing the sounds. In doing this, the children can apply their knowledge to unfamiliar words, thus developing their ability to read aloud with increasingly accurate pronunciation.

In lower key stage 2 the children can gradually be introduced to other new sounds from common letter combinations. As each lesson/unit of work is planned, it makes sense to identify key sounds in the topic vocabulary being taught, since it is this language that the teacher will want the children to use in speaking, reading and writing.

## FRENCH SOUNDS TO COVER

| Simple vowel sounds | Other vowel combinations | Nasal sounds | Tricky consonants | Silent letters |
|---|---|---|---|---|
| a / à<br>e<br>o<br>é / er / ez<br>è / ê<br>i / y<br>is / u | ai/ei<br>oi<br>ou<br>ui<br>au/eau | an/en<br>ain/in<br>ien<br>ion<br>on<br>un | ç<br>ch<br>ll<br>j<br>r | ent (at the end of words)<br>th<br>h<br>consonants at the ends of words such as: s,p,t |

A helpful rule when it comes to pronouncing consonants at the ends of words is to remember to be CaReFuL. If the final consonant appears in the word 'careful' then it is generally pronounced but otherwise remains silent. While this is a helpful rule, there are some exceptions: *huit, mars, août* have final letters pronounced; *six* and *dix* also follow this rule, although the 'x' is silent when they precede another word (*six pommes*).

## MEMORY HOOKS

It is helpful to use familiar words as memory hooks for remembering sound–spelling links. As children learn each new sound, they can be encouraged to make word lists in the back of their exercise books or on classroom wall posters, to which they can add other words with similar sounds. If, for example, the topic in French is animals and they have learnt the word for cat (*chat*) they could have a picture of a cat and stick other words that have the French *ch* sound, perhaps on Post-it notes. A homework task could be to find words used in English that have the 'ch' spelling but the French pronunciation (chalet, chef, champagne, Charlotte, machine).

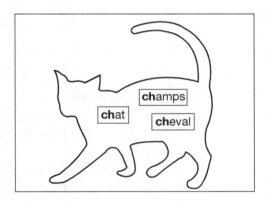

In French the days of the week and numbers contain several vowel combinations and other common phoneme–grapheme representations that can be useful as memory hooks for these different sounds.

| Days of the week | Numbers |
|---|---|
| lundi<br>mardi<br>mercredi<br>jeudi<br>vendredi<br>samedi<br>dimanche | 1. un<br>2. deux<br>3. trois<br>4. quatre<br>5. cinq<br>6. six<br>7. sept<br>8. huit<br>9. neuf<br>10. dix<br>11. onze<br>12. douze |

## Liaison

Liaison (the carrying over of the final sound from one word to the initial sound of the following word) is very important for making spoken French sound smooth. The following letters (*d, n, s, t, x, z*) are usually silent at the end of a word but can be sounded when they are followed by a vowel (*a, e, i, o, u* and *y*) or a silent *h*. Example: *les animaux, dans un camping, il est au café*. An important exception to this rule is the word *et* (and), where the *t* is never sounded.

## Sounds French/Spanish or English?

Another way to raise awareness of the different ways in which sounds are pronounced in the target language is to have a poster of two famous people (one English and one from the country where the target language is spoken) with a speech bubble coming from each. Post-it notes with the letter combinations written on them can be added to each speech bubble and the children can practise saying them as if they were each character – thus applying their knowledge of English phonics and the phonics for the target language.

## TONGUE-TWISTERS

These are an excellent way of practising sounds and can be set as a challenge to a class/group or individual children.

### French

> *Les chaussettes de l'archiduchesse, sont-elles sèches? Archi-sèches!*
> Are the socks of the archduchess dry? Extra dry!

> *Trois tortues trottaient sur un trottoir très étroit.*
> Three tortoises trotted along a very narrow pavement.

> *Cinq chiens chassent six chats.*
> Five dogs chase six cats.

### Spanish

> *A mí me mima mi mamá.*
> My mother is miming to me.

> *Tres tristes tigres comían trigo en un trigal.*
> Three sad tigers were eating wheat in a wheatfield.

## PHONICS GAMES AND ACTIVITIES

Initially, it is important for the children to listen and identify the new sounds. Songs, poems and rhymes are helpful here. At this stage the children are not concerned with seeing the written representation. They just need to make a non-verbal response when they hear the sound. There are a variety of ways in which they can be asked to do this: pass a teddy or other object from one to another (around a circle or table group)/stand up/sit down/take a step around the room/touch head/tap nose. Later, when the sound–spelling link needs to be taught, a game can involve passing a picture of an object with the sound written on it. For example, if practising the *oi* sound, a cut-out croissant could be used as the object is passed from one person to the next.

### Grapheme spotter activities

Once the children are familiar with the sound, they can spot the grapheme representation. Many traditional song texts are good for this activity, lending themselves to highlighting different graphemes. Some are recommended in the 'Hitting the right note' chapter.

www.momes.net is a useful website for stories, poems and rhymes which could be helpful texts for grapheme work. For example, see below the French text for 'The little red hen', which is used for sounds: *ou / é / er*.

### Sound buttons

Children have boards divided into columns, with a space at the top to write the grapheme being practised, together with a red button symbol, which could be a red circle drawn with a marker pen. For instance, if focusing on differentiating nasal sounds in French, there would be three columns with the headings: *un*, *in* and *on* and three red circles for buttons next to each sound. The teacher calls out one of the phonemes at random, whereupon the children pretend to press the correct button. Older children could be asked to keep a tally chart.

| ● | ● | ● |
|:---:|:---:|:---:|
| un | in | on |

The children can write the phoneme they hear in the correct column. As a further development, the teacher could read a word containing one of the phonemes for the children to write it in the appropriate column (*mon / ton / son / salon / brun / lundi / lapin / jardin*).

### Sound stations

Cards containing the sounds children are learning to read (for example, *un*, *in* and *on*) are placed round the room. Each child is given a card with a word on it. The children take it in turns to say the word on their card and place it at the correct sound station.

**First or second?**

Children listen to two words or short phrases and are then asked to identify which one contained a particular sound. They vote for either the first or the second and can be asked to put up either one or both thumbs to indicate their choice. It is particularly helpful for the children to be shown the words/phrases afterwards, so that they can see the written sound. This sort of activity works very well in PowerPoint. After listening and then seeing the words or phrases as they are read once more, the children can practise reading other familiar and unfamiliar words containing the same sound. This might also include reading rhymes and tongue-twisters. For example, if children were focusing on the *oi* sound in French, they could use the excellent French counting rhyme:

> *Une oie* (one goose)
>
> *Deux oies* (two geese)
>
> *Trois oies* (three geese)
>
> *Quatre oies* (four geese)
>
> *Cinq oies* (five geese)
>
> *Six oies* (six geese)
>
> *Sept oies* (seven geese)
>
> *C'est toi* (it's you)

The children will gradually build up their knowledge of sounds but will need regular practice to consolidate their learning. There are many games that can be played to revise several sounds at one time. See the suggestions below.

**Finger dance mat**

Children work in pairs, taking turns. The first child touches a square and says the grapheme. The partner repeats the first child's grapheme and adds another. It is important that they touch the squares in the correct order each time while chanting the graphemes. The aim is to build as long a sequence as possible. Squares can be revisited more than once. A familiar word containing the sound is added to each square as a helpful pronunciation reminder.

SPY SCHOOL - phonics

| ien | in | ai |
| --- | --- | --- |
| chien | lapin | J'ai..ans |
| on | je | oi |
| cochon | | poisson |
| elle | eu | au |
| belle | bleu | oiseau |

## Round the circle

Graphemes written on cards are placed face down on the floor/on chairs arranged in a circle. The children dance round the room/chairs until the music stops. They pick up a card and practise reading and saying the sound. The teacher chooses several children to say their sound and invites children to think of words they know, which contain that sound.

## 'We will rock you' lesson starter

With the children's help, a grid displayed on the whiteboard can be filled with known graphemes and sung to the tune of 'We will rock you'. This makes an entertaining warm-up to a lesson. The last two graphemes in each line need to be repeated. The one below is an example. The children can also be asked to vary speed and volume in order to create additional challenge and interest.

| ou | on | ou | on | eau | ch |
|----|----|----|----|-----|----|
| un | oi | un | oi | in | in |
| eu | en | eu | en | au | oi |
| ou | on | ou | on | eau | ch |

## Phonic families (card game)

This is based on the traditional card game, in which players try to acquire phonic family sets of picture cards. All the cards are dealt as equally as possible. Play starts by the first player (usually on the dealer's left) asking for a certain card. The player must already hold one of that family and asks just one other player. If the other player does not have the card, it is then their turn to ask. If they do have the card, they have to pass it to the first player, who can ask again. As players make sets of four, they place them face down and the winner is the first player to group all their cards into sets.

The game can be adapted for any level of phonic knowledge. It could be played using alternative grapheme representations for the sounds. In French, as in English, there are different ways of writing the same sound; this is shown in the table below. However, unlike English, each grapheme is always consistent in the way in which it is pronounced. This is also true of Spanish.

The grid on the next page can be used to create a French phonic families game. The aim of the game is to collect four different-coloured cards (red, blue, yellow and green) for the sound represented by each column. To make the card attractive, a small picture could be added, illustrating a word containing that sound.

We would suggest a total of twenty-four cards representing the six sounds grouped into four colour families. The six sounds being practised could be written on the board to remind children what they should be asking for.

To collect the whole *an/en* family, a child would have to collect the following cards:

- *an rouge*
- *an bleu*
- *an jaune*
- *an vert.*

It is also a good idea to teach the children to ask for the cards in the target language.

> *Est-ce que tu as le 'an' rouge?* or *As-tu le 'an' rouge?*
> (Have you got the red 'an'?)

| an | au | in | oi | é | ou |
|----|----|----|----|----|----|
| en | eau | yn | ois | ez | |
| | o | | | er | |

The game can be simplified for a younger age group where fewer sounds have been learned. It could be played as a paired game with only four families (*an/en, au, oi, ou*).

## Phonic lotto – Loto phonique

A photocopiable master for this game is included at the end of the chapter. For a class set, the teacher needs to:

- photocopy each of the pages of lotto cards three times, on card (this will provide thirty-six cards);
- cut out individual lotto cards;
- photocopy the word grid three times, on card (this will provide 120 words); and
- cut up the word grids, putting the words in an envelope.
- It is worth laminating the cards to make the resource more durable.

The rules of play are that:

- each child is dealt a lotto card; alternatively, a pair could share two cards and work together;
- the teacher picks a small card from the envelope and reads the word;
- the first child to recognise that s/he has the grapheme for that word on their card must raise a hand, without calling out;
- the teacher chooses the first child s/he sees;
- that child must call/spell the correct phoneme to win and place the word card over the grapheme;
- the winner is the person who covers all four graphemes on his/her card and calls out 'loto'.

Alternatively, teachers could make a different version of the game, which works equally well. Phonemes are called by the teacher and the children have to identify any word on their lotto card that contains the sound.

In this chapter, we have discussed reasons for children to learn the alphabet in the new language, given ideas for practising new sounds, looked at memory hooks and suggested a range of phonic games and activities for further practice.

**LOTTO CARDS**

| in | on | ou | on | e | an |
|----|----|----|----|----|----|
| en | au | oi | in | ez | eu |
| an | in | en | ez | eau | in |
| ou | oi | o | oi | in | oi |

| eau | ez | ou | en | on | e |
|-----|----|----|----|----|----|
| in | e | ez | oi | ez | oi |
| ez | eau | on | eu | en | en |
| on | an | au | eau | an | eau |

**WORD GRID**

| intelligent | toi | janvier | regardez |
|-------------|-----|---------|----------|
| oiseau | deux | pingouin | jardin |
| éléphant | cinq | mois | école |
| enfant | moi | beau | écoutez |
| stylo | jeudi | bateau | bonbon |
| trousse | dimanche | marchez | danse |
| crayon | rouge | café | coucou |
| jaune | lapin | château | tout |
| vendredi | serpent | sautez | consonne |
| singe | poisson | cinéma | vous |

# 5 Fun with grammar

## RATIONALE

It is generally recognised that if primary children become familiar with grammatical terminology and looking in detail at how words and sentences are formed, this will have the following advantages in that

- they will understand and use their own language better;
- confidence in reading familiar and new words will be improved;
- awareness of word derivation can help with spelling and expand vocabulary;
- children's thinking skills will also be developed; and
- they will be able to build on this knowledge, both at secondary level and in the future.

The key stage 2 languages programmes of study (DfE, 2013) state that children should

> understand basic grammar appropriate to the language being studied,
> including (where relevant): feminine, masculine and neuter forms and
> the conjugation of high-frequency verbs; key features and patterns of
> the language; how to apply these, for instance, to build sentences; and
> how these differ from or are similar to English.

Children are also required to 'describe people, places, things and actions both orally and in writing'. In order to achieve this, sentence structure, punctuation and grammar need to be taught consistently and progressively across key stage 2.

In the primary school children are discovering so much about English, learning the different purposes of sentences – whether a sentence is a statement, a question, a command or an exclamation. They also learn to differentiate word classes and how to use different sentence starters as well as using a variety of sentence structures.

Teachers cannot assume that children understand the conventions of punctuation and sentence structure in the new language. As one child said: 'I know that we have sentences in English, but I didn't realise they have sentences in French as well!'

Meeting the same grammatical terms and developing an understanding of grammar in another language should enhance their knowledge and understanding in English. This chapter sets out ideas that can be used across key stage 2 to build progression in children's use of language.

## PUNCTUATION

It is important to encourage children to use the correct punctuation in the new language.

For example, an important difference between English and other European languages, such as French, Spanish or Italian, is that the days of the week and months start with an upper case letter in English and a lower case in the other languages. German, like English, takes an upper case letter. Indeed, in German all nouns have an upper case letter, whatever their position in the sentence.

If learning Spanish, children will be fascinated by the inverted punctuation at the start of questions and exclamations. The teacher can explain that the Spanish believe that questions and exclamations have to be contained between two question or exclamation marks. As a link with ICT, children also need to know how to find the inverted question and exclamation mark by selecting 'Insert symbol'. They could be given some words to type and practise finding the correct symbols. This could be linked to using different fonts, font sizes and colours for effect, as in the example below:

In French, when looking at story books, the children will be interested to see that when a new person starts speaking in a conversation it is indicated with a dash (–).

Another punctuation mark useful to compare in French and English is the apostrophe. In lower key stage 2 children should know that in English the apostrophe is used for two reasons: omission and possession. In French, the apostrophe for omission exists but is used for a different purpose – to make words easier to pronounce (*parce qu'il / elle*). The *e* at the end of *parce que* is dropped in order to make the liaison smoother. There is no use of the apostrophe in French to show possession; instead, they use *le chat de Pierre* (literally, the cat of Peter, meaning Peter's cat).

## ACCENTS

Children are fascinated by the accents found in words in other languages. It is good to arouse children's curiosity about accents. If there are any children with English as an additional language (EAL) in the class, it may be worth asking if they have an accent in their written name and how it alters the sound. Children need to understand that *a* and *à* and *e*, *é* and *è* are all different keys on a French keypad because they represent different sounds, while in Spanish the same applies to n and ñ. An accent (over an *á*, *í* or *ó*) is to put emphasis on the letter. Refer to the 'Sounds different' chapter for ways to practise these sounds.

Let us take the French accents as an example. Since this knowledge will help greatly with pronunciation, it is worth taking time to let children practise the sounds é and è.

Finding words they already know, such as *école* (school) and *éléphant* (elephant), or *père* (father) and *frère* (brother) will help.

The teacher could also train the children's ear by reading four sounds, of which three are similar and one is different (example: *é é è é*). The children need to raise their hand to say which number is different or even put a tick on a pre-prepared chart. They find it amusing when the teacher reads words as if they merely have an *e* (uh) sound – for example *éléphant* without the accents.

Children need to know that sometimes accents are used to differentiate meaning – for instance, *a*, as in *il a* (he has), is different from *à Paris* (in/to Paris).

The circumflex always arouses children's interest. They enjoy knowing that in old French there used to be an s in some words instead of a circumflex and English has kept many of these words, such as island (*île*), hostel (*hôtel*), forest (*forêt*). Children may already know *âge*, where the circumflex lengthens the vowel.

The c cedilla (*ç*) is also much easier for the children to understand if the class investigate words containing it to see whether they can make up a rule about the vowel following it and what it does to the sound. Examples: *garçon, voici, comme ça, parce que*. They can be led to see that the cedilla softens a *c* when followed by *a, o* or *u*, but that it is not needed when *i* or *e* follow the *c*.

At upper key stage 2, the teacher could see whether pairs of children can spot the missing accents in a known text.

In Spanish, the most commonly used accent is over a vowel and puts the stress on that letter or syllable: *á é í ó ú* (Examples: *Sofía, té, ratón*). Its direction never changes. The other accent, the tilde over the n (*ñ*), changes the sound of n to 'enyeh'.

## ARTICLES AND NOUNS

Nouns in French and Spanish are determined as masculine or feminine by the article. It is therefore important that we teach children nouns with the correct form of the article. As previously mentioned, whether the teacher chooses to use 'the' or 'a' before the noun will depend on the type of sentences that s/he wishes the children to create. It is therefore important to spend time thinking about this when planning lessons.

Inevitably, a lot of the earlier teaching at KS2 will start with articles and nouns. The concept of nouns being a particular gender is very different for English children. A good lead-in is to draw and reinforce their understanding of English nouns that have different words for masculine and feminine jobs (e.g. actor/actress). The children find the whole concept of gender fascinating and are generally very capable of grasping the concept from the start. It is very helpful for visual learners if the teacher uses coded flashcards to signify gender.

Any colour or symbol can be used as long as the children know what each represents. Remember that red may be difficult for any child who is colour-blind and might be best used in conjunction with another symbol (statistics show that one in ten boys is colour-blind). Some teachers also use different walls of the classroom to separate masculine and feminine nouns, when displaying them for children to learn.

Another technique for teaching and embedding children's knowledge of gender is to link the nouns with people. This can be done in French by introducing the nouns as *Monsieur/Madame*. For example: *Monsieur Chocolat/Madame Pizza*. They could even be pulled from different bags – one representing girls and the other representing boys.

An idea that came from children in one class was to connect proudly with each noun that was taught. They instigated a competition to compete for different nouns. For example, the boys called out: 'We've got chocolate' while the girls replied: 'We've got pizza'. This can be a fun approach and can even be taken a stage further with class posters to display the masculine and feminine words.

Another memorable way to teach gender is to tell stories about the nouns. The nouns either form part of the girl's story or the boy's story, as suggested by Biriotti (1999). This can be adapted to any topic, and to other languages such as Spanish or Italian. The authors have themselves used this idea in a unit of work on food and adapted the stories for that purpose. Their example is below:

### The girl's story

A little girl was very hungry. She ate a *pizza*. Later, she was still hungry so she went into the kitchen and ate an *ice cream*. She topped it with an *apple*, a *banana* and a *strawberry*. Then she watched television.

### The boy's story

A boy went to a shop and bought a *cake*. At playtime he saw his friend and swapped the cake for a *sweet* and a *biscuit*. He put them in his bag to eat on the bus.

After each story, ask the children to work in pairs to recall the items that were mentioned. Then invite a volunteer to come to the front of the class, with back to the board, and say the words in the order they occur in the story. As each one is remembered, the teacher can say them in the new language, emphasising their gender, and recording each on the board, as shown in the French example below.

| The boy's story | The girl's story |
|---|---|
| un bonbon | une pizza |
| un gâteau | une pomme |
| un biscuit | une banane |
| | une fraise |
| | une glace |

It is useful to build in opportunities to sort and group words that the children have learnt. There are many ways of focusing their attention on sorting masculine and feminine nouns. The children can be asked to sort cards physically in two houses (these can literally be houses made very cheaply and easily from A4 paper boxes with slits cut in the top, for posting cards through, or by using coloured hoops to represent each house). Packs of picture flashcards can be shuffled and one by one drawn for the children to categorise. Individual children can also be asked to decide where to place the card. If unsure, they can be invited to ask the class to vote (likening it to 'ask the audience', as in the well-known TV game show). This physical sorting activity can be checked by counting the number of correctly placed cards, in the target language, at the end of the activity. Alternatively, the same sorting exercise can be done on the interactive whiteboard (further details are given in the 'Technology tools' chapter).

A good way to ensure an individual response from each child is to issue double-sided cards with masculine and feminine articles on each side (*un/une* for French, *un/una* for Spanish). As the children hear nouns called by the teacher or look at a flashcard representing a noun, they hold up the correct article. This is also a very visual form of assessment for the class teacher. It is worth making the point that using the correct grammatical terminology here will greatly help the children since they are currently expected to identify all word classes, including articles, in national tests at the end of key stage 2.

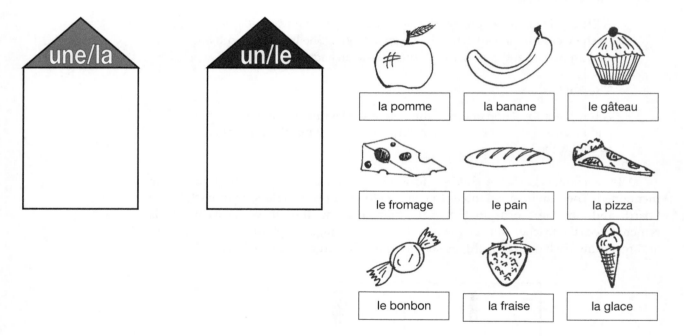

Giving children lists of nouns (familiar or unfamiliar) written with the article and asking them to group them in two houses (masculine and feminine) will help embed knowledge of the masculine and feminine articles, in addition to providing an opportunity to look for patterns in the words.

Suffixes can give clues as to the gender of nouns. In French there are certain endings that are typically masculine and others that are typically feminine. Typical masculine endings are: *oir, ou, eau*. Typical feminine endings are : *ette, ée, ion*. Generally, but not always, feminine nouns end in an *e*.

In Spanish, words ending in *-o, -aje* and *-or* are generally masculine. Those ending in *-a, -dad, -ción and -sión* are usually feminine.

## Plurals

A good way of teaching plurals is to show pictures of nouns with the word next to them and the number as a digit.

| 1 lapin | 2 lapins | 3 lapins |

The children can spot any changes in spelling patterns between a singular item and plural items. They can note any similarities and differences with English. In French they will be able to see that an *s* is often added to a word to make it plural but, unlike English, the *s* is silent. It is helpful for the children to practise reading these words aloud and to make a physical striking gesture with their hand to remind them that the consonant at the end is silent.

A game that allows children to practise this further is 'treasure hunt', based on the traditional game of 'battleships'. This is illustrated in 'The magic of games' chapter but would need to be adapted to show numbers on the horizontal axis and singular/plural nouns (for example *chat(s)*, *chien(s)*, *lapin(s)*) on the vertical axis.

## ADJECTIVES

At lower KS2, it is very useful to teach the place of common adjectives, such as 'big' and 'small' (*grand* and *petit*) before the noun. Children get a lot of practice and enjoyment from working with these. Teachers sometimes refer to the big red 'e', which makes an adjective feminine.

Children do not readily accept that many adjectives follow the noun in other European languages. To help them, one idea might be to imagine a space alien, who has landed in the classroom and turned everything green (Biriotti, 1999). The children can be asked to creep around the room in pairs, describing as many objects as they can in English but using the French word order (for example, a table green, a chair green).

### Adjectival endings and examples

It is also helpful to build phrases in French using nouns, represented by objects or picture flash-cards, and colour adjectives, represented by small coloured cubes or coloured squares of card. The nouns can be drawn from one bag and the adjectives from another; this works well as a 'pass the parcel' game. The children then hold or place the objects in the correct order and practise chorusing the French phrase, for example, *un cochon rouge* (a red pig).

After the children understand the rules for adjectival position, they can practise making the correct adjectival agreement. If they have already met the big red 'e' being added in French to make *grand* or *petit* feminine (*grande, petite*), that will be the foundation upon which to build for making all adjectives agree with the noun they describe.

An excellent story that models adjectival agreement and position is: 'Va-t'en Grand Monstre Vert', which is available in several languages. It is a story about a scary monster where the different body parts are described in terms of size and colour. It is ideal for any topic teaching body parts and adjectives. Linking with the theme of the book, grammatical knowledge of adjectival position and agreement could be practised by asking the children to create their own monsters and describe them.

Writing a poem based on a fantasy or magical country can also be an engaging writing opportunity, allowing children to practise adjectival position with colours. They could be asked to describe unusually coloured animals or objects that can be found there, as shown below:

> *Au pays magique*
>
> *Il y a*
>
> *Un cheval bleu*
>
> *Un cochon rouge*
>
> *Une poule jaune et*
>
> *Une vache verte.*

## PREPOSITIONS

Because of the nature of prepositions, active learning is easy to devise when teaching them. Children can do actions for each preposition (*sur* (on), *sous* (under), *dans* (in), *devant* (in front of), *derrière* (behind)) and then show understanding by getting into the appropriate position. The basic prepositions can also be taught by singing them while performing hand actions representing each position.

| **Preposition song (Tune of London Bridge)** | |
| --- | --- |
| • Sur, sous, dans | • On, under, in |
| • Devant derrière | • In front, behind |
| x3 | x3 |
| • Sur, sous, dans | • On, under, in |
| • Devant derrière | • In front, behind |
| • A côté de | • Next to |

As the different prepositions are sung, the teacher keeps one hand flat and stationary, while the other is placed on top, underneath, in between the fingers of, in front of and behind the stationary hand. At the end of the song, both hands are brought together so that the thumbs touch. Initially, the children can be invited to join in with the hand actions, while the teacher sings. Before they are confident with the words, they can sing slowly. The song can be sung at a faster tempo once the actions and words have been mastered.

A mischievous animal is also another way of bringing prepositions to life in the classroom. For example, the teacher could describe the location of a naughty frog that is jumping on, under, in front of and behind various objects.

| | |
|---|---|
| *Où est la grenouille?* | (Where is the frog?) |
| *Sur la table* | (on the table) |
| *Sous la table* | (under the table). |

The children can be invited to bring in their own toys from home and make up a story about them. They can work in pairs and take photographs of their toys in different places; this can then make an attractive class book. The example below is one page of a class book entitled: 'Our toys' day out!'

Où est Léo?

Léo est dans l'arbre

## POSSESSIVE ADJECTIVES

These are easy to teach in the context of family. To avoid complex family situations, this vocabulary might be best taught through a fictional one, for example, a well-known cartoon family. The children can be asked to imagine that they are now a member of the chosen family. In this way, they can learn how to refer to all the different family members: *mon père, ma mère, mon frère, ma soeur,* and so on. The possessive adjectives can be practised to the well-known tune of 'Frère Jacques'.

| | |
|---|---|
| *Mon, ma, mes* | ×2 |
| *Ton, ta, tes* | ×2 |
| *Son, sa, ses* | ×2 |
| *Mon, ma, mes* | ×2 |

To help the children learn the correct form of the possessive adjective, the teacher calls out a noun and the children reply with the correct possessive adjective. Alternatively, they can sort nouns into different groups – *mon, ma, mes* (maybe designating different coloured hoops for each adjective).

The children can also act out a pretend argument in pairs over an object on their table:

| | |
|---|---|
| *C'est ma gomme!* | (It's my rubber!) |
| *Non, c'est ma gomme!* | (No, it's my rubber!) |
| *Non, c'est ma gomme. C'est à moi!* | (No, it's my rubber. It's mine!) |
| *Mais non, c'est à moi!* | (But no, it's mine!) |
| *C'est ma gomme!* | (It's my rubber!) |
| *D'accord. Voilà!* | (OK. There you are!) |

## Snakes and ladders – Le jeu de l'oie

A grammatical version of the game 'snakes and ladders', created by Mary Higgins and Jo Peach, is excellent for practising possessive adjectives: *mon, ma, mes* with the correct noun. Counters are needed, but no dice. A set of cards with pictures of family members or clothing is prepared and placed face down in a pile. In turn, children take a picture card. If child A turns over a picture of a father (*père*), s/he puts the counter on the first correct matching word (*mon*) that s/he finds on the bottom row, starting from *Départ*. Child B then turns over a different picture and searches for the first correct possessive adjective on the board. There are snakes and ladders, as always, to make the game more exciting.

A variant on this game is for practising *du/de la/de l'/des* with the correct noun instead. Children turn over pictures of food and match to the squares. For example, if a child turns over a picture of soup (*soupe*), they move the counter on the board to the first square labelled *de la*, and so on.

There are photocopiable masters for both games of 'snakes and ladders' at the end of the chapter.

## CONNECTIVES

As in English, the most useful connective to teach first is *et* (and) to help children extend their sentences. *Voici un chat et un chien* (Here are a cat and a dog). *Je voudrais un café et un biscuit* (I would like a coffee and a biscuit) with a sentence ending would be even better *s'il vous plaît!* (please). At a later stage, using *aussi* (also), *mais* (but), *parce que* (because) and *donc* (therefore) enables children to build both compound and complex sentences.

## Making sentences

In English, children are taught to think about writing sentences and how we can create different sentence structures (simple, compound, complex, compound-complex). They are expected to think of a variety of ways in which to start their sentences. Similarly, we want children to learn to construct sentences in their new language. Most topics will begin with the teaching of some relevant nouns, but teaching a large number of nouns on their own is not helpful. From the start it is useful to teach a basic sentence structure and show children how they can make simple sentences in the new language. As mentioned above, helpful sentence openers might include: it is; here is/are; there is/are. These will enable children to make simple statements.

The next step would be to think about ways of getting children to extend their sentences, first by the use of 'and' (they pull two things out of a bag and link them: *Voici une pomme et une banane*). The 'I went to market and I bought . . . ' game is also adaptable to a theme park or other topics.

## Phrases magiques

This activity has been adapted from an original by Pete Jones of Pine Ridge secondary school, Ontario. The aim is for each child in a pair to make up a sentence by starting with *Je* and moving in any direction (either horizontally, vertically or diagonally) via touching squares until they reach a full stop. If they exit at a square marked with stars, they score two points for the sentence, otherwise one point.

| mange | *****Je***** | chante | bien |
|--------|--------------|--------|------|
| au | vais | joue | au |
| cinéma | avec | à | football |
| *****amis***** | mon | avec | Paris |
| deux | mes | frère | *****Paul***** |

Progression to third person verb forms will allow them to talk about a friend: *Il aime les pommes / Elle aime les bananes*. Equally, they can talk using *on* for 'we'; this is typically French and much easier to use at this stage. The verb ending is spelt in the same way as the third person singular: *on aime* (we like).

## QUESTION FORMS

Children should be given opportunities in the new language to listen for and recognise question forms. It is also important that they have practice in asking questions – this is an essential skill for taking part in conversations. As the key stage 2 languages programmes of study (DfE, 2013) state, children should 'engage in conversations, ask and answer questions, express opinions and respond to those of others, seek clarification and help'.

In French, there are three ways to form a question. The first, as in English, is through rising intonation, which turns a statement into a question. Second, the opener *Est-ce que* can be used. A third way is through inversion of subject and verb (*Es-tu?* Are you?).

Children can be taught to listen for rising intonation at the end of a sentence, which is the most basic way of asking a question. They can then imitate the model. An enjoyable activity is for the teacher to prepare a set of cards on a topic. For example, the teacher could use famous people to practise names. The children are familiar with the people on the cards and can make statements such as: *Je m'appelle Harry Potter*. Next, a child is chosen to be the guesser. One of the cards is selected and the child must guess which one, using rising intonation: *Je m'appelle James Bond?* This can initially be done as a whole class activity, which can be extended to pair work, giving plenty of opportunity for all children to ask and answer questions.

The use of *est-ce que* is very common in French. For example, it can be used for asking permission: *Est-ce que je peux . . . ?* (Can I . . . ?). It can be introduced at any stage, although some teachers may prefer to introduce it after the children have practised rising intonation. Children can remember the sound by pronouncing the word 'ask' in a very posh voice. A positive statement such as *Tu aimes le fromage* (You like cheese) is made into a question by prefixing it with the word 'ask', pronounced as explained above.

Inversion of the verb and subject (*As-tu?*) can be introduced as a sound through its similarity with a sneeze: 'Atchoo!' Children love this!

## MAKING SENTENCES NEGATIVE

Using the negative form means that children can construct twice as many sentences! Although this is more complicated in French than in other European languages (in that there are two parts *ne . . . pas*), children can have great fun learning to use the negative if it is taught in an imaginative way.

### Teaching ideas

One idea is to introduce *ne* and *pas* as the 'negative twins'. This can be demonstrated with children in a line, representing different words of a sentence. The naughty twins come in, one each side, to jostle the verb. As an extension to the above whole class teaching activity, children can practise creating positive sentences in small groups by arranging themselves into a line, each holding a word card in the correct position to form a sentence. Meanwhile, two children, appointed to be *ne* and *pas*, take their cards and attempt to gatecrash one of the sentences, as soon as it is formed. Their aim, as the naughty twins, is to destroy the positive sentences by positioning themselves around the verb. Once they have successfully made each sentence negative, the children in the group write it on mini-whiteboards. As a class, they look at the negative sentences that have been created.

### Activities to practise positive and negative sentences

#### Passez le sac!

A variation on the traditional party game, 'pass the parcel', used by the Qualifications and Curriculum Authority (2000), involves two bags being passed round the class to music, one containing verbs, the other nouns. When the music stops, the two children who are holding the bags each draw a card. If the two match, the class chants them as a positive sentence; if not, they make the sentence negative.

#### Matching cards

Noun and verb cards are separated into two piles. Children are invited to pick a card from each pile. If they match, a positive sentence is created. For example, in the context of tropical rainforests, the children describe the movements made by the different animals: *le serpent glisse, le lion bondit, le poisson nage, le singe se balance, le perroquet vole, la grenouille saute, la fourmi marche*, before going on to create negative sentences. If the two cards turned over are *le perroquet* and *vole*, the sentence is: *Oui, le perroquet vole*; (Yes, the parrot flies); if the two cards turned over are *le perroquet* and *nage*, the sentence is: *Non, le perroquet ne nage pas* (No, the parrot does not swim). It is agreed in advance that the animals can only perform one action.

#### Venn diagrams

As a wider range of nouns and verbs are introduced, children could group the animals according to the various ways in which they move, the food they eat and their habitats. A helpful way of doing this is to use a Venn diagram to help children create positive and negative sentences. This activity also provides scope for children to create extended sentences using the conjunctions *et* (and) and *mais* (but). This has the advantage of using/reinforcing mathematical skills.

## CONJUGATING VERBS

As the children progress further and have a deeper understanding of pronouns and verb forms in English, they can be taught to use other parts of verbs and to conjugate some high frequency verbs in the new language that they are learning.

Two of the most common high frequency verbs 'to have' and 'to be' are irregular verbs in French. One way of introducing the different parts of these verbs is through catchy songs in which all parts of the present tense of *avoir* and *être* can be chanted. The 'Pink Panther' tune is particularly good for *avoir* (*j'ai, tu as, il a/elle a/on a, nous avons, vous avez, ils ont/elles ont*) or *être* (*je suis, tu es, il est/elle est/on est, nous sommes, vous êtes, ils sont/elles sont*). The verb *être* also works well to the *EastEnders* tune. Other high frequency verbs that the children might encounter are: *porter* (to carry/wear) and *aller* (to go). There are also some excellent ideas, including using ten cool verbs, in the book *Le Français par le rythme et la musique de Monsieur* (Hicks, 2005).

### Using dice

Dice activities are good for practising different parts of a verb, for example, *aller* (to go). Children have cards with a numbered list of subject pronouns. A dice is thrown and the children say the correct conjugation of the verb to match the subject pronoun.

1 Je
2 Tu
3 Il/elle/on
4 Nous
5 Vous
6 Ils/elles

For example, if a 3 is thrown, representing *il/elle*, the child would say *il va/elle va* or *on va*. Higher attainers might finish the sentence with a phrase, for example *elle va à la disco/elle va à la plage* (She is going to the disco/to the beach).

### Spinners

Hexagonal cardboard spinners can be used to help the children practise the present tense. Children work in pairs with two spinners. One has subject pronouns (*je, tu, il/elle/on, nous, vous, ils/elles*) and the other some common –*er* infinitives, such as *danser, manger, jouer, acheter, marcher, monter*. Alternatively, the spinner could be used to practise high frequency irregular verbs, such as *avoir* and *être*. Sharpened matchsticks are used through a hole to spin the spinners. If one lands on '*tu*' and the other on '*être*', the partner has to say '*tu es*' to get a point. For differentiation, some children could create their own spinner, with other verbs.

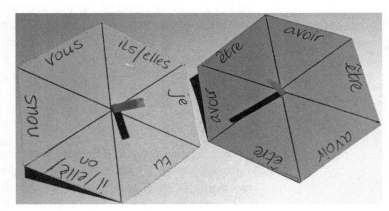

## Beanbag relay

Some verb forms in different tenses can be taught. They could be taught as discrete vocabulary items, which the children will learn and accept. The verb *avoir* can also be practised by setting up teams with equal numbers (six or eight) standing in the hall. The person at the front says *J'ai* and passes the beanbag over his or her head. The second says *Tu as*, passing the beanbag through his or her legs, and so on through the team. The last person runs to the front, and starts the verb again as s/he passes the beanbag.

## Past tense

It is important to choose commonly used verbs which will give the children more opportunities to recycle known language in new contexts. For example these verbs would be useful in describing a daily routine or a holiday: *j'ai mangé* (I ate / I have eaten), *j'ai bu* (I drank / I have drunk), *j'ai joué* (I played / I have played). At this stage, in upper key stage 2, children can learn these as discrete items of vocabulary. Poetry would be a good way to practise using the past tense, for instance, linked to a healthy eating topic. The children could write poems about food / exercise, for example, *j'ai mangé, j'ai bu, j'ai joué* in the form of a diary, using the days of the week:

> *Lundi, j'ai mangé une pomme*
> (On Monday I ate an apple).
>
> *Mardi, j'ai mangé deux bananes*
> (On Tuesday I ate two bananas).

In lower key stage 2, children understand that stories are generally written in the past tense. They learn spelling rules about the suffix '-ed' being added to make verbs past tense. They also learn that not all verbs are regular and therefore do not follow the same pattern. By the time the children are in upper Key Stage 2 they should have a good understanding of verb tenses in English and therefore be in a position to understand that all languages need different tenses to communicate more precisely.

## Future tense

There are further similarities between some languages in forming a basic future tense with the present tense of 'to go' and the infinitive, for example, *Je vais manger* (I am going to eat). A diary is also an excellent way of practising this structure: *Lundi, je vais jouer au cricket* (On Monday, I am going to play cricket).

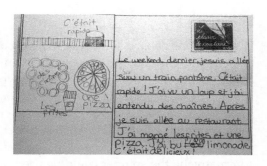

## Imperfect tense

Having learned *Il y a* and *C'est* as sentence starters in lower key stage 2, teachers could introduce discretely taught phrases: *Il y avait* . . . (There was / were . . . ) and *C'était* . . . (It was . . . ) in upper key stage 2. This allows children to write simple descriptions of days out, such as a school trip, visit to a zoo or, as in the examples on the right, an outing to a theme park.

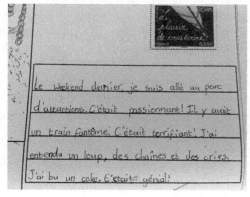

**ADVERBS**

These can provide active and enjoyable practice activities. We suggest that the children may already have met *rapidement* and *lentement* in classroom instructions. Children in lower key stage 2 will be familiar with adverbs in literacy and will therefore be aware that they tell us more about a verb. They will be developing their understanding of the different types of adverbs and their purpose. When the children are shown the written words for adverbs, they can spot the pattern in their spelling (often the *-ment* suffix in French and *-mente* in Spanish). This can be likened to the '-ly' ending in English. However, just as in English we have 'fast', there are exceptions in French and Spanish, too (for example, *vite* (fast) in French).

Adverbs can be practised through using a parachute in the school hall. See the section on parachute games and activities in the chapter 'The magic of games'. Other PE warm-up activities could include asking children to move round the hall in different ways: *Marchez lentement comme une tortue* (Walk slowly like a tortoise). *Courez rapidement comme un guépard* (Run fast like a cheetah).

At upper KS2, children can be taught other adverbs, such as *fièrement*, *timidement*, *modestement*; these can be incorporated into games where a child acts out an adverb on a card and the others guess.

The children can also be asked to compare the position of adverbs expressing how the action is performed. In French adverbs generally come immediately after the verb, whereas in English this is not always the case. For example, in French one would say: *Je joue bien au football*, but in English: 'I play football well'.

**Adverbial clauses**

As the children deepen their understanding in English of the type and purpose of adverbs, it is logical to mirror this learning in the new language, the two being mutually supportive. If the children are writing about their home town and they have learned how to name landmarks and form simple sentences using *Il y a* as a sentence starter: *Il y a une cathédrale*, they can be taught to extend their sentence, using an adverbial opener such as: *A Bristol, il y a* . . ./*Dans ma ville, il y a* . . . (In Bristol there is . . ./In my town there is . . . ). When familiar with the spoken structure, children can create a short text, using an adverbial opener, as shown in the year 4 child's poem on the right.

## WORD CLASSES

Children can be asked to identify the different word classes by miming an action for each type of word class they hear/see. They could be asked to do the following actions:

- one hand on their head for a pronoun/noun;
- two hands on their head for a proper noun;
- make a funny face for an adjective;
- link arms together for a connective;
- run on the spot for a verb;
- run on the spot and make an addition sign with their two index fingers for an adverb.

### 'Jigsawing'

Asking the children to jigsaw words together to form sentences with familiar vocabulary (from a song/story or topic sentences) helps to develop their knowledge and understanding of sentence structure. In addition, words can be colour-coded according to their word classes, which helps children understand that different languages do not all construct sentences in the same way. *Je porte une robe jaune* literally means 'I am wearing a dress yellow' because the adjective follows the noun in French.

This works well as a human sentence activity (in which individual children hold the cards and arrange themselves in order) or as a group activity with several sets of word cards to make different sentences. Children can work together, arranging the cards within a specified time limit, before moving to another table with a new set of cards to arrange. Children can also be asked to record the finished sentences on mini-whiteboards or in exercise books.

In conclusion, children need grammatical knowledge to be successful in both spoken and written language. Although sometimes thought of as a dry subject, many children find it fascinating; they are naturally curious about language and can quickly become language detectives, comparing and contrasting both languages. In this chapter we have tried to enliven the teaching of grammar through mime and action, games and activities.

**PM 5.1** *LE JEU DE L' OIE* **PRACTISING** *MON, MA, MES*

| | | | | | | | | |
|---|---|---|---|---|---|---|---|---|
| 91 ma | 90 mes | 71 mon | 70 mes | 51 ma mes | 50 ma | 31 mon | 11 mon | 10 mes |
| 92 mon | 89 ma | 72 mes | 69 ma | 52 | 49 mon | 32 ma | 12 mes | 9 ma |
| 93 ma | 88 mon | 73 ma | 68 mes | 53 mon | 48 ma | 33 mon | 28 mes | 8 mon |
| 94 mes | 87 ma | 67 ma | 54 ma | 47 mes | 34 ma | 27 ma | 13 ma | 7 mes |
| 95 mon | 86 mon | 75 mes | 66 ma | 55 mon | 46 mon | 35 mes | 15 ma | 14 mon | 5 mon |
| 96 ma | 84 mes | 76 mon | 65 mes | 56 ma | 45 ma | 36 ma | 26 mes | 16 mes | |
| 97 mes | 77 ma | 57 mon | 44 mon | 37 mon | 25 mon | 24 mes | 17 ma | 4 mes |
| 98 mon | 83 mes | 78 mon | 63 ma | 58 | 38 mon | 18 mes | 3 ma | |
| 99 ma | 82 mon | 79 mes | 59 mon | 42 ma | 39 | 22 mon | 19 mon | 2 mon |
| 100 Fin | 81 ma | 80 ma | 61 ma | 60 mes | 41 mes | 40 ma | 21 mes | 20 ma | 1 Départ |

© 2017, *The Really Useful Primary Languages Book*, J. Wright and A. Taylor, Routledge

## PM 5.2  *LE JEU DE L'OIE* PRACTISING *DU, DE LA, DE L', DES*

| | | | | | | | | | |
|---|---|---|---|---|---|---|---|---|---|
| 91 du | 90 des | 71 des | 70 de l' | 51 de la | 50 des | 31 de la | 30 du | 11 de la | 10 du |
| 92 de la | 89 de l' | 72 de la | 69 du | 52 des | 49 de l' | 32 des | 29 des | 12 des | 9 de l' |
| 93 des | 88 du | 73 du | 68 de la | 53 du | 48 de l' | 33 des | 28 de la | 13 de l' | 8 des |
| 94 de l' | 87 des | 74 des | 67 | 54 de l' | 47 du | 34 du | 27 de l' | 14 du | 7 de la |
| 95 du | 86 de la | 75 du | 66 de la | 55 de la | 46 des | 35 de la | 26 du | 15 des | 6 |
| 96 de la | 85 | 76 de la | 65 du | 56 du | 45 de l' | 36 de l' | 25 des | 16 de la | 5 des |
| 97 des | 84 de l' | 77 de l' | 64 des | 57 des | 44 du | 37 des | 24 de l' | 17 de l' | 4 de l' |
| 98 du | 83 des | 78 des | 63 des | 58 de l' | 43 | 38 du | 23 | 18 de la | 3 du |
| 99 de la | 82 de la | 79 du | 62 de l' | 59 | 42 du | 39 | 22 de la | 19 du | 2 de la |
| 100 Fin | 81 du | 80 de la | 61 des | 60 du | 41 des | 40 de l' | 21 du | 20 des | 1 Départ |

# 6 Allons-y! ¡Sí sí sí!
# Using target language

## RATIONALE

Speaking in the target language

- encourages children to listen attentively and increases their concentration;
- maximises opportunities for children to assimilate new language;
- gives them the chance to use the language for a real purpose;
- helps children understand their own language better through making comparisons;
- reinforces skills and concepts, learnt in the mother tongue, through playing games;
- encourages children to express themselves through mime and gesture; and
- gives them a door into a new culture through learning rhymes, songs, poems and stories.

KS2 children are good mimics of any new language we introduce into our teaching. They enjoy saying words and phrases in another language and can quickly make them part of their repertoire, through careful repetition and by having fun.

The atmosphere of the primary classroom where languages are being taught needs to be relaxed and stress-free. We realise that there can be a great difference between the foreign language skills of teachers but, for the non-specialist, it is perfectly possible to encourage spontaneous use of the target language by children through repetition and using words in context. There are many materials available where the teacher can hear accurate pronunciation and thus build up confidence. The authors have mentioned some in the chapter 'A helping hand'.

At the end of this chapter, some useful target language has been included in French and Spanish and the book's accompanying eResource provides sound files recorded by native speakers.

## ADDRESSING TEACHERS' CONCERNS

Let us consider some of the issues that teachers think will arise if they use more target language in the classroom:

- *My own French/Spanish is not good enough for me to model it!*

  — If you limit what you need to say and ensure that it is as good as it can be through checking, or using published materials, this can really help. Actions and mime are very important, too.

- *But I am afraid of losing the attention of the children if they can't understand me.*

  — If you use short phrases and a lot of gestures, and keep the phrases in context, then the children will quickly become involved. They understand much more than you imagine!

- *Will I have to speak in the target language all lesson? Can I use English at all?*
  - Of course there are times when you need to use English – to explain something, or to reassure children. Try to build up to using more French/Spanish gradually – you could even make it a class competition to see how long you can use the target language in a lesson.

- *But what if there is a major problem in the classroom?*
  - Just use English. You could use French or Spanish for minor problems.

- *Maybe I could just say everything in two languages?*
  - If you translate everything as you go, children stop concentrating because there is no point in trying to understand.

- *So how can I encourage the children to use the target language?*
  - By modelling it yourself;
  - by setting up situations where they will want/need to use it (for instance, the teacher deliberately makes a mistake in writing the date and waits for a child to say: *Erreur, Madame/Monsieur*;
  - by giving praise and some tangible rewards when children use it spontaneously (for example, children could be awarded stars or stickers to put on a class chart);
  - by setting up a graffiti wall where the children can add words and phrases as they learn them.

## STARTING OUT: WHAT TARGET LANGUAGE SHOULD I TEACH?

We would suggest that certain phrases are introduced in year 3 and gradually added to in subsequent years. However, all teachers and classes differ and teachers should feel free to introduce as much target language as the children can cope with. It is usually far more than teachers think! All the examples referred to here in French are also in Spanish at the end of the chapter.

Apart from greetings and praise words, the first really useful type of language is classroom instructions. These can be modelled with images and/or gestures and practised through a well-known game such as 'Simon says' (in French, *Jacques a dit*, or Spanish, *Simón dice*). The children mime what the teacher says only when they hear the words *Jacques a dit* or *Simón dice* before the instructions.

Consider using the following instructions, which can be learned passively, although children really enjoy giving commands as well:

> *Entrez! ¡Entrad!*
>
> *Ecoutez! ¡Escuchad!*
>
> *Répétez! ¡Repetid!*
>
> *Regardez! ¡Mirad!*
>
> *Levez-vous!* (*Lève-toi!* to one child) *¡Levantaos!* (*¡Levántate!*)
>
> *Asseyez-vous!* (*Assieds-toi!* to one child) *¡Sentaos!* (*¡Siéntate!*)

If a child notices the difference (i.e. *Assieds-toi!* rather than *Asseyez-vous!*) this would be a good moment to explain that in French (and Spanish) there are two ways of saying 'you', one which is singular, more informal and used for people you know and one which is plural or used to be polite, to an adult, for example, a teacher.

Children can also be encouraged to put their hands up by saying:

*Levez le doigt!*    (for younger children)

*Levez la main!*    (for older children)

Praise words are easily understood and children love hearing that they have done something well. It's probably a good idea to use a range of praise words so that when *Excellent!* is used they will know that it is really good.

Other commands can be added once the basic ones are known. Children will enjoy using these in the *Jacques a dit / Simón dice* game.

Greetings are easy for children to understand. When used as part of the class routine, they will quickly get into the habit of using them to the teacher and, if encouraged, to each other.

The language of games is really useful for children to use and has been included at the end of the chapter, together with other categories mentioned above.

## ENCOURAGING THE CHILDREN TO SOUND MORE FRENCH/SPANISH

As already stated earlier, children are good mimics of language and this applies equally to the way in which they speak. If we can encourage them to adopt French/Spanish gestures in the primary languages classroom, then these will become embedded and make them sound and appear much more authentic at later key stages and on visits abroad.

### Gesture

Try to use video clips to let the younger children see how French or Spanish people use gesture as a natural part of speaking.

### Hesitation phrases

If we can enable and encourage children as early as year 3 to have fun with a number of phrases which they can use when not sure what to say next, then this will increase authenticity. Great fun can be had with little phrases such as *euh; eh bien; bon, ben; et alors; et voilà* (in Spanish, *pues; eh*) at the start of sentences to give thinking time. Once they are known, the teacher could even take an easy phrase like *Je m'appelle Robert* and, using a stopwatch, see which child can make the phrase last longest by putting in hesitation words at the start of the sentence. Children could also sit opposite each other in pairs to practise the phrases. This is much better than having children continue to use 'um', as they would in English.

## GROUP TALK

If children are taught key phrases at KS2, and encouraged to practise them in a group context, they will eventually be able to hold spontaneous discussions with others in the class.

Once children can say some of the phrases, a stimulus is needed in the form of a picture or an object that can produce a variety of opinions and feelings, leading to a lively exchange of views. This could be a photograph of a celebrity, an emotive picture, or a selection of toys (real/catalogue/pictures from a website in the target language).

The following chart of phrases, adapted by Liz Black from the original by Greg Horton, could be built up over time and eventually used for group talk. The additional chart beneath provides further phrases for expressing feelings.

### KS2 group talk – key phrases

| Exchanging and responding to basic likes and dislikes (French) | Learning outcomes Children can | Exchanging and responding to basic likes and dislikes (Spanish) |
|---|---|---|
| C'est . . .<br>Ce n'est pas . . .<br>J'aime<br>J'adore<br>Je déteste + parce que c'est/<br>ce n'est pas . . .<br>Je n'aime pas<br>Je n'aime pas ça | State simple likes and dislikes and give a reason | Es<br>No es<br>Me gusta<br>Me gusta mucho<br>Odio . . . porque es/no es<br>No me gusta |
| Et toi?<br>Tu aimes (+ raised intonation)?<br>Est-ce que tu aimes . . . ?<br>Que penses-tu de . . . ?<br>Qu'est-ce que tu en penses?<br>Quelle est ton opinion? | Ask a friend if s/he likes something | ¿Y tú?<br>¿A te ti gusta . . . ?<br>¿ Qué piensas de . . . ? |
| Oui, moi aussi<br>(Je suis) d'accord<br>Et oui, moi aussi<br>Ah oui, c'est vrai<br>Moi non<br>Non, pas moi<br>Tu rigoles!<br>(Je ne suis) pas d'accord | Express simple (dis)agreement | Sí, yo también<br>De acuerdo<br>Ah sí, yo también<br>Yo no<br>No, yo no |
| A mon avis, c'est/ce n'est pas . . .<br>Je pense que c'est/ce n'est pas . . .<br>Je trouve . . . | Express simple opinions | Para mí, . . . |
| Je ne sais pas, moi<br>Bof, peut-être | Express uncertainty Maybe | No sé<br>Quizá |

## OTHER USEFUL FRENCH/SPANISH TARGET LANGUAGE

### The language of games

| A toi | Your turn | Te toca a ti |
|---|---|---|
| A moi | My turn | Me toca a mí |
| J'ai gagné | I've won | He ganado |
| Tu triches | You're cheating | ¡Tramposo!/¡Tramposa! |
| Avance! | Go forward | ¡Avanza! |
| Recule! | Go back | ¡Retrocede! |
| Choisis! | Choose | ¡Elige! |

### Language for children to use

| Présent/présente | Present | Presente |
|---|---|---|
| Absent/absente | Absent | Ausente |
| Oui | Yes | Sí |
| Non | No | No |
| S'il te plaît/s'il vous plaît | Please | Por favor |
| Merci | Thank you | Gracias |
| (J'ai un) problème | I've a problem | (Tengo un) problema |
| J'ai fini | I've finished | He terminado |
| Pardon | Sorry | Perdón |
| Je ne comprends pas | I don't understand | No entiendo |
| Est-ce que je peux . . . aller aux toilettes/aller au bureau/boire de l'eau? | Can I . . . go to the toilet/go to the office/get a drink of water? | ¿Puedo ir . . . al baño/a la oficina/a coger agua? |
| Je n'ai pas de . . . | I haven't got a . . . | No tengo . . . |

### Guardian of the phrase

When phrases are introduced and in the process of being mastered, the teacher can observe children who are quick to remember and appoint them as guardians of a particular phrase. This means that they are the people whom others consult when they can't remember the phrase.

### Expressing feelings

| Je suis . . . | I am . . . | Estoy . . . |
|---|---|---|
| content/contente | happy | contento/contenta |
| triste | sad | triste |
| surpris/surprise | surprised | sorprendido/sorprendida |
| choqué/choquée | shocked | escandalizado/escandalizada |
| fâché/fâchée | angry | enojado/enojada |
| terrifié/terrifiée | terrified | aterrorizado/aterrorizada |
| **Je me sens . . .** | **I feel . . .** | **Siento . . .** |

## Classroom objects

| le tableau (interactif) | the board (IWB) | la pizarra (interactiva) |
|---|---|---|
| la porte | the door | la puerta |
| la fenêtre | the window | la ventana |
| un stylo | a pen | un boli |
| un crayon | a pencil | un lápiz |
| un crayon de couleur | a coloured pencil | un lápiz de color |
| un feutre | a felt-tipped pen | un rotulador |
| un taille-crayon | a pencil sharpener | un sacapuntas |
| un cahier | an exercise book | un cuaderno |
| un livre | a book | un libro |
| du papier/une feuille | paper/worksheet | un papel |
| une trousse | a pencil case | un estuche |
| une gomme | a rubber | una goma |
| une règle | a ruler | una regla |
| un mini-tableau | a mini-whiteboard | una mini pizarra |
| des ciseaux | scissors | unas tijeras |

## The language of grammar and literacy

| un mot | a word | una palabra |
|---|---|---|
| une phrase | a sentence | una frase |
| un consonne | a consonant | una consonante |
| une voyelle | a vowel | una vocal |
| un syllabe | a syllable | una sílaba |
| un nom | a noun | un nombre |
| un nom propre | a proper noun (e.g. name) | un nombre propio |
| un adjectif | an adjective | un adjetivo |
| un verbe | a verb | un verbo |
| un adverbe | an adverb | un adverbio |
| un point | a full stop | un punto |
| une virgule | a comma | una coma |
| point d'interrogation | a question mark | un signo de interrogación |
| point d'exclamation | an exclamation mark | un signo de exclamación |

## Teacher language: greetings and leave-takings

| Bonjour | Hello | ¡Buenos días! |
|---|---|---|
| Salut | Hello (more casual) | ¡Hola! |
| Je vais faire l'appel | I'll take the register | Voy a pasar lista |
| Il/elle est malade? | Is he/she ill? | ¿Está enfermo/enferma? |
| Qui mange à la cantine? | Who's having school lunch? | ¿Quién come en el colegio? |
| Bon appétit! | Enjoy your meal! | ¡Que aproveche! |
| Au revoir | Goodbye | Adiós |
| A bientôt | See you soon | Hasta pronto |
| A demain | See you tomorrow | Hasta mañana |
| Bon week-end! | Have a good weekend! | Buen fin de semana |
| Bonnes vacances! | Have a good holiday! | Buenas vacaciones |
| Calmez-vous! | Quieten down! | ¡Calmaos! |
| Calme-toi! | Calm down! (one child) | ¡Cálmate! |
| Un peu de silence! | Silence! | ¡Silencio! |
| Arrêtez de bavarder! | Stop chatting (class) | ¡Dejad de charlar! |
| Arrête de bavarder! | Stop chatting (one child) | ¡Deja de charlar! |
| En rang | Get in line | En fila |
| En cercle | Get into a circle | En un círculo |
| Passe-moi . . . | Pass me . . . | Pásame . . . |
| Posez vos crayons/stylos | Put your pencils/pens down | Los lápices/bolis en la mesa |
| Mettez-vous par deux | In pairs | En parejas |
| Trouve un(e) partenaire | Find a partner | Busca una pareja |
| Rangez vos affaires | Put your things away | Recoged |

## Introducing the lesson objective and transitions

| Aujourd'hui on va écouter/parler/lire/écrire/jouer/chanter/faire    Today | we're going to listen/speak/read/write/play/sing/make | Hoy vamos a escuchar/hablar/leer/escribir/jugar/cantar/hacer |
|---|---|---|
| Maintenant . . . | Now . . . | Ahora . . . |
| Quelque chose de différent | Something different | Algo diferente |

## Praise

| Oui, c'est ça/c'est correct | Yes, that's right | ¡Sí, eso es!/es correcto |
|---|---|---|
| Bien | Good | Bien |
| Bravo | Well done | Bien hecho |
| Très bien | Very good | Muy bien |
| Génial | Nice/very good | Genial |
| Super | Very good | Estupendo |
| Fantastique | Fantastic | Fantástico |
| Excellent | Excellent | Excelente |

## Language for use in physical education (PE)

| marchez | walk | caminad |
|---|---|---|
| courez | run | corred |
| sautez | jump | saltad |
| sautez à cloche-pied | hop | saltad a la pata coja |
| marchez sur la pointe des pieds | walk on tiptoe | caminad de puntillas |
| c'est parti | start | adelante |
| arrêtez | stop | parad |
| changez de direction | change direction | cambiad de dirección |
| lentement | slowly | despacio |
| rapidement/vite | fast | rápido |
| doucement | quietly | sin hacer ruido |
| prudemment | carefully | con cuidado |

## Language for use in maths

| et/plus | plus | más |
|---|---|---|
| moins | minus | menos |
| multiplié par | multiplied by | multiplicado por |
| divisé par | divided by | dividido por |
| égal | equals | igual |
| combien de faces? | how many faces? | ¿cuántas caras? |
| combien de surfaces? | how many surfaces? | ¿cuántas superficies? |
| combien de contours? | how many edges? | ¿cuántas aristas? |
| combien d'angles? | how many angles? | ¿cuántos ángulos? |
| combien d'arêtes? | how many corners? | ¿cuántas esquinas? |
| combien de sommets? | how many vertices? | ¿cuántos vértices? |

Teachers can develop their use of target language in the classroom by choosing an area from the list to work on each week. There is a chart at the end of this chapter which teachers can use as a record of the intended language to be used and the start date. Teachers might like to tick each star when their use of the target language is consistent. The areas to include are:

- greeting and saying goodbye to the children;
- praising them;
- giving them classroom instructions; and
- encouraging children who spontaneously use the target language.

In conclusion, this chapter has looked at the importance of using target language wherever possible. Children usually find it fun, and it demonstrates to them that language is real.

## PM 6.1 TARGET LANGUAGE CHART

I will use the target language for...

# 7 The magic of games

## RATIONALE

With few exceptions, games are universally enjoyed. They are certainly very much part of the learning experience in the primary classroom and effective for the following reasons:

- their repetitive nature is excellent for consolidating vocabulary;
- games often involve an element of chance, taking the pressure off an individual child to perform;
- they give scope for working individually, in pairs, in a small group or as a class;
- games give children the chance to try out the target language;
- and, last but not least, they are fun!

## USING LANGUAGE GAMES AND ACTIVITIES

The chance element of many games is important in that it encourages children to take risks. Any answer is not seen as 'wrong' and since the game is non-threatening, it allows even the least confident of children to participate. For example, flashcard prediction and 'battleships' type games, both described later in this chapter, allow learners to use the language they know.

Games involving pictures (flashcards or images) provide a natural level of differentiation. A picture can allow children to respond with varying amounts of language at word, phrase or sentence level.

It is a good idea to refer to the games in the target language in that this provides a further opportunity for listening to French/Spanish. Names can easily be converted to any other language. Once the game is familiar, the children will be able to respond quickly without the need for explanation of the rules. Furthermore, the names are easy to reference in lesson planning, and it is also more fun to give names in the new language.

Games can be used:

- at the start of a lesson to revisit/recap previous learning;
- as a core part of main teaching to practise new vocabulary;
- as an assessment tool to review new learning (mini-plenary/plenary).

There are many tried and tested games, some traditional, some new, and the authors have included a variety of games for different situations. Many of them involve flashcards, which can be used to show pictures or words, depending on the skill being practised. The more they are played, the more both teachers and children alike find ways to make subtle changes, adapt and reuse them. This keeps them fresh and can give ownership of the game to particular individuals. However, in order to help teachers get started, a few useful games have been listed under the skills headings and directly linked to those specifically mentioned in the 'Developing skills' chapter. Others have been grouped according to their type or category.

## LISTENING COMPREHENSION

### Stations – Stations

Pictures are placed round the room to represent stations. Children run to one of the 'stations'. The teacher or a child randomly selects a picture/word from a bag and calls it out. All children at that station are out and they then become the helpers. The game continues and those who are out point to the station they think is correct the next time, to help the others. They can also volunteer to call out the next station.

### Touch the board – *Touchez le tableau!*

Put the children in two teams, with a fly swat for each team. Name the team (numbers/colours/letters/animals). Pictures of the vocabulary being practised are displayed in front of the class (either physical flashcards or on the interactive whiteboard). One member from each team comes to the board and when the teacher calls an item of vocabulary, both children compete to swat it first. Count the points in the target language afterwards.

### Fruit salad – *Salade de fruits*

The children sit in a circle on chairs. They are given a French name (a fruit or an animal). Several have the same name. When their name is called, they must stand up and change places. The teacher has a collective noun (for example, salade de fruits, transport, sport) when everyone must change places.

## SPEAKING GAMES

### Orchestra – *Orchestre*

Display the picture flashcards for the vocabulary being practised. One person is chosen to be the conductor; his/her job it is to point to the cards in turn and conduct the class. As the class chant the vocabulary, the conductor can signal for the pitch/tempo/volume to be changed. This game provides an opportunity to repeat and practise the words as a whole group, while having fun.

### Kim's game – *Qu'est-ce qui manque?*

This traditional party game works really well in PowerPoint, using images of the vocabulary taught, although the game can also be played with physical picture flashcards and Blu-Tack. Children have to say which picture has been removed. They can be encouraged to 'call out' in order for them to gain confidence at having a go because they feel less self-conscious when several are speaking at the same time.

### Prediction – *Prédiction*

Six items of topic vocabulary are hidden. These could be on the whiteboard, or physical pictures covered up. Each one is given a number/colour/letter. The aim is to predict all six items correctly against the clock. This is a good game for quick revision of previously learned vocabulary.

## PRONUNCIATION AND INTONATION

### Secret signaller – *Code secret*

The children sit in a circle. A volunteer, the detective, goes out of the room. While s/he is out, someone is chosen to be a signal giver (the signal might be tapping the nose, leaning on one arm, touching the head). When the detective comes back in, the children repeatedly chant the first phrase until the signal giver indicates that they should go on to the second phrase, and so on. The detective needs to watch carefully in order to discover the identity of the signal giver. It is usually best to have a time limit for each round.

### Noughts and crosses – *Morpion*

This can be played as a whole class, or in pairs. Words or phrases are displayed in a grid. Children have to pick a numbered square and read the text aloud. If correct, the team rereads it to earn a nought or a cross. The first team to have a line of three is the winner.

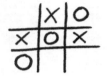

A variation is to give first letter clues, for example:

J_ p_ _ _ _ u_ p_ _ _ _ _ _ _
(*Je porte un pantalon*).

As an extension to practise reading, the game can be played with a display of phrases or sentences round the edge of the grid; the children link these to a specific number and hope they match. The teacher has a master plan!

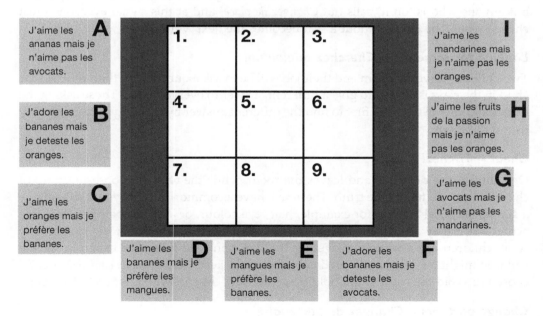

**A** J'aime les ananas mais je n'aime pas les avocats.

**B** J'adore les bananes mais je deteste les oranges.

**C** J'aime les oranges mais je préfère les bananes.

**D** J'aime les bananes mais je préfère les mangues.

**E** J'aime les mangues mais je préfère les bananes.

**F** J'adore les bananes mais je deteste les avocats.

**G** J'aime les avocats mais je n'aime pas les mandarines.

**H** J'aime les fruits de la passion mais je n'aime pas les oranges.

**I** J'aime les mandarines mais je n'aime pas les oranges.

| 1. | 2. | 3. |
| 4. | 5. | 6. |
| 7. | 8. | 9. |

### Beat the clock – *Contre la montre*

A person tries to read a list of words, phrases or text clearly and quickly so that others can understand before the time runs out.

## READING COMPREHENSION

### Pelmanism game – *Jeu de mémoire*

Sets of text and picture cards are placed face down on the table. Children take turns to reveal pairs of cards in the hope of finding a pair. In doing so, they practise reading the cards in the target language.

### Dominoes – *Dominos*

An adaptation of the traditional game but created as a set of rectangular cards, each of which shows a picture on one half and a piece of text on the other (the text and picture on a card do not match). The cards are shared between the children. The first person lays down a card and the others take turns to link one of their cards by creating a chain that has pictures correctly connected to the matching text.

## QUESTION AND ANSWER GAMES

Children need plenty of opportunities both to ask and answer questions. These games will provide valuable practice.

### Change places – *Changez de place!*

Children sit on chairs in a circle, except one who becomes the first volunteer. The volunteer then leaves the room and the teacher chooses three children to be 'on it'. The volunteer comes in and asks each child in turn a question. Most answer the question but anyone who is 'on it' calls out *Changez de place!* and at this signal everyone must change seats. The child without a seat becomes the next 'volunteer'.

### Looking for someone – *Cherchez quelqu'un!*

Two children leave the room and their job will be to ask a question on their return. One child in the class is chosen to give a different answer to everyone else. Those asking the question compete to be the first to find the different answer by asking questions quickly round the room.

### Cheat – *Trichez!*

One child is the detective and leaves the room, while the teacher chooses a group of children to avoid telling the truth. These will have a common link (they will either have a similar physical feature, for example, hair/eye colour, or agree to perform the same action when they answer the question). The detective must work out the reason why some children are avoiding answering the question truthfully. For example, all the children might be given a coloured cube and are asked: *C'est de quelle couleur?* A child chosen to avoid the truth might hold up a blue cube, but answer: *C'est vert* (It's green).

### Change partners – *Changez de partenaire!*

This game involves one group of children remaining stationary and the other group rotating.

They could sit in an inner and outer circle/horseshoe or two lines facing each other. One group practises asking the question, the other giving the answer. The teacher signals when it is time for the rotating group to move on one person. When everyone has practised their role, the two groups swap over.

### Start again – Recommencez!

A dialogue is prepared with alternative answers to each question. One person is chosen to leave the room while the class chooses which answer to each question will be correct. The person re-enters the room and the dialogue begins. The class asks the questions and the person chooses a reply. If it is correct, the dialogue continues, but, if incorrect, the class shouts *Recommencez!* and the conversation begins once more from the start. Every time an incorrect reply is given, the dialogue must begin again. This game can also be played in pairs.

### Letters – Lettres

Write a question(s) on coloured card(s) and some sample answers on differently coloured cards. Put children in groups of six and ask them to sit in a circle, leaving enough space to place the cards in the middle. These will serve as writing prompts. The children are given blank pieces of paper on which they write their letters or notes to each other. The aim is for the children to write, fold the paper over and deliver it to another child in the group. Everyone must receive just one letter or note. The recipients write a reply and papers are swapped again. They must not pass consecutively between the same two children. At the end the children could share some of their favourite questions and answers from their writing.

## WHOLE CLASS GAMES

### Repeat if it's true – Répétez si c'est vrai!

This is a game to practise listening and repetition. Children must repeat a statement if it is true. The teacher holds up a flashcard or object, or performs a gesture, making either a correct or incorrect statement in the target language to describe it. If both match, the children repeat it; if they do not match, the children must remain silent. Younger children can be asked to put their finger on their lips to reinforce the silence. For example, the teacher points to a picture of a dog, saying: *C'est un lapin* (It's a rabbit). Or the teacher crosses his/her arms, saying: *Levez la main!* (Put up your hand). The class can score a point by remaining silent at the correct times and the teacher gains a point if s/he catches the children out. This game can be turned into a Class versus Teacher competition.

### Tennis – Tennis

The teacher and whole class (or children working in pairs) take it in turns to 'bat' vocabulary items back and forth. The same language might be batted between partners in order to practise correct pronunciation, or items of vocabulary could be said in sequence, such as numbers, days of the week, months of the year or verbs. The game can be developed for asking and answering questions. For example, in a whole class setting, child A asks child B a question; child B then replies and asks child C a different question.

### Yes or no – Oui ou non

A series of flashcard pictures is displayed face up on the board or on the interactive whiteboard. Under each is a small card with a word on the back. All cards except one have the word *Non* and one has the word *Oui*. Children take turns to say the item of vocabulary on one of the cards before it is revealed. The child who finds the card with *Oui* wins a sticker.

## Whispering game – *Chuchotez!*

Each child is given a card with a picture or a word. They stand up and move round the room, whispering their words. The aim of the game is to find other people with the same word. This is a good game for grouping children together for other activities. Since the whispering game is quiet, it is good for children who are shy or feel less confident practising speaking on their own in front of the class.

## Keep it moving – *Allez!*

Cards or objects are given out to approximately a third of the class. In order to obtain an item, a child must ask or tell the child holding the item something in the target language. At that point, the card or object must be handed over immediately. The child who has handed over the item should then try to obtain another item. On the teacher's signal, everyone must freeze and those holding an item are awarded a point. Several rounds of the game can be played. Each child can only hold one item at any one time, and items cannot pass twice consecutively between the same two people. The value of this game is in giving children time to practise with different partners.

## Make a list – *Faites une liste!*

The traditional version of this game is 'I went to market and I bought . . . '; items are cumulatively added to the list as it is repeated over and over again by the class. Individual children can be chosen to add each new item or they can be drawn from a bag at random. The game can be played in smaller groups; this would allow for a greater degree of participation, with individual children repeating the sentence each time.

> *Dans mon panier, il y a une pomme*
> (In my basket, there is an apple).

> *Dans mon panier, il y a une pomme et une banane*
> ( . . . and a banana).

> *A la plage, j'ai vu un bateau*
> (At the beach, I saw a boat).

> *A la plage, j'ai vu un bateau et une mouette*
> ( . . . and a seagull).

## Eleven – Onze

Children stand behind their chairs. They count individually and consecutively round the class, until the child who has to say *onze* is out and sits down (e.g. child A might say 1, 2; child B 3, 4, 5; child C 6, 7; child D 8, 9, 10; child E 11). The winner is the last person standing.

## Follow me – Suivez-moi!

Use this game to practise whatever questions and answers have been taught in the new language. The teacher prepares cards that have the answer to a question, followed by a new question. Children listen carefully to see if the answer to a question is on their card. If it is, the child answers and then asks the question on his/her card. Example: *Deux plus deux?* A child with the right card would say *Quatre* and then ask his or her question.

### Walk the plank! – *Sur la planche*

This game is a version of 'hangman'. A plank from a pirate ship to the sea is drawn on the whiteboard. The teacher puts up dashes to represent a word in the new language and the class guess, letter by letter. For every letter that is wrong, a part of a body is drawn and if the class fails to guess the word before the person walking the plank is complete, s/he falls into the sea.

### Heads down, thumbs up – *La tête en bas, les pouces en l'air*

Children put their heads down and thumbs up. Four children representing animals, fruits or family members are 'on it' and hold an appropriate flashcard to show their identity. Each gently touches or squeezes the thumbs of one person. All children look up and the four who were touched must guess who touched them by naming the flashcard.

## PARTY GAMES

### Pass the parcel – *Le sac surprise*

Ask the children to sit in a circle. Put a few vocabulary items (pictures, objects or text cards) into a bag or box and play some music. While the music is playing, the children pass the bag/box round the circle. When the music stops, the class asks: *Qu'est-ce que c'est?* and the person holding the bag or box pulls out one of the items. The child or class names or reads it. This game can also be used for spelling words by removing a letter each time the music stops. The child whose turn it is can choose to speak on their own first for the class to repeat all together; alternatively, it could be agreed that the same child counts: *Un, deux, trois,* signalling that the whole class should chorus together.

### Musical chairs – *Chaises musicales*

Flashcards are placed upside down round the room on each child's chair. They circulate to music. Each time the music stops, children move to a different chair, turn over the card and practise the language with the nearest child.

## CIRCLE GAMES/ACTIVITIES

### Hot or cold? – *Chaud ou froid?*

A child goes out of the class and the others decide where to hide a flashcard. When the child comes back in, everyone chants the word quietly and then more loudly as the seeker approaches the hidden card. The game works well if children are sitting on chairs in a circle (one child sits on the card) but if this is not possible, the card can be hidden anywhere in the room. However, ensure that a small part of it is revealed, or a time limit imposed!

### Throw the ball – *Jetez le ballon!*

This is a good game for practising asking and answering questions. Children stand in a circle. The teacher or a pupil in the middle asks a question and throws a soft ball to someone in the circle, who replies and throws the ball back. Later the ball can be thrown from one to another round the circle as they ask and answer questions.

**TEAM GAMES/ACTIVITIES**

### Imagine – *Imaginez!*

When drilling new vocabulary, the teacher holds two flashcards with both hands behind his/her back and says: *Imaginez . . . c'est un . . . ou un . . . ?* (Imagine, is it a . . . or a . . . ?). Children are in two teams and someone from each team in turn is chosen by the teacher to guess which one will be revealed in his/her right hand. If correct, the teacher says: *Un point*. (The children always think the teacher is cheating but it is a surprise for the teacher as well when the card is revealed!) This game works particularly well with difficult items of vocabulary, which need to be practised a great deal. After a few turns, the teacher changes to two other flashcards.

### Who wins? – *Qui gagne?*

In this game, the teacher plays against the class. After introducing new vocabulary, the teacher drills the hardest four items by sitting down and hiding the images under the table, having shown the class the four possibilities. A child is chosen to guess which card has been selected. If the child is correct when the card is revealed, the teacher looks disappointed and puts it on the table, saying: *Un pour la classe* (One for the class). If the child is wrong, the teacher looks delighted and puts it on a different pile, saying: *Un pour moi!* (One for me!). When all four have been guessed, the teacher gives the score. Example: *trois pour la classe, un pour moi* (three for the class, one for me). A volunteer teacher is then chosen to repeat the game.

### Mexican wave – *La hola*

The teacher says a sentence and starts a Mexican wave round the room, either individually or in groups. When it is their turn, each person/group repeats the sentence, while doing a Mexican wave with their hands.

### Chinese whispers – *Le téléphone arabe*

This game is excellent for developing children's listening and speaking skills. Divide the class into teams arranged in a straight line, five or six in each team. At the front of the line there is a table with cards or objects. The teacher gives the first person in each team a word or phrase. For example, it might be: *Tengo dos conejos* (I have two rabbits). When the teacher signals to start, the person at the back whispers the vocabulary to the next person and so on down the line. The last person collects the corresponding card or object from the front; the first person to pick it up wins a point for the team.

### Sorry – *Pardon*

This is a good game for developing strategies to ask for help when something is unclear. A word or phrase is passed through the team. Each person must ask for the word or phrase to be repeated before they can, in turn, pass the word or phrase on. They can use the following for clarification: *pardon/encore/répétez, s'il vous plaît*.

### Rapido – *Rapidement*

A child from each team collects a word from the teacher. S/he must then go back to the group and make the object from Play-Doh/plasticine. As soon as someone in the team guesses the object, that person can go to the teacher, say the word and collect the next one.

### Pictionary – *Pictionary*

Similar to the game above but the child draws a picture to be guessed.

### Team bingo – *Loto en équipe*

Children are placed in teams of five or six and members are given French words (all teams have the same number of words in total). The teacher calls the English word or shows a picture and children holding the relevant cards sit down. The first team to have everyone sitting wins.

### What is it? – *C'est quoi?*

The children are put in teams. The teacher holds up a flashcard and the teams compete to win a point by someone on their team being the first person to stand up and give the answer. If the teacher holds up a picture card, the French word is given. If it is a word card, the English meaning is given. This game is good for revising new vocabulary.

### Treasure hunt – *La chasse au trésor*

This is a version of 'battleships' created on the interactive whiteboard. Small pictures of treasure chests can be placed at random on a grid; shapes are used to cover all the squares. The children play in teams and seek treasure which gives them points. Each team searches for treasure by saying the coordinates for the square where they think the treasure is hidden. The coordinates are labelled with vocabulary in the target language. This game also helps to reinforce the mathematical or geographical skill of reading coordinates (*x* before *y*).

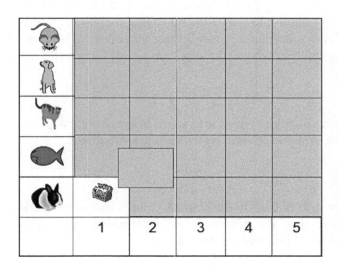

## Mrs Red – *Madame Rouge*

The aim of the game is to get children to listen for specific words or phrases in the target language. Children are placed in teams that sit in straight lines facing the teacher. The same vocabulary is allocated to members in each team who compete against each other. The teacher tells a story in English (or the target language) about Madame Rouge; this could be adapted to any context, such as a shopping trip or an outing to the zoo. The story includes the key vocabulary that the children need to listen for. When the children hear their words, they must stand up, run all the way round their team and back to their place. The first person to sit down wins a point for the team.

## PARTNER AND GROUP GAMES/ACTIVITIES

Many of the card and dice games described later are also good for children practising language in pairs.

## Guess the mime – *Devinez ce que je mime!*

In pairs children mime a word or phrase for their partner to guess.

## Fastest finger! – *Le doigt champion*

A small group version of *touchez le tableau!*, this is a quick way to practise vocabulary. Children work in threes. One is the caller; the other two are competitors. The competitors have a board each. When the caller calls out a word, the two competitors race to point to the correct picture.

## DRAMA GAMES/ACTIVITIES

## Zip zap – *Zip zap*

All children stand in a circle, and vocabulary in the target language is given an action and a direction for passing (person to the right/left/across the circle, miss one person to the right). One person begins by pointing to a person and saying the correct word. That person repeats the word with the action before passing on another word. The game can be competitive by eliminating children who hesitate or pass words incorrectly.

## Listen to me – *Ecoutez-moi!*

A child is chosen to perform a short dialogue with the class. S/he performs in such a way as to demonstrate a particular emotion/character; the class tries to guess.

## Who is it? – *C'est qui?*

One child stands at the front with his/her back to the class. A child is chosen to speak in the target language in a disguised voice. The child at the front attempts to guess who spoke. The game is repeated until the child guesses who spoke.

### Musical statues – *Statues musicales*

The children dance or move round the room. When the music stops, the teacher says something in the target language for the children to mime, in a 'freeze' position. Any child seen moving is out or misses a turn.

### Charades – *Jeu de mimes*

A child mimes a word or phrase for the class to guess.

### What am I doing? *Qu'est-ce que je fais?*

This activity trains children to listen carefully rather than following somebody's actions. Children stand in a circle and one person begins by asking the person on the left a question. That person replies but mimes a different answer by performing the wrong action, for example, s/he mimes a banana but says 'I would like an apple'. The person who asked the question begins miming an apple and the first person stops miming. The next person to the right repeats the question to the person now miming the apple, who will give a different answer.

### DICE GAMES/ACTIVITIES

### Say it with feeling! – Emotion!

For this game use small picture cards and emotion dice. In pairs or small groups, children practise new vocabulary, taking it in turns to say a word in a voice showing a particular emotion.

### Dingo – *Loto calcul*

Two or three dice are rolled and the numbers added together. Children with that number on their grid cross it out. This is a good cross-curricular link with maths.

### Beetle – *Scarabée*

Draw or construct a picture according to the number thrown on the dice. A reference card is needed to list the item of vocabulary for each number. For example, to build a monster, throw 1 for the eyes, 2 for the nose, 3 for the ears and so on. Variations on this could include setting the table (with 1 being a plate, 2 a fork, 3 a knife) or designing a bowl of fruit. To extend the game, set a time limit and see how many pictures the children can draw; alternatively, they can be asked to make their pictures disappear by throwing the dice and striking out each item.

| Throw a 6 to start and draw **le corps** |
| :--- |
| 1. les yeux |
| 2. le nez |
| 3. les oreilles |
| 4. la bouche |
| 5. les cheveux |
| 6. la tête |

### Team relay – *Relais d'équipe*

This game allows all four skills to be practised. Numbered vocabulary cards are hidden round the classroom or in the corridor. Each one is numbered to correspond to the numbers on the dice. Children work in A B pairs; A rolls the dice and finds the matching text to read and memorise. A tells B who then writes or draws what s/he has heard. For example, if they have learned body parts and colours, they could be reading, speaking, listening to and writing or drawing a description of a monster.

## CARD GAMES

### Bingo – *Loto*

Children have a game card (a six square grid) on which they have numbers, pictures or words. If they hear the vocabulary on their card called, they cross it out. The first person to cross everything out is the winner. A simplified version of *loto* is when the children write or draw three objects from a recent topic: the teacher calls out the French and the first person to cross out all three is the winner.

### Snap – *Bataille*

This is similar to the childhood game of 'snap'. A pack of cards with two copies of each individual card is dealt. Children take turns to place one of their cards on the pile. They must then call out what is shown on matching cards to win the pair.

### Guess what? – *Devinez!*

In pairs children are given a pack of cards. One child tries to guess the card the partner is looking at in the pack. As soon as s/he guesses correctly, that card is placed face down and the game continues with the child guessing the next card and so on. They keep a tally of the number of guesses. Whoever has the lowest number of guesses wins the game.

## LARGE SPACE GAMES

### Mr Wolf – *Monsieur Loup*

One person stands at the end of the playground or hall, facing away from the other children. They ask the Wolf a question, for example: *C'est combien, Monsieur/Madame?* The Wolf says: *Deux*. Children take two steps forward. When the Wolf shouts *Dix*, s/he turns and runs towards the other children until one is caught and becomes the Wolf. This can be adapted to many topic areas, including the traditional *Quelle heure est-il, Monsieur le Loup?* The Wolf can answer any time on the clock and the children creep forward. When the Wolf shouts: *Il est l'heure du déjeuner!* (It's dinner time!), the children scatter and one is caught. This child then replaces the Wolf. A classroom version, which the authors have seen played, involves children standing in front of their chairs. They take the equivalent number of steps on the spot before they can sit down. The last person to sit replaces the Wolf. In the context of ordering food, if the Wolf says: *Je voudrais cinq bananes* (I'd like five bananas), the children would do five marching steps on the spot and sit down as fast as they can.

## Little pig – *Petit cochon*

This is a game based on 'piggy in the middle'. One child is the *petit cochon* (little pig) and stands between two other children. They must try to pass the ball to each other by throwing it around or over the *cochon* whose aim is to intercept the ball. If successful, the *petit cochon* changes places with the child who threw the ball. In this game, items of vocabulary are stuck on the ball and, with every throw, the child chooses something different to call out.

## PARACHUTE GAMES/ACTIVITIES

Parachute games are excellent for reinforcing language in an engaging and active context, in addition to encouraging cooperative play and turn-taking. Here we have suggested a few favourites for practising new language. The initial warm-up activity below is useful to ensure that the children are all listening carefully before starting any games, as well as providing an opportunity for them to follow instructions in the target language.

## Warm-up activity

Children hold the parachute and circle round, following the teacher's instructions: *Marchez vite/lentement! Courez! Sautez! Changez de direction!*

## The storm – *La tempête*

Children listen to the weather and move the parachute appropriately (with a soft toy in the middle) as the storm brews. At the start, the teacher says: *Bon voyage!*

> *Il fait beau* (it is fine) . . . *la mer est calme* (the sea is calm) . . . *il fait du vent* (it is windy) . . . *un peu de vent* (there is a breeze) . . . *beaucoup de vent* (there is a strong wind) . . . *il fait mauvais* (it is bad weather) . . . *c'est un orage* (it's a storm) . . . *l'orage passe* (the storm passes) . . . *la mer est calme* . . . *il fait beau.*

## Find – *Cherchez*

The teacher places two bags of objects (for example, plastic fruit or clothes) under the parachute. Children are in two teams, holding opposite sides of the parachute; each child has a number. If the teacher calls out *numéro deux* and asks for a pair of trousers (*un pantalon*) or an apple (*une pomme*), the first child with that number to dive under the parachute and bring the object to the teacher gets a point.

## Change places – *Changez de place!*

If what the teacher calls out is true for individual children, they change places before the parachute falls. For example, *changez de place . . . si tu n'aimes pas le rugby/si tu aimes le football mais tu préfères le rugby* (change places . . . if you don't like rugby/if you like football but you prefer rugby).

## GAMES BASED ON TV SHOWS

### Champion – *Champion*

Children practise questions and answers, using the multi-choice approach of the game show that involves phoning a friend. A series of questions with alternative answers are given. Children all record the letter representing the correct answer while one child is the contestant at the board. At any stage the contestant can use one chance to 'phone a friend', that is, ask an individual child the answer or 'ask the audience', that is, take a class vote.

### Cross the grid – *Traversez la grille!*

Using the grid on an interactive whiteboard, children compete in teams to be the first to cross the board, either vertically or horizontally, by responding correctly in turn to the pictures on the board.

### Find the money – *Trouvez l'argent!*

- A selection of numbered flashcards (suggest six) is displayed and a volunteer chosen to be the contestant. Each card is assigned a monetary value (suggest range in euros is: 5000, 2000, 1000, 200, 50, 1). There are three high and three low cards: €1 is the one the contestant wishes to avoid!
- The contestant chooses one card, which is set aside from the others. S/he hopes this is the highest value card.
- The contestant selects each card in turn, practising the vocabulary on the card. In the context of sport, s/he might respond to a picture of someone playing tennis with *le tennis, je joue au tennis* or *je joue au tennis parce que c'est mon sport préféré* (remember that picture flashcards provide natural differentiation).

- The amount on the card is then revealed and the game continues until there are only two cards left, one in play and the other chosen at the start by the contestant.
- At that stage the value of the last two cards is unknown and the contestant must decide if s/he wishes to keep the original card or swap with the remaining card. Will the contestant win the jackpot or end up in the euro hall of fame? The class can be asked to help the contestant decide.

In conclusion, this chapter suggests a variety of games and activities, which can be adapted to suit different skill areas, groupings and languages. If the games are referred to in the target language it saves time and provides interest. Enjoy the magic!

# 8 What's the story?

## RATIONALE

Everyone loves a good story and this is particularly true of children. It is a natural way for them to learn language and, hopefully, one that will be familiar to them from learning their first language. Well chosen stories in the target language also engage and capture the imagination. The key stage 2 languages programmes of study (DfE, 2013) state that 'pupils should be taught to appreciate stories . . . in the language'.

## CONTEXT

A story may be used for pure enjoyment, or because it links well with a theme or topic being taught. On the other hand, a story can be fully exploited; it can become the vehicle for an entire unit of work, from which a teacher can develop further language skills in listening, speaking, reading and writing, based on or around the new language in the story.

## CHOICE OF STORIES

This will depend on the age and ability level of the children, the learning objectives and intended outcomes. Teachers often make judgements about the usefulness of a text or the need to amend it, in order to make it more accessible to the learner. While there are often good reasons for adapting an original text, it is also important to provide opportunities for children to 'understand and respond to spoken and written language from a variety of authentic sources' (DfE, 2013). According to the Oxford University Press *English Language Teaching Global Blog* (OUP, 2014), an authentic text is generally accepted to be one that has not been written for the 'language classroom' but one that 'retains its original vocabulary and grammar' and has not been 'changed or simplified'.

## FAMILIAR STORIES

Using a familiar story in the new language (such as 'Little Red Riding Hood', 'The enormous turnip', 'Jack and the beanstalk') is often helpful because the children can draw on their prior knowledge of the story to help them understand and decode the new language. However, it is best not to rely on every child being familiar with the story (especially those children who have English as an additional language) and it is generally a good idea to recap the English version, prior to introducing the foreign text. Learning the same story in a different language also provides an opportunity for the children to recognise similarities between the two stories. Furthermore, these stories can be used to develop children's knowledge and understanding of grammar and sentence construction. The use of 'well loved' tales is particularly suitable for lower key stage 2 learners, whereas other familiar stories, such as Aesop's fables, may be used for upper key stage 2.

## ACTIVITIES FOR DEVELOPING READING SKILLS

- Show some picture flashcards representing the story characters or places and ask if the children can guess what the story might be.
- Look at the book cover and discuss the title. For example, 'Le Petit Chaperon Rouge' ('Little Red Riding Hood'), 'La Barba Azul' ('Blue Beard') will lead to discussions about adjectival position and the use of the article 'the' in French and Spanish, which is not used in the same way as in English.
- Use an electronic copy of the book or a visualiser so that the text can be projected on to a whiteboard, allowing the children to follow the text as they listen.
- Give the children specific words in English to listen for and remember later in the new language (a character's name or repeated phrase). Well loved tales are excellent in this respect.
- Discuss the purpose and effective use of repetition (i.e. how it helps language learning).
- Ask children to respond when they hear a word they understand or think they have understood – for example, by putting their thumb up to respond.
- Agree mimes or actions to fit with the story vocabulary – children perform these while listening.
- Encourage children to join in with repetitive phrases.
- Ask the children to predict what might happen next.
- Prepare cards with words/phrases/sentences from the story and ask children to hold them up or wave them when they hear the words (differentiate by the amount of language they are expected to recognise).
- Ask the children to follow the text and carry on reading when the teacher stops.
- Cover a word or words and ask children to recall them.
- Ask for volunteers to perform the story (repeat several times to give as many children as possible the opportunity) and use simple costumes and props.
- Assign individual speaking parts/choral speaking.
- Give children a short passage from the text and ask them to annotate it – highlighting words they know, words they can work out and words they do not yet understand.
- Reread the story.
- Make sets of jumbled sentences from the story – one word per A4 card for the children to arrange. Use these for groups to complete a 'jigsaw' activity; this develops their grammatical knowledge of word classes and sentence structure. Refer to the 'Fun with grammar' chapter for further explanation about this activity.

Another approach is to teach the children some key vocabulary from the story before they hear/see it for the first time. If specific actions or mimes are practised with the words, these can be used by children as they listen to and join in with the story. Alternatively, a simple thumbs-up response could be used when they understand. If children are following a written text, it is helpful for them to practise the strategy of using cognates to aid understanding. Pre-teaching some vocabulary is usually appropriate when using an unfamiliar story or an authentic text, which contains a high percentage of unknown or more complex language. In many cases, nouns will be pre-taught.

It is important, however, for children to realise that they are not expected to understand everything, and younger children are often more accepting of this fact. The situation can be compared to a very young child having a story read to them in English. They enjoy listening but at first do not understand all the vocabulary. They gradually learn more and more until eventually, they learn to read for themselves. The process takes time, and reading skills begin with gist comprehension; this is acquired through listening and practice in looking at words and pictures. At a later stage, children are able to remember more words and learn to work out their meaning within a sentence.

## STORIES LINKING WITH TOPICS OR THEMES

Choosing a story to link with a topic can provide an opportunity for some cross-curricular language teaching. There are some suggestions for this in the chapter 'A helping hand'. For example, *The Very Hungry Caterpillar*, which has been translated into many languages, links very well with a topic on mini-beasts, life cycles or food.

If teachers are visiting the country in which the target language is spoken, it is a good idea to visit a bookshop and spend some time perusing the children's section. The search may result in the discovery of an authentic text that will prove successful in the primary classroom. For the authors, a trip to France resulted in finding a book telling the moving story of war from a child's point of view. The story might be about any child living in a worn-torn country; it is sympathetically told and provides an opportunity to focus on emotions. The book, *Chez moi c'est la guerre* (Sharafeddine and Dubois, 2008), was subsequently used for integrating some language teaching into an upper key stage 2 topic on war. The story has cognates that aid comprehension and is beautifully illustrated; before it was shared with the children, however, they were taught some key vocabulary from the story text. On the initial reading, the children followed the text, looked at the pictures and gestured with a thumb up when they felt that they had understood a word or phrase. Some examples of children's work in other chapters were inspired by this story.

## STORIES AS A CENTRAL RESOURCE

A story text in the new language can be used as a central resource for an entire unit of work, becoming a springboard for developing children's oracy and literacy skills. The vocabulary and grammatical structures in the text might be used, or new vocabulary introduced on a relevant theme. Furthermore, a text can provide a structure, which can serve as a writing frame for the children to create their own writing. Stories can also provide material for giving a performance to another class, to parents or for a school assembly.

## ORAL STORYTELLING

In literacy, children practise telling stories orally; this improves their ability to use story language and ultimately to write stories of their own. The oral telling of a story helps to embed sentence structure and cohesion between sentences and the whole text. As children retell the same story aloud again and again, they become more fluent and confident in their use of language. As an aide-memoire, the children use picture prompts, in the form of a story map, to help them remember the story. As they move from one picture to the next, they recall that part of the story, and actions are also added.

The success in adopting this approach in literacy teaching has been quite significant, leading to substantial improvement in children's ability to speak and write more fluently. Therefore, there is much to be gained in adopting a similar approach to storytelling in the target language.

Many children have very good memories and never cease to surprise in the way they can grasp, recite and soon remember longer pieces of spoken language. This approach allows children both to hear and speak longer utterances. The teacher initially takes the lead in telling the whole story while children listen or quietly participate with actions for some pre-taught key words. Subsequently, the children become co-tellers through the teacher pausing for the children to repeat. After several retellings, the teacher can lower his/her voice, thus allowing the children to take the lead. Ultimately, children could be asked in pairs or in small groups to retell the story.

## Preparation of a text for accessibility or to fit teaching purpose

### Adapting an existing story

It may sometimes be necessary to adapt an existing story. When creating an adaptation of the text, it is possible to use language structures and vocabulary that will be helpful for the children to master and reuse. Teachers could seek the help or advice of the local secondary school language department or subject specialist in selecting these.

Texts such as 'We're going on a bear hunt' (suitable for lower KS2) and 'Handa's surprise' (which can be adapted to be suitable for either lower or upper KS2) are good stories to use because the children are probably already familiar with them in English.

### Creating a story

Another way of introducing and reinforcing specific vocabulary or language structures is to create stories for this purpose. The authors have designed two stories with suggested ideas for teaching sequences and some supporting materials, which are included at the end of the chapter. English translations of the stories are in the Appendix. Both stories are intended to focus on oral retelling. They are repeated and rehearsed so that children can easily recall the sentences and sequence from memory, with a picture map for support.

The first story, 'On va faire un pique-nique', is written for lower key stage 2, linked to the key stage 2 languages programmes of study (DfE, 2013). It is a story about food, in the context of going on a picnic. A child is preparing a picnic basket, putting in the different items of food. Children learn to tell the story orally and therefore have considerable practice in rehearsing the useful topic vocabulary and language structures. There is an attempt to recycle familiar phrases (here it is assumed that the children might already know 'weather' vocabulary), so a weather sentence is included at the start of the story to set the scene for the picnic. The story leads to a short role-play where children practise a picnic conversation, using polite language; they later have the opportunity to use this on a French picnic. Children then write an invitation to their own teddy bears to come on the picnic. This links to the story text, which explains the idea of taking her grandfather and a bear for company because everyone else in the family is too busy to go! There is a song (sung to the tune of 'The teddy bears' picnic') to further reinforce some of the vocabulary and structures.

The second story, 'La surprise de Jean-Luc', is written for upper key stage 2, again linked to the key stage 2 languages programmes of study (DfE, 2013). It is based on a surprise, and there are actually no less than three surprises in one story! It is about a boy, Jean-Luc, who has the idea of making a fruit salad for his grandmother's birthday. It rehearses several dialogues that take place in a market where Jean-Luc is buying fruit. Each stallholder is surprised by the fact that the boy is only buying *one* of each fruit, until he explains that it is to make a fruit salad for his grandmother's birthday. Following the story, a suggested activity for year 5 is a fruit-tasting experience, providing an opportunity for them to give opinions about fruit. This includes the use of the connective *mais* (but) to practise creating longer sentences, for example: *J'aime beaucoup les pommes mais je préfère les kiwis* (I really like apples but I prefer kiwis).

It is suggested that year 6 children follow an instructional text in French to make their own fruit salad. This provides an opportunity for them to taste the fruit salad and give their opinion. Some of the story language that has been practised can be recycled, as they use descriptions of the different fruit to justify their opinion. They practise constructing sentences using the connective *parce que* (because) to create longer sentences. For example: *J'adore la salade de fruits parce qu'elle est juteuse* (I love fruit salad because it is juicy).

Both stories have the potential to lead to a performance. Older children could write and perform their own simple play-scripts. Children could also use stop motion animation to retell the story or create their own electronic books in PowerPoint (or using storytelling software such as Storybird and StoryJumper, both of which are mentioned in the 'Technology tools' chapter).

The authors have created a further story for oral storytelling; this is on a pirate theme linked to clothing vocabulary. The Spanish story follows a simple structure, using the days of the week to describe what clothes the pirate wears each day. This simple structure can easily be adapted to fit other topics and vocabulary.

In conclusion, using stories to teach new language is a natural and enjoyable way for children to hear and see the new language in a meaningful context. They provide numerous opportunities for developing both children's spoken and written language skills. In this chapter we have looked at the benefits of using familiar stories, suggested activities to develop reading skills and considered how a story can either be linked to a topic or used as a central resource for a unit of work.

**Table 8.1** On va faire un pique-nique: suggested ideas for teaching sequence

| Overview | This unit involves learning to tell a story about going on a picnic. It also includes a song and a picnic. The children write a shopping list, a picnic invitation and practise perfect picnic manners – learning a short role-play dialogue. Suitable for lower key stage 2. |
| --- | --- |
| **Story and song** | Tell the story as often as possible so that children become increasingly familiar with it. Likewise the song can be introduced and sung often – at the start/end of lessons and at other times during the week. |

| Objectives/outcomes | Content/vocabulary | Suggested teaching activities: **Going on a picnic** | Resources |
| --- | --- | --- | --- |
| **PoS 1, 8** | *un nounours* (a teddy bear) | Prepare a story sack (picnic basket) containing clues about the story the class is going to learn to tell in French. Suggested items: a blanket, a radio, a shopping receipt … Can they guess what the story is about? | Picnic basket and objects as story clues |
| Children will: | *le panier* (the basket) | | Picture flashcards for story nouns |
| recognise and begin to say words for teddy bear, basket and picnic foods | *le beurre* (the butter) | Ask questions such as: Who would you take with you on a picnic? What would you take with you? How would you feel if everyone was too busy to go with you? Who/what could you take? Reveal Monsieur Nounours (a small teddy bear) from a *sac surprise* (a surprise bag). | *\*On va faire un pique-nique'* story text for teacher |
| have joined in a French story | *le miel* (the honey) | | \*'Teddy bears' picnic song |
| | *les chips* (the crisps) | | |
| | *un couteau* (a knife) | Pass the small teddy bear round the class, giving children the opportunity to greet the bear: 'Bonjour, Monsieur Nounours!' Ask them to greet him as if they are planning to take him on a picnic with them. Explain that the class will be preparing to go on a French picnic. | |
| | *une radio* (a radio) | | |
| | *Papa* (Dad) | Use colour-coded flashcards and **varied repetition** techniques to introduce the story nouns: basket, butter, honey, crisps, knife, radio, Mum, Dad, brother and sister. Add a mime for each. Go through the **miming sequence** so that children practise all the agreed mimes for the story vocabulary. | |
| | *Maman* (Mum) | | |
| | *mon frère* (my brother) | | |
| | *ma sœur* (my sister) | Children listen to the teacher telling the story in French and participate by miming the words they know. The teacher prompts and supports less confident children. | |
| | Also story vocabulary (refer to English translation, if needed) | During the week introduce the 'Teddy bears' picnic song' – ask the children to do some actions for some of the key words and phrases in the song. | |

**Table 8.1** continued

| Objectives/outcomes | Content/vocabulary | Suggested teaching activities: Shopping lists | Resources |
|---|---|---|---|
| **PoS 1, 2, 5, 7**<br><br>Children will:<br><br>know some words for food in French and be able to read them aloud with increasingly accurate pronunciation<br><br>be confident with some French sounds and spelling links<br><br>be more confident in joining in with a French story | *le panier* (the basket)<br><br>*le beurre* (the butter)<br><br>*le miel* (the honey)<br><br>*les chips* (the crisps)<br><br>*un couteau* (a knife)<br><br>*une radio* (a radio)<br><br>*une limonade* (a lemonade)<br><br>*un jus d'orange* (an orange juice)<br><br>Also story vocabulary (refer to English translation, if needed) | Display the story map for 'On va faire un pique-nique'. The teacher retells the story using the map and actions. Teacher pauses appropriately for children to repeat the story after him/her.<br><br>In pairs, the children remember the order of the items put into the picnic basket.<br><br>The teacher introduces some new words for additional picnic items: *la limonade, le jus d'orange*.<br><br>The teacher introduces text cards for each item of food and drink. Children repeat the words after the teacher and match them to the picture flashcards. Ask the children what they notice about the pronunciation of the letters *ch, i and s* in the French word *chips*. Draw attention to the 'ain' grapheme and its pronunciation in the French word *pain* and the *eu* grapheme in the French word *beurre* and the *ou* and *eau* graphemes in the French word *couteau*.<br><br>Practise two of the French sounds met in the story vocabulary.<br><br>Hold up the grapheme card and ask the children to listen carefully to two words. They should indicate whether the grapheme is in the first or second word they hear. They could hold up a number fan or the correct number of fingers. Show the words once the children have made their choice. Here are some words that could be used:<br><br>*ain: Alain/Paul, main/bouche, certain/possible*<br><br>*eu: trois/deux, rouge/bleu, peu/beaucoup*<br><br>Play '**stations**' to practise reading the French food words. Teacher calls the word in English and children run to the French word. Before moving to the next word, all the children practise reading the word aloud.<br><br>Children are given a list of food (12 items) which includes the items for the picnic. Ask them to find and highlight the food needed and match it to the correct picture. Anyone who finishes early can look up the meaning of the other items on the shopping list. If the children are using a bilingual dictionary, and have not used one before, the teacher will need to show the children how to use the dictionary. Alternatively, the children could make their own word search, using the story vocabulary. | *Story map for 'On va faire un pique-nique'<br><br>*Story text for 'On va faire un pique-nique' for teacher use<br><br>Food picture and text flashcards<br><br>Grapheme cards<br><br>Shopping list |

**Table 8.1** continued

| Objectives/outcomes | Content/vocabulary | Suggested teaching activities: Picnic manners | Resources |
|---|---|---|---|
| **PoS 4, 5, 12** | Food vocabulary | Play 'prédiction' to revise the food vocabulary. | Puppet/class mascot |
| Children will: | *Bonjour* (Hello) | The teacher has a conversation with a puppet/class mascot to model a polite conversation. | Feeling flashcards |
| have practised questions linked to a picnic conversation | *Ça va?* (How are you?) *Ça va bien, merci* (I am well thank you) | – *Bonjour* <br> – *Bonjour* <br> – *Ça va ?* | Food flashcards |
| know some polite language | *Et toi?* (And you?) | – *Ça va bien merci. Et toi?* | |
| (please and thank you) | *Ça va mal* (I am not good) | – *Ça va bien merci* | |
| have met the c cedilla accent | *Comme ci comme ça* (OK) | – *Passez-moi le pain, s'il vous plaît* | |
| | *Passez-moi . . .* (Pass me . . . ) | – *Voilà le pain* | |
| | *S'il vous plaît* (Please) | – *Merci* | |
| | *Voilà . . .* (There's the . . . ) | The teacher asks the children what they think the conversation was about. Use **varied repetition** to practise the different feelings. Children repeat sentences, adding actions. Play '**chaud ou froid**' to rehearse these further. | |
| | *Merci* (Thank you) | Ask the children to practise passing a food flashcard round the table but before the item passes the person must request it. For example, if the bread card is being used, the child will say: *Passez-moi le pain, s'il vous plaît* (Pass me the bread, please). Once it is passed, the child will say: *Merci* (thank you). | |
| | | Display the dialogue on the whiteboard. See the oracy section for suggested sequence in rehearsing it and using the disappearing dialogue technique to help children remember. The teacher can talk to the children about the use of rising intonation to form the question *Ça va?* Ask higher attainers to add to or change the dialogue. | |
| | | Discuss the c cedilla accent (*Ça*) makes the c soft here because followed by an 'a' (refer to Chapter 5 'Fun with grammar' for further information). | |

Table 8.1 *continued*

| Objectives/outcomes | Content/vocabulary | Suggested teaching activities: Picnic invitations | Resources |
|---|---|---|---|
| **PoS 7, 8, 10, 12** | *Bonjour, mon nounours* (Hello, my teddy bear) | Sing the 'Teddy bears' picnic song'. | *Teddy bears' picnic song |
| The children will: | *Viens à un pique-nique!* (Come to a picnic) | Tell the story 'On va faire un pique-nique' together, encouraging children to take the lead. | French birthday party invitation |
| have had the opportunity to read an authentic text | *heure* (hour) | Teach the children the days of the week (look at 'Hitting the right note' for a suggested song to help them learn this vocabulary). Show the children the days of the week, written without capital letters. Ask what they notice about the way they are written in French. French uses | *Writing frame for the picnic invitation |
| written invitation | *lundi* (Monday) | lower case letters for days of the week unless they begin a sentence. | *Story map 'On va faire un pique-nique' |
| be more familiar and confident with telling the French story from memory | *mardi* (Tuesday) | If possible, find some images online of children's birthday party invitations written in French. Ask the children in pairs to discuss what sort of text it is and what they can understand. | |
| | *mercredi* (Wednesday) | | |
| | *jeudi* (Thursday) | | |
| | *vendredi* (Friday) | | |
| | *dans les bois* (in the woods) | | |
| | | Children use the simplified writing frame to invite their bears to the picnic. The teacher will need to go over the new vocabulary with the children and show which part of the invitation needs to be changed – the date and time (underline words as appropriate). Children can add the agreed date and time for their actual picnic. There is a border for the children to decorate with their own teddy bear design. | |
| | | Finish with the class story 'On va faire un pique-nique', using the story map for support. | |

**Table 8.1** continued

| Objectives/outcomes | Content/vocabulary | Suggested teaching activities: Teddy bears' picnic | Resources |
|---|---|---|---|
| **PoS 1, 3, 4**<br><br>Children will:<br><br>have been able to use the language they have learned for a purpose<br><br>have performed a French song and told a French story | No new vocabulary | The children bring their favourite teddy bear to school for the Teddy bears' picnic. Parents could also be invited.<br><br>The children perform the story 'On va faire un pique-nique' for teddy bears and any parents. Next they sing the song and then continue singing the song as they travel to the picnic. This could be marching around the class/school hall/to an outside space.<br><br>During the picnic encourage children to use polite language when asking for any food to be passed to them. For example, *Passez-moi les chips, s'il vous plaît* (Pass me the crisps, please). They can greet each other and use the role-play dialogue vocabulary about feelings.<br><br>Additonal ideas following the picnic event:<br><br>The children could draw and describe their bears attending the picnic. This would require some teaching of vocabulary for parts of the face.<br><br>The song 'Heads, shoulders, knees and toes', in French, could be used to support learning the vocabulary for parts of the body and face.<br><br>Children could then draw and label their bears. They could learn how to use the simple adjectives of size: *grand/grande* and *petit/petite* to make their descriptions more interesting. In order to support children in writing accurately when using adjectives, please refer to the sentence switchboard ideas in the chapter 'Developing skills'. | *Story map 'On va faire un pique-nique'<br><br>*Story text 'On va faire un pique-nique' for teacher, if needed<br><br>Teddy bears<br><br>Tablecloths<br><br>Picnic blankets<br><br>Picnic food<br><br>Picnic equipment |

Refer to the 'Assessment and progression' chapter for details of each programme of study (PoS). Words highlighted in bold refer to games or teaching techniques already mentioned in the chapters 'Developing skills' and 'The magic of games'.

* indicates that a photocopiable master is provided.

## PM 8.1 ON VA FAIRE UN PIQUE-NIQUE: STORY TEXT

**On va faire un pique-nique**

Aujourd'hui il fait beau.
On va faire un pique-nique.
On va dans les grands bois.
Voici mon panier neuf.
Viens préparer le pique-pique avec moi!

Dans mon panier je mets le pain
Dans mon panier je mets le pain et le beurre
Dans mon panier je mets le pain, le beurre et le miel
Dans mon panier je mets le pain, le beurre, le miel et les chips
Dans mon panier je mets le pain, le beurre, le miel, les chips et un couteau
Dans mon panier je mets le pain, le beurre, le miel, les chips, un couteau et une radio.
Voici le pique-nique!

Qui vient avec moi?
Pas Papa – il regarde la télévision
Pas Maman – elle fait de la natation
Pas mon frère – il écoute la musique
Pas ma soeur – elle fait de la gymnastique

Ah, je sais…Grand-père… et mon petit nounours!
On y va!

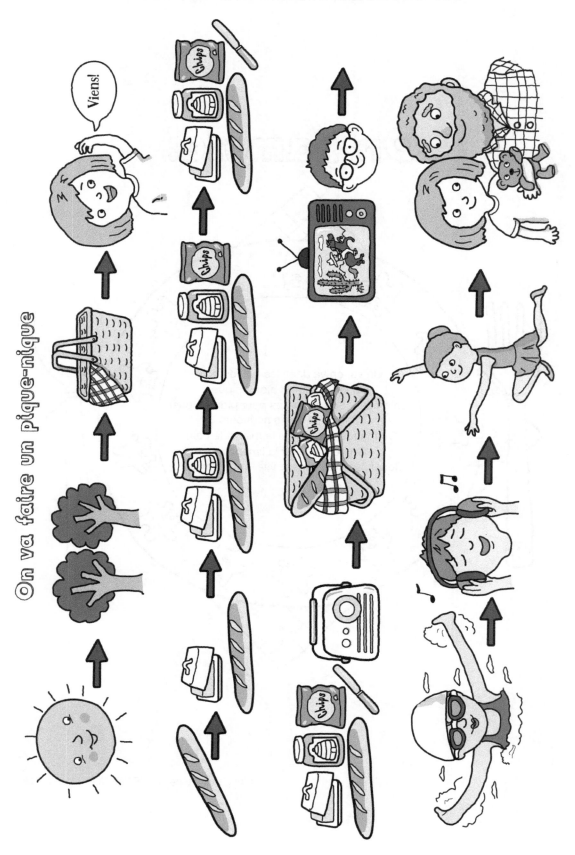

# On s'amuse!

On va, on va dans les grands bois
On fait un grand pique-nique
On a beaucoup de temps pour pique-niquer
Avec nos petits nounours
On mange, on mange le miel et le pain
On boit, on boit la limonade
Jouez, sautez, dansez vite – on s'amuse!

(Sung to the tune of THE TEDDY BEARS' PICNIC.)

## PM 8.4 TEDDY BEARS' PICNIC INVITATION

Bonjour, mon nounours!
Viens à un pique-nique
vendredi 5 juillet
à 11 heures
dans les bois

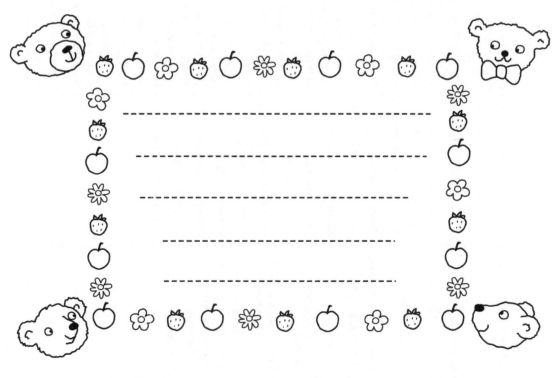

**Table 8.2** La surprise de Jean-Luc: suggested ideas for a teaching sequence

| Overview | The children learn to tell a story in French, make a fruit salad/taste some fruit and give opinions. | | |
|---|---|---|---|
| **Story and song** | Tell the story as often as possible (within a lesson or at other times during the week) so that children become increasingly familiar with it. Encourage children increasingly to take the lead. | | |
| **Objectives/outcomes** | **Content/vocabulary** | **Suggested teaching activities: La surprise de Jean-Luc** | **Resources** |
| **PoS 1, 2, 5, 8, 12**<br>Children will:<br><br>know some story vocabulary<br><br>have revised the use of the article in French<br><br>have practised speaking and reading aloud with increasingly accurate pronunciation<br><br>have joined in with a French story | *une banane* (a banana)<br>*une orange* (an orange)<br>*une poire* (a pear)<br>*une pêche* (a peach)<br>*une mangue* (a mango)<br>*un ananas* (a pineapple)<br>*un kiwi* (a kiwi)<br>*l'hôpital* (the hospital)<br>*l'anniversaire* (the birthday)<br>*la surprise* (the surprise) | Explain to the children that they will be learning to tell a story in French called 'La surprise de Jean-Luc'. First show the list of seven fruits that they will meet in the story (see vocabulary list). Ask if they know/can guess the meaning of these words. What do they know about the gender of these words? How do they know? (Look at the article *un/une*). Next show the words for hospital, birthday and surprise (the remaining words in the vocabulary column). What do they think these words mean? Discuss how cognates are really helpful when learning a new language. Ask children to look at the title of the story and discuss with a partner the possible plot for the story.<br><br>The teacher models pronunciation, adding a mime for each word and the children repeat and copy the actions. Explain that the mimes will later be used to help tell the story. Discuss how gesture and mime help us remember, too. Practise the fruit words in the story order (banana, orange, pear, peach, mango, pineapple, kiwi). Give the children time to practise reading the story vocabulary in pairs to each other, trying to sound as French as possible. The teacher can listen to individual pronunciation. Follow up with phonics activities, e.g. **dance mat** to consolidate these sounds (*ge/gu/an/oi/ch/aire/i/un/une*). An example of a dance mat can be found in the 'Sounds different' chapter.<br><br>The teacher tells the story of 'La surprise de Jean-Luc', adding appropriate actions for phrases and key words (for example, *Il était une fois . . .* could have the action of opening a book) while the children listen, adding actions when they hear the key words they have learned.<br><br>The teacher retells the story, this time displaying a picture map and pausing for the children to repeat. | List of fruit words<br><br>Dance mat<br><br>*Story text 'La surprise de Jean-Luc' for the teacher<br><br>*Story map for 'La surprise de Jean-Luc' |

**Table 8.2** continued

| Objectives/outcomes | Content/vocabulary | Suggested teaching activities: Yummy fruit | Resources |
|---|---|---|---|
| PoS 1, 2, 4, 7, 8, 11, 12 | une *banane* (a banana) | On mini whiteboards, the children practise spelling the story nouns using the '**look, cover, write, check**' method. They can tick or colour the word on the sheet when they spell it correctly. | Story noun sheet |
| Children will: | une *orange* (an orange) | | *Story text 'La surprise de Jean-Luc' for the teacher |
| know how to spell some French words for fruits and know their gender | une *poire* (a pear)<br>une *pêche* (a peach)<br>une *mangue* (a mango)<br>un *ananas* (a pineapple) | Practise the correct use of the article before the nouns. The teacher says a noun and the children repeat, adding the correct article. For example, the teacher says *banane* and the children respond *une banane*. | Story map for 'La surprise de Jean-Luc' |
| be able to read, understand and sequence familiar phrases and sentences from the story | un *kiwi* (a kiwi)<br>*elle est . . . (it is . . . )*<br>*juteuse* (juicy)<br>*mûre* (ripe) | Using the story map, the teacher retells the story with actions, pausing for the children to copy both words and actions.<br><br>Put the children in mixed ability groups. Give each group a set of story text cards. The children listen while the teacher retells the story and they arrange the text in order. Repeat story if necessary.<br><br>How does the story begin? What is Jean-Luc doing and why? | *Story sequencing cards for 'La surprise de Jean-Luc'<br><br>*Gap fill sheet for describing fruits |
| know some verb forms (*il/elle*) and how they are used to replace the noun | *délicieuse* (delicious)<br>*bonne pour la santé* (healthy)<br>*exotique* (exotic) | Ask the children to find the word for Why? In French. Why do the market stall holders keep asking the question Why . . . ? The sentences describing the fruit begin: *Il est/Elle est . . .* (It is . . . ). Do children know why there are two ways of saying 'it' in French? (Can they see a pattern in how they are used – when replacing the masculine/feminine nouns?) Go through each description for the fruits. What happens to Jean-Luc? Give the children two or three minutes to try to remember the order of the fruit and the description for each. Put the story text cards away. | |
| be able to say some sentences describing fruit | *il est . . . (it is . . . )*<br>*sucré* (sugary)<br>*joli* (attractive) | Ask the children if they can find the different surprises in the story (the surprise fruit salad for Grandma's birthday, the surprise fruit salad from Grandma to Jean-Luc in hospital and the surprise slip on the banana skin!).<br><br>Working in pairs or independently, children complete a gap fill task describing the story fruits.<br><br>Voici une banane. Elle est _____ .<br>Voici une _____ . Elle est _____ .<br>Voici _____ . Elle est _____ .<br>Voici _____ . Elle est _____ .<br>Voici _____ . Il est _____ .<br>Voici _____ . Il est _____ .<br><br>The teacher allocates each group a fruit and asks them to describe it. | |

**Table 8.2** continued

| Objectives/outcomes | Content/vocabulary | Suggested teaching activities: Fruit tasting Year 5 | Resources |
|---|---|---|---|
| **PoS 3, 4, 5, 10**<br><br>Children will:<br><br>be able to give opinions about fruit<br><br>use connectives *mais/et* to extend sentences<br><br>write an opinion, adapting sentences they know | *Est-ce que tu aimes ...?* (Do you like ...?)<br><br>*J'aime* (I like)<br><br>*J'aime beaucoup* (I really like)<br><br>*J'adore* (I love)<br><br>*Je n'aime pas* (I don't like)<br><br>*Je n'aime pas du tout* (I don't like at all)<br><br>*Je déteste* (I hate)<br><br>*oui* (yes)<br><br>*non* (no) | In teams, take it in turns to give the teacher a word/phrase from the story. The team who is last in wins.<br><br>Show the children the question: *Tu aimes les bananes?* What does this sentence literally mean?<br><br>You like the bananas? Discuss that in French there is an extra word (article 'the' has to be added).<br><br>Use numbered option cards (1–6) with **varied repetition** to teach the possible opinions:<br><br>*J'aime ...* (I like ...); *J'aime beaucoup ...* (I really like ...); *J'adore ...* (I love ...); *Je n'aime pas ...* (I do not like ...); *Je n'aime pas du tout ...* (I do not like at all ...); *Je déteste ...* (I hate ...).<br><br>Put the children in two teams so that they can practise giving opinions, using the fruit flashcards and numbered opinion cards. Allow children to turn over a fruit flashcard and roll the dice (to determine which of the six opinions to use). Teams take turns to give opinions linking the two.<br><br>In pairs, the children are given very small pieces of each fruit to try and give an opinion in French to their partner. The children record opinions on their fruit-tasting record sheet.<br><br>In a whole class setting, the teacher asks individual children about the fruit, using the questions:<br><br>*Tu aimes ... ?*. For example, *Tu aimes les bananes?* Children reply in full sentences, using their fruit-tasting record sheets to prompt their replies. For example, *Oui, J'aime beaucoup les bananes* (Yes, I really like bananas).<br><br>Next, the teacher models an extended sentence: *J'aime beaucoup les oranges mais je n'aime pas les bananes* (I really like oranges but I don't like bananas). Show the sentence and discuss the use of the connective *mais* (but). Model a further sentence: *J'aime les oranges mais je préfère les kiwis* (I like oranges but I prefer kiwis). Ask the children to write some extended sentences giving their opinions on the fruits at the bottom of their record sheets. | Fruits for tasting cut into small pieces<br><br>Opinion flashcards numbered 1–6<br><br>Flashcards for the 7 fruits<br><br>Dice<br><br>*Fruit-tasting opinion sheet |

**Table 8.2** continued

| Objectives/outcomes | Content/vocabulary | Suggested teaching activities: **Recipe for une coupe fruitée Year 6** | Resources |
|---|---|---|---|
| **PoS 1, 4, 7, 9, 12** Children will: be able to follow an instructional text analyse text features (layout/language) | *les mandarines* (mandarins) *les bananes* (bananas) *les framboises* (raspberries) *les pêches* (peaches) *les prunes* (plums) *les raisins* (grapes) *un demi-citron* (half a lemon) *du sucre* (some sugar) *lavez* (wash) *épluchez* (peel) *coupez* (cut) *découpez* (cut up) *mettez* (put) *pressez* (press) *versez* (pour) *saupoudrez* (sprinkle) *bien* (well) *doucement* (carefully) *morceaux* (pieces) *petits* (small) *bol* (bowl) | Ask the children to tell each other in French which fruits from the story, La surprise de Jean-Luc' they would like to put in a fruit salad. Ask a few children to tell the class which would be their favourite ingredient. Introduce the list of ingredients for the fruit salad recipe to the children, using picture flashcards (*les mandarines, les bananes, les framboises, les pêches, les raisins, du jus de citron et du sucre*). Practise the new fruits with **varied repetition**. Pass the fruit flashcards round the children, asking them to give an opinion in a full sentence before passing the card to the next person, for example: *J'aime les bananes* (I like bananas). This works well as a circle game and cards can be passed at the same time round the circle and from both directions. Introduce and practise the recipe instructions (imperative verbs) with **varied repetition** and mime. Use the **miming** sequence ('Developing skills' chapter) to ensure that the children understand the verbs. Show the written method for the recipe. The teacher reads aloud different steps and the children write the number of the corresponding instruction they hear on their mini-whiteboards. Give the children copies of the French recipe to stick in their book. Discuss the type of text and the way it is presented. Ask them to find any language they recognise or think they can work out. Discuss the method – what type of word is at the start of every sentence? Is there a pattern with the verbs? ('-ez' is a common ending for imperative verbs in French). Can they find any nouns, verbs, adverbs, adjectives or connectives? Ask children to highlight the word classes in different colours, adding a key. **Before the next lesson teach/revise sentences for expressing opinions. See first part of year 5 Fruit-tasting lesson plan for suggestions.** | Fruit flashcards for each fruit being used in the fruit salad *Recipe for *la coupe fruitée* Mini-whiteboards Highlighters/crayons |

**Table 8.2** *continued*

| Objectives/outcomes | Content/vocabulary | Suggested teaching activities: Making and tasting Year 6 | Resources |
|---|---|---|---|
| **PoS 4, 7, 11**<br><br>Children will:<br><br>have followed an instructional text to make a fruit salad<br><br>have tasted and given their opinions about the fruit salad<br><br>have practised using *parce que* to construct longer sentences | Recipe instructions<br><br>*La coupe fruitée*<br>(Fruit cup)<br><br>*J'aime . . .* (I like . . .)<br><br>*Je n'aime pas . . .* (I don't like . . .)<br><br>*J'adore . . .* (I love . . .)<br><br>*Je déteste . . .* (I hate . . .)<br><br>*juteuse* (juicy)<br><br>*mûre* (ripe)<br><br>*délicieuse* (delicious)<br><br>*multicolore* (multicoloured)<br><br>*bonne pour la santé* (healthy)<br><br>*parce que/parce qu'* (because)<br><br>These adjectives are in the feminine form and can be used to describe the fruit salad.<br><br>*If *sucré* (sugary) or *joli* (attractive) are used to describe the fruit salad, they will need to use *sucrée* or *jolie* (feminine form). | Quickly revise the recipe instructions – the teacher reads each step and children repeat with actions.<br><br>Display the recipe. In groups of six, children make the fruit salad.<br><br>The teacher shows children a range of sentences that could be used to describe their fruit salad. (*Elle est juteuse/mûre/sucrée/multicolore/bonne pour la santé*). Ask children what each sentence means. Remind them that the pronoun *elle* is used to replace the fruit salad, which is feminine. The teacher explains that these descriptions can be used to explain why we like the fruit salad. Ask the children how to improve two short sentences: *J'aime la coupe fruitée. Elle est sucrée.* Discuss joining them with the word 'because': *J'aime la coupe fruitée parce qu'elle est sucrée* (I like fruit salad because it is sweet).<br><br>Display a copy of the speaking frame on the board to support sentence construction. Pass a picture of fruit salad to different children to express possible opinions about it.<br><br>In their groups, the children share out the fruit salad to taste. They use the vocabulary practised to write a sentence under their recipe saying if they like it/do not like it and why. The children choose different friends in the class to give their opinions about the fruit salad in French. | * *La coupe fruitée* recipe:<br>– displayed on the whiteboard<br><br>– small copies for children's books (if not already in books from previous lesson)<br><br>Enough of the fruit ingredients for children to work in groups of six (probably 5x recipe ingredients for a class)<br><br>Equipment to prepare and taste the fruit salad<br><br>*Speaking frame to help children give opinions and reasons<br><br>Fruit salad flashcard |

Refer to the 'Assessment and progression' chapter for details of each programme of study (PoS). Words highlighted in bold refer to games or teaching techniques already mentioned in the chapters 'Developing skills' and 'The magic of games'.

* indicates that a photocopiable master is provided.

## PM 8.5 LA SURPRISE DE JEAN-LUC: STORY TEXT

**La surprise de Jean-Luc**

Il était une fois, un petit garçon qui s'appelait Jean-Luc.

Un jour, c'est l'anniversaire de sa grand-mère
Il décide de faire une surprise pour sa grand-mère - une belle salade de fruits.

 Il va au marché…

Bonjour Monsieur, je voudrais une banane, s'il vous plaît.
Pourquoi **une** banane?
C'est l'anniversaire de de ma grand-mère et je vais faire une salade de fruits.
Voici une banane. Elle est bonne pour la santé.
Merci, au revoir.

Bonjour Madame, je voudrais une orange, s'il vous plaît.
Pourquoi **une** orange?
C'est l'anniversaire de ma grand-mère et je vais faire une salade de fruits.
Voici une orange. Elle est juteuse.
Merci, au revoir.

Bonjour Monsieur,je voudrais une poire, s'il vous plaît.
Pourquoi **une** poire?
C'est l'anniversaire de de ma grand-mère et je vais faire une salade de fruits.
Voici une poire. Elle est mûre.
Merci, au revoir.

Bonjour Madame, je voudrais une pêche, s'il vous plaît.
Pourquoi **une** pêche?
C'est l'anniversaire de de ma grand-mère et je vais faire une salade de fruits.
Voici une pêche. Elle est délicieuse.
Merci, au revoir.

Bonjour Monsieur,je voudrais une mangue, s'il vous plaît.
Pourquoi **une** mangue?
C'est l'anniversaire de de ma grand-mère et je vais faire une salade de fruits.
Voici une mangue. Elle est exotique!
Merci, au revoir.

Bonjour Madame,je voudrais un ananas, s'il vous plaît.
Pourquoi **un** ananas?
C'est l'anniversaire de ma grand-mère et je vais faire une salade de fruits.
Voici un ananas. Il est joli.
Merci, au revoir.

Bonjour Monsieur,je voudrais un kiwi, s'il vous plaît.
Pourquoi **un** kiwi?
C'est l'anniversaire de de ma grand-mère et je vais faire une salade de fruits.
Voici un kiwi. Il est sucré.
Merci, au revoir.

A la maison, il prépare la salade de fruits. Quelle belle salade de fruits!
En route chez sa grand-mère, il glisse sur une peau de banane!
La salade de fruits tombe par terre.

Plus tard à l'hôpital, sa grand-mère arrive.
Bonjour, Jean-Luc.
Bonjour, Mamie.
J'ai une surprise pour toi, Jean-Luc. Voici une belle salade de fruits!
Une salade de fruits! Quelle surprise!

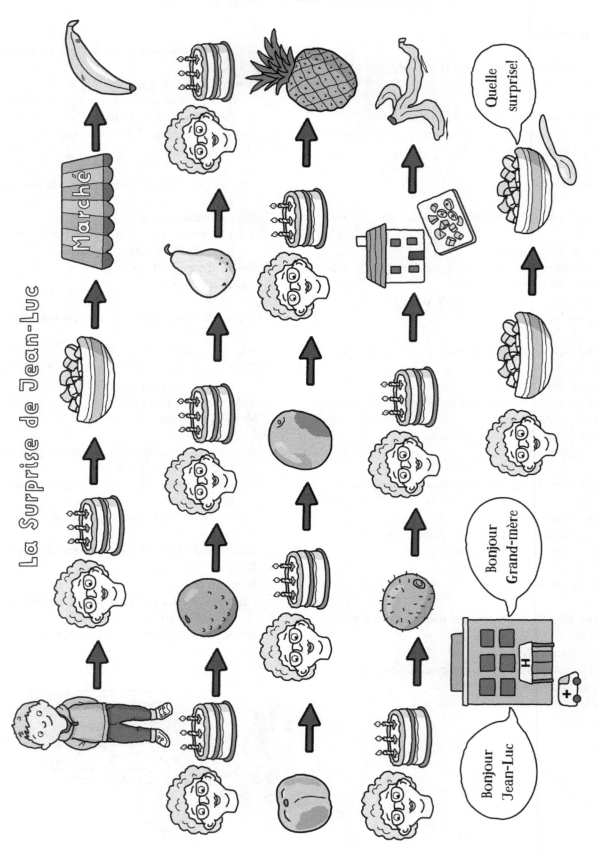

| |
|---|
| Il était une fois, un petit garçon qui s'appelait Jean-Luc. |
| Un jour, c'est l'anniversaire de sa grand-mère. |
| Il décide de faire une surprise pour sa grand-mère. – une belle salade de fruits. |
| Il va au marché... |

| |
|---|
| Bonjour Monsieur, je voudrais une banane, s'il vous plaît. |
| Pourquoi **une** banane ? |
| C'est l'anniversaire de ma grand-mère et je vais faire une salade de fruits. |
| Voici une banane. Elle est bonne pour la santé. |
| Merci, au revoir. |

| |
|---|
| Bonjour Madame, je voudrais une orange, s'il vous plaît. |
| Pourquoi **une** orange ? |
| C'est l'anniversaire de ma grand-mère et je vais faire une salade de fruits. |
| Voici une orange. Elle est juteuse. |
| Merci, au revoir. |

| |
|---|
| Bonjour Monsieur, je voudrais une poire, s'il vous plaît. |
| Pourquoi **une** poire ? |
| C'est l'anniversaire de ma grand-mère et je vais faire une salade de fruits. |
| Voici une poire. Elle est mûre. |
| Merci, au revoir. |

| |
|---|
| Bonjour Madame, je voudrais une pêche, s'il vous plaît. |
| Pourquoi **une** pêche ? |
| C'est l'anniversaire de ma grand-mère et je vais faire une salade de fruits. |
| Voici une pêche. Elle est délicieuse. |
| Merci, au revoir. |

| |
|---|
| Bonjour Monsieur, je voudrais une mangue, s'il vous plaît. |
| Pourquoi **une** mangue ? |
| C'est l'anniversaire de ma grand-mère et je vais faire une salade de fruits. |
| Voici une mangue. Elle est exotique. |
| Merci, au revoir. |

| |
|---|
| Bonjour Madame, je voudrais un ananas, s'il vous plaît. |
| Pourquoi **un** ananas ? |
| C'est l'anniversaire de ma grand-mère et je vais faire une salade de fruits. |
| Voici un ananas. Il est joli. |
| Merci, au revoir. |

| |
|---|
| Bonjour Monsieur, je voudrais un kiwi, s'il vous plaît. |
| Pourquoi **un** kiwi ? |
| C'est l'anniversaire de ma grand-mère et je vais faire une salade de fruits. |
| Voici un kiwi. Il  est sucré. |
| Merci, au revoir. |

| |
|---|
| A la maison, il prépare la salade de fruits. Quelle belle salade de fruits ! |
| En route chez sa grand-mère, il glisse sur une peau de banane ! |
| La salade de fruits tombe par terre ! |

| |
|---|
| Plus tard à l'hôpital, sa grand-mère arrive. |
| Bonjour, Jean-Luc. |
| Bonjour, Mamie. |
| J'ai une surprise pour toi ! Voici une belle salade de fruits ! |
| Une salade de fruits ! Quelle surprise ! |

Voici une banane. Elle est _____.

Voici une _____. Elle est _____.

Voici __ _____. Elle est _____.

Voici __ _____. Elle est _____.

Voici une _____. __ est _____.

Voici un _____. Il est _____.

Voici _ _____. __ est _____.

---

une banane  une mangue   une poire   un ananas   une orange
une pêche  un kiwi   juteuse   délicieuse  mûre  joli  sucré
bonne pour la santé   exotique

---

Voici une banane. Elle est _____.

Voici une _____. Elle est _____.

Voici __ _____. Elle est _____.

Voici __ _____. Elle est _____.

Voici une _____. __ est _____.

Voici un _____. Il est _____.

Voici _ _____. __ est _____.

---

une banane  une mangue   une poire   un ananas   une orange
une pêche  un kiwi   juteuse   délicieuse  mûre  joli  sucré
bonne pour la santé   exotique

## I can give my opinion in French

| 1. | J'aime ... | ☺ |
|----|----|----|
| 2. | J'aime beaucoup... | ☺☺ |
| 3. | J'adore... | ☺☺☺ |
| 4. | Je n'aime pas... | ☹ |
| 5. | Je n'aime pas du tout... | ☹☹ |
| 6. | Je déteste... | ☹☹☹ |
|    |    |    |
|    |    |    |
|    |    |    |
|    |    |    |
|    |    |    |
|    |    |    |
|    |    |    |
|    |    |    |

## My opinion on the fruits that I have tasted

_____

_____

_____

_____

_____

_____

# La Coupe Fruitée

## Ingrédients (pour six personnes)

- une banane
- 12 raisins
- 12 framboises
- 2 prunes
- une pêche
- un demi-citron
- du sucre

## Méthode

1. Lavez bien les raisins et les prunes

2. Epluchez la pêche et la banane

3. Coupez les raisins en deux

4. Découpez la pêche, les prunes et la banane en petits morceaux

5. Mettez les morceaux de fruits dans un bol

6. Pressez le demi-citron

7. Versez le jus sur les fruits

8. Saupoudrez de sucre

9. Mélangez bien les fruits

10. Voilà la coupe fruitée

## PM 8.11 SPEAKING FRAME (EXTENDING SENTENCES – GIVING OPINIONS)

| | | | |
|---|---|---|---|
| J'aime<br><br>J'adore<br><br>Je n'aime pas<br><br>Je déteste | la coupe fruitée | parce qu'elle est | juteuse<br><br>mûre<br><br>sucrée<br><br>délicieuse<br><br>multicolore<br><br>bonne pour la santé |

# Pedro el Pirata

Érase una vez un pirata que se llamaba Pedro.

El lunes se pone unos pantalones

El martes se pone unos pantalones y una camisa.

El miércoles se pone unos pantalones, una camisa y unas botas.

El jueves se pone unos pantalones, una camisa, unas botas y un sombrero de pirata.

El viernes se pone unos pantalones, una camisa, unas botas, un sombrero de pirata y un pañuelo.

El sábado se pone unos pantalones, una camisa, unas botas, un sombrero de pirata, un pañuelo y un parche.

El domingo está cansado y duerme.

## PM 8.13 PEDRO EL PIRATA: STORY MAP

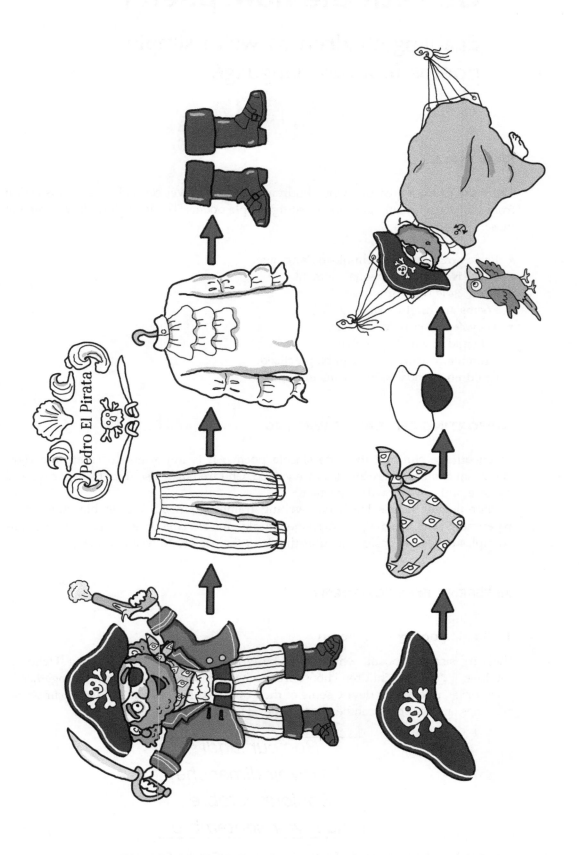

# 9 Go with the flow: poetry

## Enabling children to write simple poems in a new language

### RATIONALE

There are so many reasons why children at primary level can gain great satisfaction from playing with language and creating simple poems. The list below shows some of these:

- Poems can use small chunks of language.
- There is a strong personal element.
- Nothing is right or wrong.
- Poems are fun to write.
- They can be cross-curricular.
- All children can be involved.
- Grammatical structures can be practised.
- Children already write poems in English.

### SUPPORTING CHILDREN'S WRITING

To encourage children to write simple poems, it is important to create the right classroom climate where all ideas are valued. Children may also find it supportive and less stressful to write with a partner.

For poems at this level, use writing frames or models to enable children to experiment with language and create simple and effective poems. This chapter has examples of several basic structures that lend themselves to writing poetry.

### DIFFERENT TYPES OF POEMS

#### 'Hello ... goodbye ...' poem

The very simplest poem, which could be written as early as year 3, is a 'Hello ... goodbye ...' poem. Children choose from a bank of words things that go together in pairs, or later years can devise some of their own, working in pairs. If each pair writes two lines, a class poem can be put together. Here is an example in French:

> *Bonjour lundi*
> *Au revoir dimanche*
> *Bonjour octobre*
> *Au revoir septembre*

*Translation:* Hello Monday/Goodbye Sunday. /Hello October/Goodbye September.

## Shape poems

These are easy to construct. Children write words, phrases or sentences round the edge of a picture they are describing, as in this famous calligram by the French poet Apollinaire. There are many others available online, written in the shapes of the Eiffel Tower, a cat, or rain.

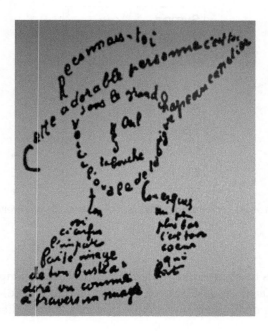

A variation on this is where children fill the image over and over again with language associated with parts of the image. The following example was written by one of Isaac Greaves' pupils (2015). The amount or complexity of the language can be varied; at the simplest level a word or simple phrase can be repeated. The use of colour within the shape can also provide meaning.

## An acrostic poem

This is where, for example, the children write the letters of their name vertically and find a word/phrase for each letter describing them/something they do. They can work in pairs and use a dictionary. Here is an example:

| |
|---|
| **S**ympa |
| **T**reize ans |
| **E**nergique |
| **F**antastique |
| **A**crobate |
| **N**age bien |
| **I**ntelligente |
| **É**légante |

Stefanie is nice/Thirteen years old/Energetic/Fantastic/Acrobatic/Swims well/Intelligent/Elegant.

## Likes and dislikes

Using simple phrases to express likes and dislikes provides a simple structure to create an effective poem. *J'aime* ... *Je n'aime pas* (I like ... I don't like) can lead to children writing a four-line poem, choosing nouns or verbs from either a word bank or a dictionary.

| | |
|---|---|
| *J'aime manger*<br>*J'aime jouer*<br>*J'aime parler*<br>*Je n'aime pas dormir!* | *Me gusta comer*<br>*Me gusta jugar*<br>*Me gusta hablar*<br>*¡ No me gusta dormir!* |

I like eating/ I like playing/ I like talking/ I don't like sleeping!

## Simile poems

A colour poem can be effective, with the colours highlighted either by hand or different coloured fonts if word-processed.

| | |
|---|---|
| *Rouge comme une pomme*<br>*Bleu comme le ciel*<br>*Jaune comme une banane* | *Rojo como una manzana*<br>*Azul como el cielo*<br>*Amarillo como un plátano* |

Red like an apple/ Blue like the sky/ Yellow like a banana.

## Pyramid poem

In years 5 and 6, children can be even more creative, constructing a pyramid-shaped poem from a basic sentence with use of additional adjectives and phrases:

> *La*
> *La chambre*
> *Dans la chambre*
> *Dans la grande chambre*
> *Dans la grande chambre jaune*
> *Dans la grande chambre jaune il y a*
> *Dans la grande chambre jaune il y a un chien*

In the big yellow room, there is a dog.

## A strange animal poem

Children enjoy creating this poem, with strange adjectives to describe animals:

> *Au zoo il y a*
> *un lion bleu*
> *un tigre vert*
> *un crocodile gentil*
> *un rhinocéros*
> *minuscule*
> *un guépard lent*

At the zoo there is a blue lion, a green tiger, a friendly crocodile, a tiny rhinoceros, a slow cheetah.

## Rhyming poems

Rhyming poems are also popular with children. Using a word bank, children could select matching names and towns, for example, *Mireille habite à Marseille . . . Jean habite à Lyon* (Mireille lives in Marseille . . . John lives in Lyon). Alternatively, family members could be linked with clothes:

> *Ma cousine Josette*
> *Porte des chaussettes*
> *Mon frère Jean*
> *Porte un pantalon*

My cousin Josette/Wears socks./My brother John/Wears trousers.

## If I were . . ., I would be . . .

*Si j'étais . . ., je serais . . .* (if I were . . ., I would be . . . ) is another structure that appeals to children. They can write two or three lines in pairs to contribute to a longer class poem:

> *Si j'étais un animal*
> *Je serais un lion*
> *Pour être fort*
>
> *Si j'étais un jour*
> *Je serais dimanche*
> *Pour rester au lit*

> *Si yo fuera un coche*
> *Sería un Porshe*
> *Para ser rápido*
>
> *Si yo fuera una fruta*
> *Sería una naranja*
> *Porque es jugosa*

*If I were an animal/I would be a lion/To be strong.*
*If I were a day/I would be Sunday/To stay in bed.*
*If I were a car/ I would be a Porsche/To be fast.*
*If I were a fruit/I would be an orange/Because it's juicy.*

The third line in each verse is optional and could be used as an extension activity for some children.

## Love poems

Writing a love poem works well in all languages. Here is a Spanish example:

> *Como un día sin sol*
> *Como un gato sin ratón*
> *Como un río sin peces*
> *Como yo sin ti*

Like a day without sun/ Like a cat without a mouse/ Like a river without fish/ Like me without you.

## Alphabet poems

These can be fun for children to write, using a dictionary or word bank. Each pair could be given a different letter of the alphabet:

> *Un alligator d'Afrique*
> *Un babouin de Belgique*
> *Un chat de Chine*
> *Un dauphin de Danemark*
> *Un éléphant d'Ethiopie*

An alligator from Africa/ A baboon from Belgium/ A cat from China/ A dolphin from Denmark/ An elephant from Ethiopia.

## Recipe poems

Children can use word banks to write a poem about, for example, a perfect day in the park:

> *Prenez le beau temps*
> *Ajoutez un enfant*
> *Mélangez avec des amis*
> *Ajoutez un vélo et un jeu de football*
> *Ajoutez aussi une balançoire et une glace*
> *Mélangez bien*
> *Faites cuire toute l'après-midi*

*Take good weather/Add a child/Mix with some friends/Add a bike and a game of football/Add a swing and an ice cream, too/Mix well/Cook for a whole afternoon.*

Differentiation can be introduced by encouraging some children to add adjectives, for example, *une balançoire rapide* (a fast swing), *une glace énorme* (an enormous ice cream).

In conclusion, children derive great satisfaction from writing a poem alone or with a partner. They see it as an easy form of writing and are helped by writing frames. Poems can be displayed either in a book of class poems, a frieze round the walls or even a 'poem of the week', enlarged for other children to see as they pass the classroom. Poems can be performed for other classes, in assembly or for parents.

# 10 Hitting the right note: music and song

## RATIONALE

Music and languages are closely linked in that they express feelings and ideas. The primary curriculum for both music and languages has many similarities: listening attentively; exploring patterns and sounds of language; enjoying singing songs and chanting rhymes which include authentic texts; and performing with increasing confidence and fluency. Musical elements and melody can all enhance primary language teaching.

## AUTHENTIC SONGS

Traditional songs in the language are useful in that they are culturally based. Songs also have the advantage of sensitising the ear. They can be used for identifying new sounds in the language and later for learning the phoneme–grapheme representations. For example, 'Sur le pont d'Avignon' is good for learning about the *on* sound. Once the children have listened and responded (see the 'Sounds different' chapter), the song text can be displayed and the different grapheme representations for this sound can be highlighted.

---

**Sur le pont d'Avignon**

| | |
|---|---|
| *Sur le <u>pont</u> d'Avign<u>on</u>,* | On the bridge at Avignon, |
| *L'<u>on</u> y <u>danse</u>, l'<u>on</u> y <u>danse</u>,* | We are dancing, we are dancing, |
| *Sur le <u>pont</u> d'Avign<u>on</u>,* | On the bridge at Avignon, |
| *L'<u>on</u> y <u>danse</u> tous <u>en</u> <u>rond</u>.* | We are all dancing in a circle. |

---

The traditional song 'Dans la forêt lointaine' is excellent for getting the children to recognise and practise the *ou* sound. One half of the class can be asked to stand when they hear *coucou* and the other half when they hear *hibou*.

For a list of some more traditional children's songs from France and Spain, refer to the chapter 'A helping hand'.

---

### Dans la Forêt Lointaine

| | |
|---|---|
| *Dans la forêt lointaine* | In the distant forest |
| *On entend le coucou* | You can hear the cuckoo, |
| *Du haut de son grand chêne* | From the top of his big oak tree |
| *Il répond au hibou:* | He answers the owl: |
| *Coucou, hibou,* | Cuckoo, owl, |
| *Coucou, hibou,* | Cuckoo, owl, |
| *Coucou, hibou, coucou,* | Cuckoo, owl, cuckoo, |
| *Coucou, hibou,* | Cuckoo, owl, |
| *Coucou, hibou,* | Cuckoo, owl, |
| *Coucou, hibou, coucou.* | Cuckoo, owl, cuckoo. |

---

## COMPOSING SONGS

When key language structures and vocabulary are set to music, many children will learn and remember them easily. While there are many commercially produced songs for teaching topic vocabulary, it is also possible for both teachers and children to compose their own songs for this purpose. This may involve composing melodies but can also be done by adopting familiar tunes, to which they set their own words.

Composing songs allows children to focus on new vocabulary around any topic or theme; this could later lead to performances, or even song competitions. There is a strong link with developing musical skills because children will need to be aware of the duration and rhythm of the words in order to make them fit the tune.

### Transition songs

Teachers might compose songs to aid daily routines and transitions. Such songs could be used at various points in the day such as lining up, making a circle, returning to tables and settling down to work. See below for examples of simple songs that could be used to make transitions smooth, while providing further opportunities to practise the new language.

---

### Lining up
#### to the tune of
#### 'London's Burning'

| | |
|---|---|
| *¡En fila!* | Line up! |
| *¡En fila!* | Line up! |
| *¡Sin ruido!* | No noise! |
| *¡Sin ruido!* | No noise! |
| *¡En fila!* | Line up! |
| *¡En fila!* | Line up! |
| *¡Sin charlar!* | No chatting! |
| *¡Sin charlar!* | No chatting! |

---

### Making a Circle
#### to the tune of
#### 'Frère Jacques'

| | |
|---|---|
| *Faites un cercle,* | Make a circle |
| *Faites un cercle,* | Make a circle |
| *En silence,* | In silence, |
| *En silence,* | In silence, |
| *Venez vite* | Come quickly, |
| *Venez vite,* | Come quickly, |
| *Doucement* | Quietly, |
| *Doucement.* | Quietly. |

---

**Days of the Week**

to the tune of 'DooDah'


*Lundi ... mardi ... mercredi*

*Oh là, oh là*

*Jeudi ... vendredi ... samedi*

*Oh là là là là*

*Samedi ... dimanche*

*Samedi ... dimanche*

*Lundi ... mardi ... mercredi*

*Jeudi ... vendredi*

---

Here is a tried and tested list of other familiar tunes, which can be used when creating songs in the new language.

### Children's songs

- Three blind mice
- Frère Jacques
- Jingle bells
- Old McDonald
- London Bridge is falling down
- Hickory, dickory, dock
- London's burning
- Twinkle, twinkle, little star
- Here we go round the mulberry bush
- If you're happy and you know it
- The wheels on the bus.

### Others

- Happy birthday
- Pink Panther
- She'll be coming round the mountain
- Hey Jude
- When the saints go marching in
- My Bonnie
- Various football songs, for example, 'Ere we go
- Yellow submarine
- Joseph and his technicolour dreamcoat.

## COMMERCIALLY PRODUCED SONGS

These often accompany a course or scheme of work, but can often be bought as separate CDs and/or song books. In addition to embedding new language, they often provide opportunities for listening to a range of different voices and accents.

## EXPLOITING SONGS

Initially the teacher may want to use a song as a listening exercise. This might follow some work on a topic and be useful in showing the children's comprehension skills by their being asked to perform an action or mime to show their understanding of key vocabulary.

When the teacher wants the children to learn a song, it is best to show the words as they hear the song being sung. In the authors' experience, children generally like to know what the song words mean and, therefore, one approach is to let children follow the words while listening to it being sung, with an accompanying English translation. Adding pictures to reinforce meaning is another way of helping the children understand the song. However, the teacher may choose to use the song text, without English, if the objective is to develop reading skills.

Adding actions for words and phrases will further reinforce the meaning and help the children remember the vocabulary. In this way, children are immediately able to enjoy joining in with the song. Children can be encouraged to sing repeated words and choruses, but verses will often need to be rehearsed. It might be necessary for the children to repeat or sing lines of the song back to the teacher, in order to help them articulate the words. It helps when the teacher points to self or the class, to indicate whose turn it is.

As part of the teaching process, it might be helpful to give different lines or verses to different groups of children to sing, with everyone joining in the chorus.

It is also possible to introduce an element of competition in this way, thereby encouraging the children to sing more confidently.

Being able to sing songs in another language gives children a sense of achievement, in addition to embedding really useful language and linguistic structures. Songs also have the added advantage of making excellent material for class performances in assemblies and to perform for parents.

## MUSICAL ELEMENTS

The benefits of using different musical elements, such as pitch (high/low), tempo (fast/slow), or dynamics (loud/soft), to make repetition of new vocabulary interesting, has already been mentioned in the chapter on 'Developing skills'. Children can be encouraged to use the musical terminology to choose how they would like to practise.

## RHYTHM

Counting the number of syllables in words and clapping them is an efficient technique for helping children to internalise and recall new language. Children can listen and identify a word or phrase from a list, which the teacher or another child has clapped. In continuous speech, clapping can also be useful for stressing particular words as an aid to good pronunciation.

### Clapping rhythms

The authors have devised the following clapping rhymes to embed specific useful vocabulary and develop good pronunciation and intonation. In these rhymes, children clap every time a word or part of a word is highlighted in bold.

*Pliez les genoux (bend your knees)*

*Pliez les genoux (bend your knees)*

*Indiquez à gauche (point to the left)*

*Indiquez à droite (point to the right)*

*Indiquez à gauche*

*Indiquez à droite*

*Indiquez en haut (point up high)*

*Indiquez en bas (point down low)*

*Indiquez en haut*

*Indiquez en bas*

*A moi moi moi (my turn)*

**Battez ici**
(Clap here - near body)

**Battez là**
(clap there - away from body)

**Sur** la jambe
(on right leg)

**Sous** la jambe
(under right leg)

**Sur** la jambe
(under left leg)

**Sous** la jambe
(under left leg)

**Battez tout autour**
(Clap all around - turn around)

This adaptation of a party game aids concentration and helps develop intonation, as the children ask who has stolen the biscuits from the big blue tin. One child's name is given and that person replies with *qui moi?* and later with *pas moi*; s/he then names the new person, after the question *qui donc?*

**Qui** prend les **bis**cuits dans la **grande boîte bleue**?

... (**child's name**) prend les **bis**cuits dans la **grande boîte bleue**

**Qui moi**? (Who me?)

**Oui, toi!** (Yes, you!)

**Pas moi** (Not me!)

**Qui donc**? (Then who?)

... (a different name) prend les **bis**cuits dans la **grande boîte bleue**
**Qui moi**? (Who me?)
(then repeat from line 4)

In Spanish, the hand-clapping song 'Toma tomate' performed by children sitting or standing in a circle, provides a fun way of saying Spanish words over a steady beat. Teachers can see it demonstrated on several different YouTube websites.

---

### Toma Tomate

*Toma tomate Tomalo*

*ia ia oh Plof*

---

Actions with rhythm are a further way of helping children to learn while enjoying playing with language. This popular Spanish rhyme is a good example.

---

### Soy una taza

| | |
|---|---|
| *Soy una taza* | (I'm a cup/mug) |
| *una tetera* | (a teapot) |
| *una cuchara* | (a spoon) |
| *un cucharon* | (a ladle) |
| *un plato hondo* | (a bowl) |
| *un plato llano* | (a dinner plate) |
| *un cuchillito* | (a knife) |
| *un tenedor.* | (a fork) |
| | |
| *Soy un salero* | (I'm a salt cellar) |
| *un azucarero* | (a sugar bowl) |
| *la batidora* | (a blender) |
| *una olla express chu chu* | (a pressure cooker) |

*Taza tetera*
*cuchara cucharon*
*plato hondo plato*
*llano cuchillito*
*tenedor salero*
*azucarero batidora*
*olla expres.*

---

## TRADITIONAL RHYMES

Traditional rhymes also help children memorise useful vocabulary, while encouraging good pronunciation and intonation in the language. The following rhyme is excellent for making children aware of special pronunciation rules for the numbers *six* and *dix* when followed by a consonant. They learn to avoid sounding the last letter of each number, as they would normally do when counting. The rhyme is fun because of the joke at the end (*dix nez* has two meanings – 'ten noses' or 'dinner').

> *Un nez, deux nez, trois nez,*
> *quatre nez, cinq nez,*
> *six nez, sept nez, huit nez,*
> *neuf nez, dix nez (dîner)*

The next rhyme is good, both for learning the days of the week and for practising speech. Children will be interested to know that the days of the week here have a capital letter because they are seen as people.

> *Bonjour Madame Lundi*
>
> *Comment va Madame Mardi?*
>
> *Très bien, Madame Mercredi.*
>
> *Dites à Madame Jeudi*
>
> *De venir Vendredi*
>
> *Danser Samedi*
>
> *Dans la salle de Dimanche*

A traditional rhyme that children love and can use to decide who will be 'out' is the nonsense rhyme below. Children form a large circle and chant the words. As they become familiar with them, the words can be chanted much faster. Whoever has a turn when *pic* is said is out and the chant restarts until only one child is left:

> *Am stram gram*
>
> *Pic et pic et colegram*
>
> *Bour et bour et ratatam*
>
> *Am stram gram pic*

### Finger rhymes

These are effective for lower key stage 2 children in that they allow them to hear and repeat several short sentences in sequence. The eventual aim is for children to perform the finger rhymes confidently, in small groups, or individually. In order to achieve this, they need to be repeated often and make good lesson starters. The suggested steps for learning are:

- the teacher asks children to watch the hand actions, while listening to the finger rhyme;
- children listen again, while copying the hand actions;
- children repeat each line after the teacher, with accompanying hand actions;
- half the class lead and the other half repeat;
- children recite the finger rhyme as a class, in groups, pairs or independently.

## ADDING SOUNDSCAPES

Another rewarding and meaningful link between music and teaching another language is to combine spoken language with musical composition.

### Stories

These can be a starting point for creating a soundscape. A bilingual story that the authors have used is 'Walking through the jungle'; this shows animals in different habitats. The actions of the person in the story and pictures of the different landscapes provide an excellent stimulus for creating a soundscape, using a variety of instruments. Children can discuss the timbre and suitability of different sounds to portray the story text and add a narration in the new language to complete the performance.

### Poetry

Reciting a poem to a musical accompaniment or adding an ostinato can be highly effective and really add to the performance. The poem 'Il pleut' by Jacques Prévert, with its short lines and suggested sound effect of rain, fits a weather topic well. Half the class can recite the poem while the other half repeat a line from the poem – *il pleut* – over and over again, thus creating an ostinato effect. It is an ideal poem for designing a soundscape.

Teachers can find or create their own poems for this purpose. Children can enhance their performance of a 'noisy' poem, either by adding sound effects, with percussion instruments or body percussion (clapping, slapping thighs, vocal sounds).

The example on the right of a 'noisy poem' could be practised by the whole class together, before children work in small groups to create sound effects. This would allow them to describe through words and sound what is happening in the different rooms of a house. At the end of this chapter there is a photocopiable master of another 'noisy' poem, written to demonstrate the increasing intensity of an approaching storm.

> **A la maison**
>
> *Dans la cuisine*
> *Mon père prépare le dîner*
> *Dans le salon*
> *Ma mère joue du piano*
> *Dans le jardin*
> *Mon frère répare sa moto*
> *Et dans la chambre*
> *Moi, je dors*

*In the kitchen/ My father is making the dinner/ In the lounge/My mother is playing the piano/In the garden/My brother is repairing his motorbike/And in the bedroom/I'm sleeping.*

## Photographs and paintings

Using photographs of places in countries where the target language is spoken, or paintings and music by artists from those countries, has the added advantage of helping to enhance and develop children's knowledge and understanding of different cultures. Photographs and paintings can provide the inspiration for creating a short narration over music. Children use their senses to list what they can see, hear, smell and taste to describe the scene in the new language. It may be appropriate to include feelings, too. The suggested vocabulary for this can be found at the end of the 'Allons-y! ¡Sí sí sí!' chapter. Music and language, when combined in this way, make for a powerful performance.

The following paintings could all provide good starting points for creating a narration over a soundscape:

- *La Grande Jatte* by Georges Seurat. This shows a scene beside water, with lots of people and action.
- *Scène à la plage* by Edgar Degas. This shows a beach scene with bathers, boating and lots of action on the sand.
- *Fight between a Tiger and a Buffalo* by Henri Rousseau shows the movement of two powerful animals in a jungle setting.
- *Afternoon Sun* by Joaquín Sorolla shows a boat, men and cows in the sea.
- *Las Meninas* by Velásquez depicts a family in a room, with their dog, and a painter who is painting the group.

Further inspiration and ideas can be found on the National Gallery website: www.nationalgallery.org.uk/noisypaintings. This has ideas for composition and creating soundscapes. Children are encouraged to compose, by choosing from a menu of mood sounds and short musical phrases to accompany paintings by Monet and Rousseau. It is possible for them to send their composition to a friend as an e-card. The examples will inspire children to create their own compositions, based on other paintings.

## MUSICAL APPRECIATION AND INTERPRETATION

### Opinions in the target language

Children can be taught appropriate vocabulary in the target language that will enable them to respond to pieces of music they hear. For example, they name the instruments they hear playing – *Il y a une trompette/J'ai entendu un piano* (There is a trumpet/I heard a piano); identify the genre of music – *C'est la musique jazz* (It is jazz music); or give simple opinions – *J'aime ça/Je n'aime pas ça* (I like it/I don't like it), *C'est super* (It's brilliant), *C'est nul* (It's no good). They could also make comments about the music, using appropriate adjectives: *C'est rapide/lent* (It is fast/slow); or give an extended answer: *J'aime la musique parce que c'est rapide* (I like the music because it is fast).

### Interpretation

The children could be asked to listen to a piece of music and imagine what the music is about – people and places or events. They could be asked to draw or write notes about what they imagine the music is describing. The themes and ideas could then form the basis for new vocabulary and descriptions in the target language, which in turn could be used to create simple poems to accompany the music. Here are some ideas:

- Saint-Saëns – *The Carnival of the Animals*;
- Dukas – *The Sorcerer's Apprentice*;
- Debussy – *La mer*, 'Clair de lune', *L'après-midi d'un faune*;
- Berlioz – *Symphonie fantastique*.

In conclusion, in this chapter we have considered how performing, composing and appreciation of music can be combined with learning the new language in a creative way. The idea of narration over a soundscape or using a piece of music as a stimulus for writing simple poems has also been explored.

## *L'Orage*

| | |
|---|---|
| *Ouvrez les portes!* | *Ecoutez le vent* |
| *Ouvrez les portes!* | *Ecoutez le vent* |
| *Il y a du soleil..* | *Fermez les portes* |
| *On va dehors* | *L'orage arrive* |
| | |
| *Regardez le ciel!* | *Regardez le ciel* |
| *Regardez le ciel!* | *Regardez le ciel* |
| *Il y a des nuages* | *Il y a du tonnerre* |
| *On va dedans* | *L'orage arrive* |
| | |
| *Ouvrez les portes!* | *Ecoutez le tonnerre* |
| *Ouvrez les portes!* | *Ecoutez le tonnerre* |
| *Il y a du soleil..* | *Moi, j'ai peur* |
| *On va dehors* | *L'orage arrive* |
| | |
| *Regardez le ciel!* | *Ecoutez la pluie* |
| *La pluie tombe* | *Ecoutez le vent* |
| *Oh non, pas ça!* | *Ecoutez le tonnerre* |
| *On va dedans* | *L'orage arrive.. Boum!* |
| | |
| *Regardez le ciel* | *J'ai peur* |
| *Regardez le ciel* | *J'ai peur* |
| *Il y a du vent* | *Sous le lit!* |
| *On reste dedans* | |
| | *L'orage arrive* |
| *Regardez le ciel* | |
| *Regardez le ciel* | *L'orage passe... c'est calme* |
| *Fermez les portes!* | *L'orage passe... c'est calme* |
| *Il siffle fort* | |

# 11 Integrating language learning

## RATIONALE

In addition to some discrete language teaching, there are many advantages in embedding the new language in school routines and linking it to other subject areas within the curriculum. The benefits include: using language for a genuine purpose, reinforcing learning, providing meaningful opportunities for children to work together creatively and gaining additional curriculum time for language learning. Adopting a cross-curricular approach can be highly motivational for many learners.

Barnes (2011: 11) acknowledges that cross-curricular approaches may not suit all children, but maintains his belief that 'creativity is best stimulated in cross-curricular and authentic contexts'. He also speaks of it encouraging the development of 'group solutions; collaborative learning; creative combinations and independent thinkers'. He suggests that the teacher's role in a cross-curricular setting becomes much more diverse; the teacher may be a 'follower, co-learner, observer, adviser or assistant' (2011: 5).

Without cross-curricular learning, teaching in the foreign language remains a discrete activity; linking language learning to another subject area has many advantages. First, planning around a topic is seen as good primary practice. It makes the learning concrete and less abstract and therefore makes more sense to young children. The *Piece by Piece* document (DfES/CiLT, 2004) supports this view:

> It is important that languages should be integrated into the curriculum rather than being a bolt-on extra. . . . There are obvious and fruitful links between foreign languages and . . . the development of listening and speaking, mathematics, geography and citizenship.

In primary teaching it is important that children develop a love of learning, and putting learning into distinct subject areas can seem less engaging for some. A child might really enjoy one subject but dislike another; therefore, if the teaching can link the two subjects, the child's enthusiasm for one may have a positive influence on the other. For example, if a child loves music and is finding learning times tables hard, it might be beneficial to use times tables' songs to support his or her learning in maths. This analogy could also be linked to languages. A child who does not enjoy maths, but loves languages, might benefit from doing some number work in another language.

Furthermore, Gardner (1993) developed the idea of multiple intelligences (linguistic, logical-mathematical, musical, bodily-kinaesthetic, spatial, interpersonal, intrapersonal) and it could be argued that cross-curricular learning helps children develop a wider range of intelligences.

A colleague referred to a story about a year 3 child, with Special Educational Needs, who had a problem counting from ten to twenty in English because counting in multiples of ten had confused him. He could not understand the difference between sixteen and sixty. Counting in Spanish helped him understand because sixteen in Spanish, *dieciseis* (literally meaning ten and six) and *sesenta* (sixty) are completely different. She commented on how wonderful it was to see him using Spanish to solve a problem in another context.

Primary teachers are creative; they are also good at working collaboratively in a cross-curricular way, to produce highly stimulating materials that help develop key skills across several subjects. Integrating language teaching with other subjects also helps the less confident teacher find a way into teaching the new language by using their strengths. For example, a music specialist is likely to love teaching language through song and a PE specialist would enjoy using the target language in PE lessons.

Finally, the primary timetable is always busy; adopting an integrated approach to language learning can actually save time.

There are different levels and ways in which languages can be integrated into the primary curriculum. Teachers may find it helpful to consider the amount of integration according to their own level of confidence and expertise. Four distinct levels may be seen as integrating the new language to:

- use in daily routines;
- link with other curriculum areas;
- reinforce learning in another subject; and
- teach new content in another subject.

## INTEGRATING LANGUAGE WITH DAILY ROUTINES

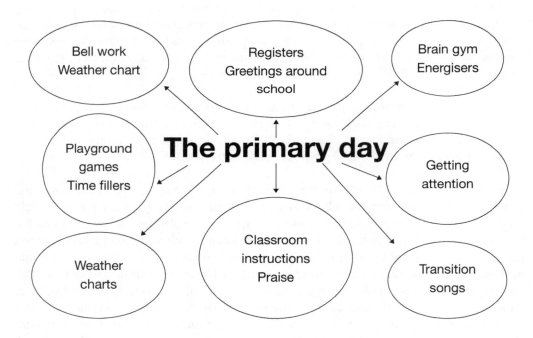

Many primary schools start the day with 'bell' or 'early' work activities. This is a prime time to revisit or consolidate learning in another language. Children can be asked to sort words into categories, spot the odd one out, arrange vocabulary in dictionary order, practise spelling some vocabulary (using the look, cover, write, check method), play a language game with a friend, which could be as simple as partner A miming a word/phrase for partner B to guess.

Greetings through the day and taking the registers (attendance and dinner) provide an opportunity to speak in the target language (please refer to the chapter 'Allons-y! ¡Sí sí sí!' for specific language) but they also give scope for further linguistic practice. The children could reply with a number, letter, day of the week, month of the year, weather phrase, an opinion or indeed any vocabulary they have been learning. Words and phrases could be written on the board, thereby providing some practice in reading aloud.

Signage in the target language to label different parts of the classroom and school building will also raise the profile of the new language and the children will benefit from further, natural exposure to the written word in context. Additionally, it is helpful in designing and labelling a plan of the school to share with a link class abroad.

Sometimes children find it hard to concentrate; they need a 'brain break' from their work, in the form of a short, energising activity. The fact that children learn better if given short breaks is highlighted by Smith and Call (2001: 131) who advocate 'experimenting with more physical movement in class' to compensate for 'a reduction in structured play'.

A favourite activity is *Passez le sac!*, which involves passing different coloured beanbags round the class to music. When the music is paused, the colour of the beanbag indicates which movement the individual holding it must perform until the music restarts. This activity comes from the 'Take 10 en français' materials (Wakely and Morrison, 2004). This excellent resource, which is also in Spanish, integrates language teaching into daily physical activity and gives many suggestions for short physical activities using the target language, as well as aerobic dance routines set to traditional songs.

---

*- Passez le sac lentement à gauche.*

*- Quand la musique s'arrête, faites l'exercice qui correspond à votre couleur.*

*ROUGE - sautez sur place, le sac entre les genoux.*

*BLEU -   Courez sur place en tenant le sac en l'air*

*JAUNE -  Asseyez-vous sur le sac, puis levez-vous d'un bond en*
*             tenant le sac en l'air.*

*VERT -   Faites un pas comme ça (a step kick), le sac derrière le*
*             dos.*

---

Linking language with movement encourages connections between the left and right sides of the brain. Activities which make a greater demand, in that they require a higher level of multi-tasking, are even more valuable for encouraging connections between the two sides of the brain. For example, a starter activity might be to present written words for colours in the target language which are written in a different colour so *azul* (blue) might be written in green. The children must call out the colour that the word is written in and not read the word itself so the children would call out *verde* and not *azul* (green and not blue).

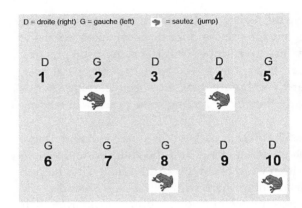

The activity on the left is another example of a surprisingly demanding task which can be used as a warm-up or 'brain break' to improve concentration and mental agility. Children chant the numbers, while raising their right/left hand for the symbols D(droite)/G(gauche). The frog signals that they should jump.

Integrating classroom commands and gaining children's attention in the target language gives children further exposure to the language they are learning, while providing a meaningful purpose for its use. These are not simply the preserve of language lessons. Many teachers ask the children to 'stop, look and listen' or count from one to five as a means of obtaining children's attention. These can easily be done in the new language. Other routines such as lining up, coming to the carpet, returning to tables and working quietly can form the basis for the use of transition songs. Please refer to the chapter 'Hitting the right note' for suggestions.

Primary language games can be used as five-minute fillers, before lunch, waiting in line, or at the end of the day. These games can be seen as a treat or reward, while subtly consolidating and reinforcing new language. This will all help children to enjoy learning another language, understand that it has a real purpose and develop a healthy and positive attitude towards language learning.

## INTEGRATING LANGUAGE WITH OTHER CURRICULUM AREAS

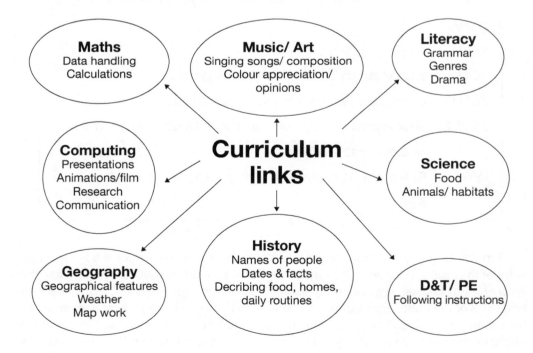

## LINKS WITH OTHER SUBJECTS

This level of integration involves finding links between the new language being taught and another subject area.

Mathematics and language can be successfully integrated. The tasks, however, must be at an appropriate cognitive level for the age and ability of the children. At primary level the children might not be able to count to a very high number in the target language; however, it is possible to create challenge through asking open questions. The examples below demonstrate how knowledge of low numbers in the target language can be used to provide different levels of mathematical challenge:

- If the question is: $? - ? = 2$, there are many possible answers, such as $5 - 3 = 2$ at a low cognitive level. A higher cognitive challenge would be to suggest that fractions could be used in the answer. This would open up possibilities for answers such as $15/3 - 3 = 2$.
- Another type of question could be: 'How many different calculations can you think of to arrive at the answer 18?'

Two further areas of mathematics that have been successfully linked to cross-curricular learning using the target language are shape and data handling. With a relatively small amount of target language, children can be taught to name and describe the properties of shapes. Surveys in the target language allow children to practise asking and answering questions on a topic, in addition to counting in the target language. Chapter 6 contains relevant mathematical terminology for calculation, shape and data handling in French and Spanish.

Looking at different text types in the new language will also provide an opportunity to discuss the layout and presentation of specific genres and seek to reinforce children's knowledge and understanding of this in literacy. Different genres also have particular language features, which are useful for comparison and to gain a deeper understanding of grammar (for example, imperative verbs and the use of adverbs in an instructional text, past tense in stories). Further benefits of linking literacy with the new language have already been mentioned elsewhere in the 'What's the story?' and 'Fun with grammar' chapters.

## LINKS THROUGH A TOPIC APPROACH

Linking language teaching with other subjects, which are often taught through a topic approach, can be effective for incorporating language topics such as daily routine, transport, animals, weather, clothes and food. In a science topic on healthy eating children could learn to

- name foods in the target language;
- talk about which foods they like;
- conduct surveys to find out which foods are the most/least popular;
- describe which foods are healthy and unhealthy;
- look at authentic recipe texts and make decisions about how healthy they are; and
- use dictionaries to find the meaning of new vocabulary found in lists of ingredients.

In a science topic on habitats, the children could learn to

- name animals,
- describe habitats, and
- say where different animals live and/or explain why.

Linking the new language with history and geography can be effective for incorporating language topics such as daily routine, transport, weather, clothes and food. The daily life of a Roman soldier or a Viking could provide the context for teaching daily routine in the target language, while creating a menu for a Tudor banquet could provide the context for learning the words for different foods and describing what we eat now and what was eaten in Tudor times.

Physical education (PE) lessons are the perfect place to use instructional language. Refer to the chapter 'Allons-y! ¡Sí sí sí!' for appropriate vocabulary that could be incorporated into lessons or warm-up/cool-down sessions. Some schools still have 'wake 'n' shake' activities each morning. This involves beginning the day with a short burst of physical activity to stimulate the brain prior to learning. The previously mentioned 'Take 10' series in French and Spanish has been used successfully for wake 'n' shake. The helpful DVD demonstrates each movement for children to copy while joining in with the songs.

A further resource that exploits the use of target language linked to cultural tradition is the *French Dance in the Primary Classroom* DVD, which is listed in the chapter 'A helping hand'. The folk dances are demonstrated on the DVD and the target language is provided on an audio CD.

Integration into daily routines and linking at a minimal level with another subject or topic allows a mixture of using the target language vocabulary and English in lessons and is therefore a suitable approach for less confident teachers. Barnes (2011: 58) speaks of much cross-curricular planning being multi-disciplinary in its approach in that it 'aims at using a single experience or theme to develop higher levels of understanding and performance in more than one discipline'. This is in contrast to 'hierarchical cross-curricular methods', which 'aim at achieving progress in one discipline by using aspects of another' (2011: 58).

## REINFORCING AND TEACHING NEW CONTENT THROUGH THE TARGET LANGUAGE

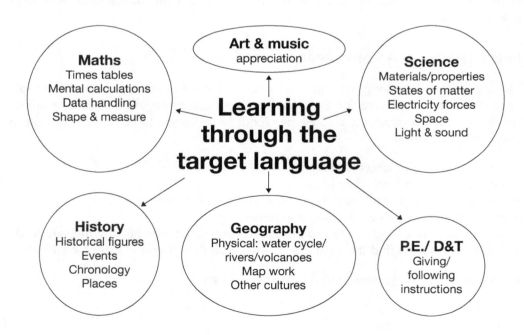

For those teachers who feel more confident in the target language, there are further levels of integration. Either subject content can be reinforced or new content taught through the use of the new language. The latter is often referred to as 'content and language integrated learning' (CLIL).

Some reinforcement of prior learning in the new language can be highly beneficial. While children need to revisit or relearn certain concepts, this can be repetitive and demotivating. A fresh approach is for them to hear it again in the new language, thereby creating new pathways in the brain. An example here would be a child who copes better with times tables in the new language. A teacher once resorted to revising all the science topics in French in preparation for SATs with her year 6 class. This proved a very successful experiment.

With careful planning, often involving shared expertise between colleagues, it is possible to teach new content in a variety of subject areas through the new language. It provides a natural context for language learning, makes excellent use of time and satisfies the principles of cross-curricularity. It can be motivational and inclusive for all abilities and helpful for children with English as an additional language in that it provides a level playing field.

Below is an example of a collaborative project, which involved lower key stage 2 children. However, the ideas would be easily adapted to suit an upper key stage 2 class.

## CROSS-CURRICULAR LEARNING: THE FIELD OF THE CLOTH OF GOLD

Traditionally studied as an A-level history topic, this is a story that can also be made accessible to primary children. It captures their imaginations and can be used to enrich their study of the Tudor period. At that time, powerful alliances were vital between countries. To that end, a meeting, near Calais in 1520, on the site now known as 'The Field of the Cloth of Gold', took place between two young kings, Henry VIII of England and Francis I of France.

The authors, together with colleagues at the University of the West of England, developed a unit of work based on this historical event, which provided an opportunity for the children to learn about life in Tudor times, the personality and behaviour of both kings and reasons for alliances between countries. The main aim was to integrate French into other curriculum subjects.

The story was written in French and in part narrated by the black trumpeter in Henry's court. Authentic images and maps were included to support the text and aid children's comprehension. The target language was carefully chosen, and cognates and familiar language were used whenever possible. Vocabulary in the target language included names, numbers, adjectives to describe the kings, food, expressing likes and dislikes, jousting (sporting) vocabulary, instructions and parts of the body.

In preparation for the unit, the children discussed the reasons for establishing friendships to better understand the concept of a need to form alliances.

The children engaged with the PowerPoint story of Henry's journey to France, the meeting of the kings, their competitiveness and rivalry, which included the design of their armour and jousting. They were fascinated by the luxury of the kings' courts with their entourage of thousands, their lavish encampments, elaborate tents and Henry's sumptuous palace erected for the occasion and hung with gold from Westminster Abbey. The copious amounts of food and drink in the English encampment amazed the children.

Each story chapter was followed by activities that provided further cross-curricular links with history, geography, music and dance, design technology and English literacy.

## Geography

The children looked at different maps and discovered that Calais was not always part of France. They mapped the route Henry would have taken to meet Francis and discussed the transport needed to carry the many thousands of people, belongings and food.

## Design and technology

There were various opportunities for links with design and technology. An enjoyable technology task was making shadow puppets by following instructions in French; these were used to practise jousting role-plays. Shadow puppets were chosen to link with a science topic on light. A photocopiable master of the instructional text for making a jousting puppet can be found at the end of this chapter.

Having learned that Francis' tent collapsed in the night, the children were interested in discussing tent design. This could have led to a project in which children designed and tested different structures. Another opportunity could have been to design a money purse to take to the banquet.

I will remember making shadow puppets and acting it out. My favourite bit was when we learned the dance to perform to the king.
Katie

I liked the jousting and learning the chanting words and learning the dance.
Lewis

## Drama

Drama and role-play were a key part of the learning in history and French. Some of the language that had been introduced in the story became the focus for role-play and a later performance for parents. Practising the target language within the context of jousting role-plays, music and dance gave meaning to language learning. Children's enthusiasm for learning about the past and using French for a 'real' purpose helped their confidence and ability to remember vocabulary and language structures.

## History

Children were encouraged to find out more about the Tudor sport of jousting at home. There is a link to an interactive tool that teaches more on the art of jousting in the eResource.

A famous painting, in the 'Royal Collection' circa 1545, depicts the scene at 'The Field of the Cloth of Gold'. This was a key image in the story PowerPoint and used as a source of evidence for discussion about life in Tudor times.

## Other links with literacy

The children received invitations to attend a Tudor banquet at which they would have to perform a dance for the kings. A reply was expected and a writing frame enabled children to do this. They also created French menus fit for the kings.

> My favourite part was when we received the invitation and had to make the puppets. I will remember the jousting part.
> Hannah

## Music and dance

The resource used for the Tudor dance was 'Jean Petit qui danse', an authentic song/dance from the period about a small man called Jean Petit who used to perform dances to entertain the king. There are several versions available online. There are also audio and video recordings of this dance, details of which can be found in the chapter 'A helping hand'. The children performed this dance with great enthusiasm, as their comments show:

> I liked doing the good dance with the marvellous music. I love the actions.
> Kirsty

> I liked the dancing best because it was quite funny as well. It was about our body parts.
> Sam

The children's final comments on their cross-curricular learning were very positive, too.

> It's more fun and encourages us to learn more. And well... I enjoy it!
> Tom

> I find it really fun! It's cool because you're doing two things at once.
> Chloe

> It's two lessons in one!
> Harry

It was evident that the children's progress in listening and reading improved significantly through the exposure to some aspects of other subjects being taught through the target language. However, the fact that there was some discrete language teaching to practise the new vocabulary aided both recall and fluency. Interestingly, some children could still produce a number of phrases from the unit after a significant time. Further details of this project can be found in the *Primary History* article (Hughes, 2007) mentioned in the References.

## MORE CROSS-CURRICULAR LINKS

More suggestions for linking languages with other popular topics/themes are included as tables at the end of this chapter. The next chapter provides another example of how a unit of work in the target language can be linked with other subjects in a meaningful and enjoyable way.

In this chapter, we have considered various ways in which a language can be integrated into the primary curriculum through: embedding it in school routines, linking with other subjects, reinforcing learning or teaching new content. We have shown in detail how the new language can be used to reinforce and extend knowledge in a cross-curricular history unit of work, and suggested some ideas for other cross-curricular topics.

## Cheval et Chevalier

**Il faut:**
- du papier noir
- un modèle d'un chevalier joutant
- un modèle d'un cheval
- un crayon
- une paire de ciseaux
- de la colle
- de la laine
- une paille
- un petit bâton

### Instructions

1. Découpez les modèles (le cheval et le chevalier).

2. Posez les modèles sur le papier noir

3. Utilisez les modèles pour dessiner un cheval et un chevalier.

4. Découpez le cheval et le chevalier joutant.

5. Collez le chevalier joutant sur le cheval.

6. Coupez dix petits morceaux de laine pour faire la crinière et la queue.

7. Collez la crinière et la queue sur le cheval.

8. Collez le cheval sur le petit bâton.

**Table 11.1** Chocolate topic

| CHOCOLATE | |
|---|---|
| **Cross curricular activities** | **Languages PoS** |
| **History/Geography**<br><br>➢ Present information about:<br>➢ Where chocolate comes from (cacao trees/countries where grown)<br>➢ History of chocolate<br>➢ French customs (bowls of chocolate and French bread for breakfast) | 1, 7 |
| **Literacy**<br><br>➢ Food/drink made from chocolate<br>➢ Phonic focus – key sounds in new vocabulary (compare with English)<br>➢ Drama – Café Chocolat role-play<br>➢ Read café menus<br>➢ Write café menu<br>➢ Explain process for making chocolate with simple phrases and actions | 1, 2, 3, 4, 5, 7, 10 |
| **Mathematics**<br><br>➢ Survey – how much chocolate eaten in a week/favourite chocolate bars | 3 |
| **Science**<br><br>➢ Ingredients to make chocolate<br>➢ States of matter – conduct experiments – temperatures to melt/solidify chocolate | 1 |
| **D & T**<br><br>➢ Follow instructions to make rice chocolate rice crispy cakes<br>➢ Design a chocolate wrapper | 1, 10 |
| **PE**<br><br>➢ Warm up hoop game. Children jump inside a hoop when they hear a country where chocolate beans are grown and outside hoop for other countries | 1 |
| **Music**<br><br>➢ Create Chocolate Chant/rap | 2, 4, 10 |
| **Useful resources**<br><br>➢ Momes.net (recettes au chocolat)<br>➢ www.bbc.co.uk/schools/primary languages (food and drink) | |

**Table 11.2** Rainforest topic

| THE RAINFOREST | |
| --- | --- |
| **Language activities** | **Languages PoS** |
| **Geography**<br><br>➢ Present information about rainforests<br>➢ Life in a rainforest<br>➢ Animals of the rainforest | 1, 7 |
| **Literacy**<br><br>➢ Describe rainforest animals (animal fact files/Power-Point presentation – size, food, movement (use third person verb structures singular/plural present tense)<br>➢ Choose one animal and create a presentation/wild life narration. This could link to work in music and art | 4, 5, 6, 11,12 |
| **PE**<br><br>➢ Warm up games involving animal movements e.g. marchez lentement comme un éléphant (walk slowly like an elephant) | 1 |
| **Music**<br><br>➢ Compose a soundscape for the jungle – using a painting (Rousseau jungle paintings)/photograph/children's own art as a stimulus<br>➢ Compose/Sing a jungle song | |
| **Art**<br><br>➢ Discuss the work of French artist Rousseau (Jungle paintings).<br>➢ Children learn vocabulary based on paintings – say what they can see/hear/ smell/feel/using first person verb structures<br>➢ They give simple opinions on the paintings<br>➢ They create watercolour Jungle paintings. | 4, 11 |
| **Useful resources**<br><br>➢ www.youtube.com/watch?v=wddaWE3HZTs names of animals<br>➢ Marchant à travers la Jungle' (Walking through the Jungle bilingual story) www.arts-wallpapers.com/galleries/henri_rousseau/imagepages/image62. htm work of Henri Rousseau | |

**Table 11.3** War topic

| WAR | |
|---|---|
| **Language activities** | **Languages PoS** |
| **History**<br><br>➢ Life as a child/evacuees<br>➢ Food and rationing<br>➢ Wartime clothing<br>➢ Political messages on posters | I, 4, 7, II |
| **Literacy**<br><br>➢ Postcard home describing country life (I see/hear/smell/eat/drink/play)<br>➢ Diary entry – an evacuee leaving home<br>➢ War poem re. feelings<br>➢ Read wartime literature: posters/accounts/story<br>➢ In pairs children role play a conversation on a train between two evacuees (might include opinions and the use of connectives) | 3, 5, 6, 7, 9, 10, II, 12 |
| **PE**<br><br>➢ Teach some dance steps to wartime music | I |
| **D & T**<br><br>Follow instructions in French to:<br><br>➢ make cakes/pies<br>➢ make a sock puppet (make do and mend) | I |
| **Music**<br><br>➢ Play some French wartime music such as songs by Edith Piaf ('La Vie en Rose')<br>➢ Compare song texts in English and French<br>➢ Listen for rhyming words in the song | I, 2, 7, 8 |
| **Useful resources**<br>➢ French wartime posters<br>➢ 'Chez moi, c'est la Guerre'<br>➢ Song lyrics for 'La vie en Rose' | |

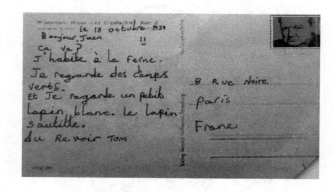

**Table 11.4** Ancient Greece topic

| ANCIENT GREECE | |
| --- | --- |
| **Cross curricular activities** | **Languages PoS** |
| **History/Geography**<br>➢ Present information about Ancient Greece<br>➢ Learn about the life of a sailor<br>➢ Ancient Greeks in Marseille and their legacy (wine and olives)<br>➢ Trading (routes and commodities)<br>➢ Piracy in ancient times | 1, 3, 7, 9, 11 |
| **Literacy**<br>➢ Read in English/French the Greek legend of Gyptis and Protis (explaining how Marseille was founded)<br>➢ Read information about Marseille<br>➢ Dictionary skills<br>➢ Drama – write/perform market trading role play<br>➢ Write a cartoon story about a pirate attack (use second person plural imperative verbs)<br>➢ Jigsaw recipe text (this could include looking at word order/classes) | 3, 5, 7, 9, 10, 12 |
| **PE**<br>➢ Warm up game to practise daily working routine on board a ship | 1 |
| **D & T**<br>Follow instructions in target language:<br>➢ To make olive cakes<br>➢ Food tasting and opinions | 1, 7 |
| **Useful resources**<br>➢ La Légende de Gyptis et Protis, available as a photocopiable master, with an English translation in the eResource<br>➢ Facts about modern day Marseille written in simple French<br>➢ 'Take10 en Français' (see references) for daily routine on board a ship<br>➢ Recipe for gâteaux aux olives (olive cakes), available as a photocopiable master, with an English translation. | |

| Market Role-play Ancient Greeks in Marseille | |
| --- | --- |
| Pelayo | Bonjour, Monsieur. |
| Client | Bonjour. Je voudrais acheter du vin. |
| Pelayo | Du vin rouge ou du vin blanc? |
| Client | Du vin blanc, sil vous plaît. |
| Pelayo | C'est 3 drachmas. |
| Client | Voilà. Merci, au revoir! |

## La légende de Gyptis et Protis

Un jour, des Grecs sont partis en bâteau. Leurs capitaines s' appelaient Simos et Protis.

Ils sont arrivés sur la côte de la région qui est maintenant la Provence.

Les habitants de la région, les Ségobriges, ont accueilli les Grecs. Les Grecs ont offert aux Ségobriges des spécialités de la Grèce - des vignes pour produire du vin et des oliviers pour la production de l'huile d'olives.

Pour dire 'merci', Nannus, le roi des Ségobriges, a invité les Grecs à un banquet.

La fille de Nannus, Princesse Gyptis, devait offrir une cruche d'eau à son mari futur. Gyptis a choisi de se marier avec Protis.

Le roi Nannus a offert un territoire aux Grecs. Sur le territoire les Grecs ont construit une ville qui s' appelait Marssila.

Aujourd'hui la ville s' appelle Marseille.

## Gâteaux aux olives

### Ingrédients

- Une tasse de farine (200g)
- Du beurre coupé en morceaux (50g)
- Du fromage râpé (50g)
- 10 olives coupées en petits morceaux
- Du lait (120 ml)

### Méthode

*Préchauffez le four à 220°C (thermostat 7-8)

1. Mettez la farine dans le bol.
2. Coupez le beurre en morceaux.
3. Ajoutez le beurre.
4. Mélangez la farine et le beurre du bout des doigts.
5. Coupez les olives en petits morceaux.
6. Ajoutez les olives et le fromage.
7. Mélangez encore.
8. Ajoutez le lait et mélangez encore.
9. Étalez bien.
10. Faites des ronds.
11. Faites cuire 12 à 15 minutes

# 12 Mission Impossible

This chapter is about a versatile, cross-curricular spy school project, designed initially for year 6 children; it was trialled with two year 5 classes in a South Gloucestershire primary school but could be adapted to suit a younger class. The project was taught over four hour-long lessons and led to a virtual day trip to Paris in the school hall. Inevitably, the teaching was quite concentrated; however, it could be extended to form a term's teaching and might also be an excellent Bridging Unit between key stages 2 and 3. Key stage 3 teachers might consider teaching this unit to lead to a virtual Paris trip.

The idea for the project sprang from a previously successful KS3 spy project designed at the University of the West of England for gifted and talented KS3 students. This project had been centred on the use of French and maths skills. A survey of year 6 children had also highlighted the fact that many wanted to know how to use transactional language that would be useful to them abroad and the project aimed to combine the personal and the transactional. The ideas can be adapted for another language and the spy mission set in Barcelona, Berlin or Rome.

## RATIONALE

Everyone is fascinated by the idea of spying – and young children are no exception. A spy theme ran throughout the project, from having code names, aliases and a spy school song to seeking clues to solve a mystery, and the final spy school certificate awarded in a whole school assembly.

The language content of the spy school project was intended to revise much of what had already been learned and also to teach new vocabulary. The aim was to motivate from the outset through creating an atmosphere of mystery and intrigue, building up to the excitement of the virtual Paris trip. By using language in context for real purposes, it was hoped that the children would be more likely to retain the vocabulary. They would also learn about cultural landmarks in Paris, involving art, in addition to experiencing other aspects of cross-curricular learning by building structures (design and technology) and decoding a secret message in a letter, using numerical skills.

## THE AIM OF THE MISSION

The overt aim of Mission Impossible was for children to work out the name of a kidnapped band, the reason for the kidnap, when it had happened, who had kidnapped the group and where they were being held. They were to do this on a virtual trip to Paris by searching for clues in each of five Paris landmarks (called 'stations' in the chapter) and using their French in the process. There was an opportunity for the children to use different language skills at each station.

## LANGUAGE CONTENT

This covered colours and adjectival endings, numbers and shapes, names and personal information, asking for and understanding directions round the town, ordering food and drink in a café, asking questions about someone's identity, descriptions of people, buying tickets and expressing likes and dislikes.

We shall now take you through the various stages of spy training, as experienced by the children.

## SPY TRAINING PART 1: CODE NAMES

As children came into the classroom, they were greeted by two well-known characters walking round in dark glasses and raincoats, with typical spy music playing on a phone in a teacher's pocket. Although the characters were represented in this case by two teachers, it would be perfectly possible for only one teacher to be involved. The project was then announced by the teachers, who told the class that they were looking for spies to help them in their mission. It was stressed that good pronunciation would be very important as they would need to pass as spies in France. There was indeed great emphasis on phonics during the mission.

The children were enthusiastic as they were introduced to the spy school song, which was to form a necessary part of the mission. The song was written to teach key vocabulary and set to a known tune. The words were circulated and children impressed the teachers by their efficiency in spotting cognates and guessing words and phrases in context. This song was then sung enthusiastically before each spy training session.

Giving the children code names was very successful. Animals and colours had been combined and a small card prepared for each child (for example, *cochon bleu, cheval rouge, oiseau jaune*). Names of animals and colours were practised and children had to whisper their code name to a partner. They then recorded it in their spy training booklet, which was also used for making notes after each session.

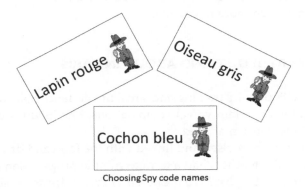

Choosing Spy code names

### Children's evaluation of Spy training part 1

Small evaluation sheets were given out following each lesson on which the children wrote their code names. There was universal enthusiasm for the lesson, which some described as 'amazing' and the 'best fun'. Children liked the spy theme, the song and repetition, using different voices. The favourite part of the lesson tended to be picking their code name; a few liked the song best and some the games. There were no suggestions for improvement, apart from longer or more frequent lessons.

## SPY TRAINING PART 2: LIVING IN FRANCE

After whispering their code name, the children were asked to choose a French alias from a bag. The small card contained their name, age (ages were chosen from nine to fifteen) and the town they came from. Children practised the aliases and circulated, getting to know the other spies through question and answer work. This links with the key stage 2 programmes of study (DfE, 2013) which state that learners should have opportunities to practise language through conversation and in presentations. They completed an individual ID card with the new information (it is important to have the child's English name on the back so that they can be taken in and redistributed). The children were then taught how to buy items of food and drink in a café and this was practised through a treasure hunt game. The session ended with singing the spy school song and making up their spy booklets.

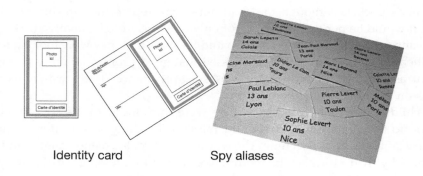

Identity card                    Spy aliases

## Children's evaluation of Spy training part 2

Again, the children said they had really enjoyed the lesson and learned to say different foods and drinks. They appreciated practising through games and using their spy role. When asked how it could have been better, there were a variety of answers; although many said 'nothing' one wrote 'listen better', another wanted a school trip to Paris and one felt it could have been more interactive.

## SPY TRAINING PART 3: OUT AND ABOUT IN PARIS

The session began with phonics training and small finger dance mats were used in pairs to practise the sounds of certain vowel combinations. The 'Sounds different' chapter shows a picture of the dance mat used.

Likes and dislikes were revised and linked with the food and drink items in a café. This could be extended if teachers had a term to run the project. Names of places to be visited in Paris were also taught (*la Tour Eiffel, le Louvre, l'Arc de Triomphe, Notre Dame, le parc Euro Disney*). Simple directions were reinforced through a 'dance', in which all children participated. Originally the idea of a Wiltshire languages teacher, this was similar to line dancing – and very popular : *à gauche, à gauche; à droite, à droite; tout droit, tout droit; reculez, reculez*. Children then had to follow directions on a map of Paris to see which buildings they were visiting and in which order. As usual, the spy song was sung and booklets filled in at the end of the lesson. To learn even more, they again suggested longer lessons or more regular lessons.

**Plate 1** Talking to my new friend

**Plate 2** Fun with spelling: look, cover, write, check

**Plate 3** Stephen Shepherd/*TES*, 2 May 2008

**Plate 4** Making a sentence with the negative twins

**Plate 5** La belle au bois dormant

**Plate 6** Who's the suspect?

**Plate 7** Trainee spy notes

**Plate 8** Finger puppet role-play

**Plate 9** Ready for Mission Impossible

**Plate 10** Newspaper headline: Groupe pop en danger!

**Plate 11** Eiffel Tower: construction work

**Plate 12** Can I check your ID card, please?

**Plate 13** Notre Dame: admiring the Rose Window

**Plate 14** Café Champs-Elysées: time for a croissant

**Plate 15** At the Louvre: what a picture!

**Plate 16** Anyone for *boules*? Whole school competition!

## Children's evaluation of Spy training part 3

The lesson was described as 'great fun' or 'interesting'. The children valued learning directions and following a map to find certain landmarks. Suggestions were to have more games and even more activities to play in bigger groups each week. Again, the children wanted further French lessons during the week.

## SPY TRAINING PART 4: EVERYONE'S A SUSPECT

After a quick revision of previous learning, the class was taught how to describe someone's hair and eyes in French. They also had to see pictures of celebrities and ordinary people in order to answer the question: *Tu connais cette personne?* In this session, the names of rides at Euro Disney were taught and the children quickly learned these. Children were reminded that the virtual trip was approaching. With more time, the teaching in this final part of the spy training could be more fully developed.

## PLANNING THE VIRTUAL TRIP TO PARIS AS SPIES

A letter was sent to parents, telling them that there would be a virtual mission to Paris for their spy sons and daughters. They were to dress as tourists but were encouraged to wear, or have with them, a small clue to indicate that they were really spies. They also needed to have their identity card with them. Feedback and comments were welcomed from parents about how their child had been motivated by the project; there was also a suggestion that they might like to follow this up by encouraging their child to find out more about Paris.

## SETTING UP THE VIRTUAL TRIP TO PARIS: PRACTICAL POINTS

Extra staff need to be involved during the day, some taking responsibility for one of the five activity stations. These could be teaching assistants, sixth formers from a nearby secondary school or parent helpers. If the day were run as part of a transition project, it would be an excellent idea for the head of year 7 in a neighbouring secondary school to be involved.

Although use of the school hall is ideal (apart from having to clear away for school lunches and setting up again in the afternoon), the virtual trip could also be run using two classrooms, if two classes were involved. The space for the event should be decorated as the centre of Paris with the key landmarks round the room, for example, with posters representing each place that they would visit during the day (different activity stations).

## THE MISSION IMPOSSIBLE DAY

Before going to Paris, the children assembled outside Spy HQ (a classroom with seats repositioned to represent an aircraft). In the queue to board the plane they were issued with their ID cards and spy notebooks for recording information. Officials checked their French aliases through questioning and the children then boarded the plane.

Once seated, the children were told that they had passed spy training and were now ready for their qualifying mission. They were given a newspaper report and briefing, setting the scene for the mission. In pairs they studied and annotated this, using cognates to help them understand the French.

They then listened to announcements by an air steward in each language and experienced take-off and landing, with sound effects simulated on a PowerPoint and aerial views which gave the impression of flying over the English Channel.

On landing in Paris, some had their identity cards checked by the French police (in this case, the head teacher in disguise) and later by the senior spies who were in charge of each small group (six if one class, twelve if two classes together). The senior spy also gave each trainee spy a map and their location. They listened to an announcement and followed directions to the place where they would start their mission. Each group was directed to a different landmark to begin their investigation and find clues. The five landmarks and the activities for each are shown below.

### Landmarks and activities: the five 'stations'

The spies spent thirty minutes at each station, completing the required tasks before moving on to the next. On arrival at a new station, the children checked in with the senior spy by giving their code names.

To allow for some groups being ready to move before others, word searches were created on a theme linked to each station. These proved to be so popular that children were keen to take them home to show their parents. Below is a summary of the activities, which took place at each station:

### *La Tour Eiffel*

- Follow an instructional text in French to construct shapes from Polydron. The first will show the building where the kidnap took place.
- Complete a word search on shapes and colours.

**Constructing Paris landmarks with Polydron**

**Travail de construction 1**

➤ Prenez 9 triangles équilatéraux verts
➤ Prenez 9 triangles équilatéraux bleus
➤ Prenez 9 triangles équilatéraux rouges
➤ Prenez 9 triangles équilatéraux jaunes

➤ Formez un grand triangle vert
➤ Formez un grand triangle bleu
➤ Formez un grand triangle rouge
➤ Formez un grand triangle jaune

➤ Formez un pyramide des 4 grands triangles

Qu'est-ce que c'est?

un triangle équilatéral

The glass triangle at the Louvre

Building the Arc de Triomphe

### Notre Dame

- Buy a boat ticket.
- Watch the video of a boat trip on a *bateau-mouche* down the Seine.
- Listen to a recorded message to discover why the kidnap took place.
- Make a replica Rose Window of the one in Notre Dame.
- Complete a word search on places and directions.

### L'Arc de Triomphe

In this French Internet café on the Champs-Elysées:

- Order a croissant and a drink from French menus (and eat/drink it!).
- Ask questions to discover who did the kidnapping (using photographs of different suspects).
- Write a short email to Spy HQ, with a description of the person (using a writing frame).
- Complete a word search on food and drink.

### Le Louvre

- Give opinions on famous paintings in the Louvre (children circulate, discussing what they like and/or dislike).
- Crack a mathematical code in a letter to discover where the band had been hidden.
- Complete a word search on French artists.

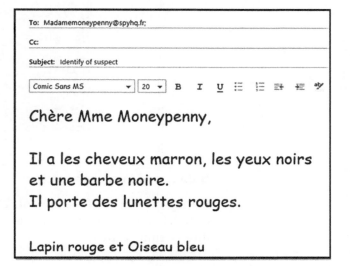

Email to Spy HQ

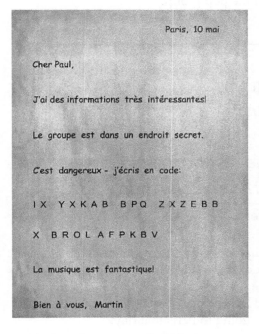

Cracking the secret code at the Louvre

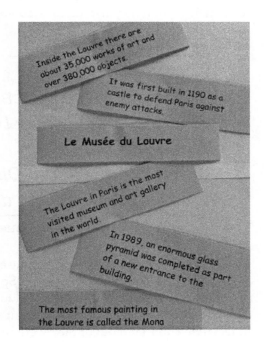

Interesting facts about the Louvre

### *Euro-Disney*

- Read a postcard, written by the criminal, to discover two facts: when the band was kidnapped and the name of the band.
- Write a postcard home from Euro-Disney.
- Complete a word search on Euro-Disney rides and adjectives.

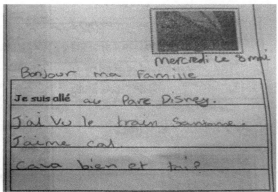

Tom's postcard home from Euro-Disney

### Balance of language skills

During the course of the mission, all four language skills were practised. The children completed two listening activities, two speaking activities, three reading activities and three writing activities.

### The debriefing

Children were then taken back to the classroom, where they were asked to reveal the secret information they had discovered about the pop group.

**Who?** *Thierry Henri*
**Kidnapped?** *One Direction*
**Where kidnapped?** *Le Louvre*
**When?** *8th May*
**Where hidden?** *Euro-Disney – ghost train*
**Why kidnapped?** *Sing at Thierry's birthday party*

The dénouement

Some were interviewed as part of the evaluation and all then joined a whole school assembly where they were awarded a Spy Certificate for having completed Mission Impossible. Two children also described to the whole school what they had been doing all day. There was still an air of excitement and children had clearly suspended disbelief. In fact, two children thought they were really going to Paris that day!

## EVALUATIONS OF THE DAY

### Children's evaluation of the day

Comments by the children showed that they had become very involved in what was a cross-curricular day with a lot of French being heard, spoken, read and written. Among the most popular activities were buying a croissant and making the Rose Window.

They took home their ID cards and completed spy notebooks containing all the language learned and notes made on the day. They also kept an individual Rose Window and several word searches.

### Teachers' evaluation

In that this successful project was trialled with classes we did not know and in unfamiliar surroundings, we believe that it could be successful in many schools.

In conclusion, we have tried in this chapter to set out the way in which a spy school mission was pre-taught in French and set up as a virtual trip to Paris, making use of other areas of the curriculum, such as music, art, design and technology.

### Photocopiable masters

Resources for Mission Impossible, including a list of vocabulary that the children should be taught and be confident with in preparation for the event, are included as photocopiable masters following this chapter, with the exception of those listed below:

### eResource

- Initial dialogue presenting the Spy Project;
- letter to parents;
- word searches;
- message giving directions through Paris;
- mobile message (why the kidnap took place).

## Mission Impossible song

(Sung to the Oompa Loompa tune from *Charlie and the Chocolate Factory*)

Bonjour, bonjour, je m'appelle …

Si tu m'écoutes, j'ai un puzzle pour toi!

Bonjour, bonjour, comment tu t'appelles?

Fais bien attention, et regarde-moi!

Où est-ce que tu vas?

Moi je vais à Paris

Qu'est -ce que tu vas faire? Je vais chercher des indices.

Voir les monuments et manger un croissant,

C'est dangereux et j'aime.. bien.. ça!

Je suis es - pi - on français!

Bonjour, bonjour, je m'appelle …

Si tu m'écoutes, j'ai un puzzle pour toi!

Bonjour, bonjour, comment tu t'appelles?

Espion! Espion! Espion.. français!

# PM 12.2 SPY SCHOOL TRAINING VOCABULARY

## Spy school training vocabulary

### Code names

Comment tu t'appelles?
Je m'appelle...*I'm called...*
Il s'appelle...*He's called...*
Elle s'appelle...*She's called...*
Je m'appelle...*I'm called...*
Il s'appelle...*He's called...*
Elle s'appelle...*She's called...*
un lapin *a rabbit*
un chat *a cat*
un chien *a dog*
un oiseau *a bird*
un poisson *a fish*
un hamster *a hamster*
un cheval *a horse*
un cochon *a pig*

bleu *blue*
rouge *red*
vert *green*
jaune *yellow*
rose *pink*
gris *grey*
Je m'appelle 'oiseau rouge' -
*I am called 'red bird'*

### Greetings

Bonjour *Hello*
Au revoir *Goodbye*
A bientôt *See you soon*

### Age/prices/numbers

Quel âge as-tu? *How old are you?*
J'ai... ans *I am...years old*

C'est combien? *How much is it ?*
Ça fait... euros *it is... euros*
1. un  2. deux  3. trois
4. quatre  5. cinq  6. six
7. sept  8. huit  9. neuf
10. dix  11. onze  12. douze
13. treize  14. quatorze
15. quinze  16. seize
17. dix-sept  18. dix-huit
19. dix-neuf  20. vingt

### Shapes

un rectangle *a rectangle*
un cercle *a circle*
un triangle *a triangle*
un carré *a square*

### Café

Vous désirez? *What would you like?*
Je voudrais... *I would like*
C'est tout ? *Is that everything?*
oui / non  *yes / no*
merci *thank you*
S'il vous plaît  *please*
Monsieur *Sir*
Madame *Madam*

un croissant *a croissant*
un sandwich *a sandwich*
un sandwich au fromage – *a cheese sandwich*
un sandwich au jambon – *a ham sandwich*
un gâteau *a cake*
une glace *an ice-cream*
au citron *lemon*
à la fraise *strawberry*
à la vanille *vanilla*

un jus d'orange *an orange juice*
une limonade *a lemonade*

### Directions

Pour aller...? *How do I get...?*
à la tour Eiffel *to the Eiffel Tower*
à l'Arc de Triomphe
*to the Arc de Triomphe*
au Louvre *to the Louvre*
au musée *to the museum*
au cinéma *to the cinema*
au café *to the café*
au marché *to the market*
la rue *the street*

Tournez à droite *Turn right*
C'est à droite *It's on the right*
C'est à gauche *It's on the left*
C'est devant *It's in front*
C'est derrière *It's behind*
C'est à côté de *It's next to*

### Describing people

Tu connais cette personne? *Do you know this person ?*
Oui, je connais cette personne
*Yes, I know this person*
Non, je ne connais pas cette personne
*No, I don't know this person*
C'est qui ? *Who is it?*
C'est... *It is*

Il a *He has*
Elle a *She has*
Il porte *He is wearing*
Elle porte *She is wearing*
les cheveux *hair*

les yeux *eyes*
une barbe *a beard*
des lunettes *glasses*
un chapeau *a hat*
noir(e)(s) *black*  gris(e)(s) *grey*
bleu(e)(s) *blue*  jaune(s) *yellow*
rouge(s) *red*  marron *brown*

### Opinions

Tu aimes ça? *Do you like this?*
J'aime ça *I like this*
Je n'aime pas ça *I don't like this*
Je préfère ça *I prefer*
beaucoup *a lot*
pas beaucoup *not much*

### Visiting a theme park

Je suis alle(é) au parc
*I went to the park*
J'ai vu *I saw*
le grand huit *the rollercoaster*
le carrousel *the merry-go-round*
le train fantôme *the ghost train*

Reactions
C'était fantastique/super/
rapide/terrifiant/passionnant
*It was fantastic/great/
fast/terrifying/exciting*

# GROUPE POP EN DANGER!

Un groupe de chanteurs célèbre a été kidnappé à Paris.
On cherche des indices.

Il y a des questions importantes.

- Qui a kidnappé le groupe?
- Quand est-ce qu'ils ont été kidnappé?
- Pourquoi?
- Comment s'appelle le groupe?
- Où est le groupe maintenant?

Si vous avez des informations, appelez
la police (numéro de téléphone:12)

C'est dangereux! Faites attention!

Les criminels ont laissé des
indices dans les monuments
célèbres de Paris.

## La Tour Eiffel
### Clue to discover
## Where?

1. Report in with your nom d'espion – whisper to the chief spy
2. Use 'Travail de Construction' cards 1 and 2 to make famous buildings in Paris
3. The first building you make will tell you where the kidnap took place
4. Make up your Spy booklet – note the answer to the clue and an interesting fact about the place
5. Complete the French 'shape' word search, if you finish early

## Le café Champs-Elysées
### Clue to discover
## Who did it?

1. Report in with your nom d'espion – whisper to the chief spy
2. Have two conversations – follow the role play cards to help you, and remember to sound really French!
3. Work in pairs to email Spy HQ with the criminal's identity, using the writing frame to help you
4. Order something to eat and drink in the café
5. Make up your Spy booklet – note the answer to the clue and an interesting fact about the place
6. Complete the French 'food' word search, if you finish early

## Le Parc Euro-Disney
### Clues to discover
## Who was kidnapped? When?

1. Report in with your nom d'espion – whisper to the chief spy
2. Read the postcard written by the criminal on the day of the kidnap – and find his/her favourite ride to discover the group's identify
3. Make up your Spy booklet – note the answer to both clues and an interesting fact about the place
4. Write a postcard to your family – use the criminal's postcard to help you know what to say!
5. Complete the 'Euro-Disney' word search, if you finish early

## Notre-Dame de Paris
### Clue to discover
## Why?

1. Report in with your nom d'espion – whisper to the chief spy
2. Listen to the criminal's mobile phone message to discover why the kidnap happened
3. Create your own Notre-Dame stained glass Rose Window
4. Make up your Spy booklet – note the answer to the clue and an interesting fact about the place
5. Complete a French 'places' word search if you finish early

## Le Louvre
### Clue to discover
## Where?

1. Report in with your nom d'espion – whisper to the chief spy.
2. Read the coded letter which has been found here; this gives information about where the criminal has hidden the group. Work in pairs and use the alphabet strips to crack the code
3. Make up your Spy booklet – note the answer to the clue and an interesting fact about the place
4. Walk round the exhibition with a partner and give opinions about the paintings in French e.g. J'aime ça/Je n'aime pas ça!
5. Complete the 'French artists' word search, if you finish early

# Café Champs-Elysées

## Menu

| | |
|---|---|
| un jus d'orange | 2 euros |
| une limonade | 2 euros |
| | |
| un sandwich | 4 euros |
| (fromage, jambon) | |
| | |
| un croissant | 3 euros |
| une glace | 3 euros |
| (fraise/citron/vanille) | |

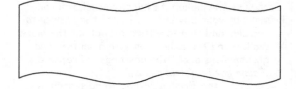

## Café Role-play 1

- **Bonjour Monsieur/Madame**
- Bonjour
- **Tu connais cette personne?** (spy kid shows photograph)
- *(Answer each child)* Non, je ne connais pas cette personne
  *(Then look again at the one with the hat).* Attends! Oui, je connais cette personne. Il s'appelle …………

## Café Role-play 2

- Vous désirez?
- **Je voudrais un croissant et un jus d'orange, s'il vous plaît**
- Voilà
- **C'est combien?**
- 3 euros, s'il vous plaît
- **Voilà** (spy pays)
- Merci

# Describing the suspect

| | | |
|---|---|---|
| Il a<br>Elle a | les cheveux<br>les yeux | bleus<br>marron<br>noirs |
| | une barbe | grise<br>noire |

| | | |
|---|---|---|
| Il porte<br>Elle porte | un chapeau | rouge<br>jaune |
| | des lunettes | noires<br>rouges<br>bleues |

## PM 12.8 SUSPECT PHOTOGRAPHS

# Travail de construction   1

> ➤ Prenez  9  triangles  équilatéraux  verts
> ➤ Prenez  9  triangles  équilatéraux  bleus
> ➤ Prenez  9  triangles  équilatéraux  rouges
> ➤ Prenez  9  triangles  équilatéraux  jaunes

> ➤ Formez un grand triangle vert
> ➤ Formez un grand triangle bleu
> ➤ Formez un grand triangle rouge
> ➤ Formez un grand triangle jaune

> ➤ Formez un pyramide des 4 grands triangles

Qu'est-ce que c'est ?

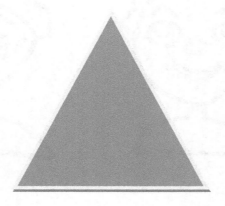

un triangle équilatéral

# Travail de construction 2

## Les colonnes verticales

➢ Prenez 8 rectangles (4 bleus, 4 rouges)
➢ Prenez 4 carrés rouges
➢ Faites un cuboïde de 4 rectangles bleus et 2 carrés rouges
➢ Faites un deuxième cuboïde

## Le toit

➢ Prenez 14 carrés verts ou jaunes
➢ Utilisez les carrés pour construire un cuboïde

les colonnes – the columns

le toit – the roof

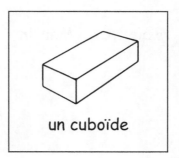

un cuboïde

Qu'est-ce que c'est ?

Cher Paul,

J'ai des informations très intéressantes!

Le groupe est dans un endroit secret.

C'est dangereux - j'écris en code:

I X   Y X K A B   B P Q   Z X Z E B B

X   B R O L A F P K B V

La musique est fantastique!

A bientôt,  Martin

Bonjour la famille,

Je suis allé(e) au parc Disney.
J'ai vu le train fantôme.
C'était fantastique!
Ça va bien – et toi?

A bientôt

Bonjour la famille,

Je suis allé(e)

# 13 Assessment and progression

## RATIONALE

Assessment is essential in order to ensure good progression in children's learning. There are two types of assessment: formative, which is ongoing assessment (assessment *for* learning), and summative, which is a more formal assessment at a given point in time (assessment *of* learning). Within primary languages, formative assessment is used much more in everyday teaching, although summative assessment can be useful. The assessment tasks, later in this chapter, could be used for formative or summative assessment.

The main reasons for assessing learning are that:

- teachers use it to inform their future planning and ensure that there is a good balance between support and challenge;
- children can celebrate their progress, which will lead to an increase in confidence and motivation;
- it helps children to manage and take more responsibility for their own learning;
- parents/carers need to follow their child's progress; and
- transitional links with secondary schools can be strengthened by exchanging information on children's attainment.

Progress made in primary languages may also be considered by those responsible for leadership and management within the school (the subject leader, head teacher, governors, Ofsted).

The key stage 2 languages national curriculum (DfE, 2013) sets out twelve programmes of study for learners. These include learning in all four skills (listening, speaking, reading and writing), in addition to grammar. By the end of key stage 2, children are expected to 'know, apply and understand the matters, skills and processes specified in the relevant programmes of study'. In order to ensure that the children meet the expected end of key stage 2 attainment, it is important to track and record their progress across the key stage and to know the types of activities that can be used to assess each skill.

In the last decade, several official documents such as key stage 2 Framework for Languages (DfES, 2005), *Making and Marking Progress on the DCSF Languages Ladder* (OCR, 2010), key stage 2 schemes of work for languages: French/Spanish/German (QCA, 2000) have guided teachers in planning, progression and assessment. Schools may still have copies of some of these documents and find them helpful.

In order to support teachers in planning for progression and assessment, the authors have created a skills progression table based on the key stage 2 languages programmes of study (QCA, 2000). In creating this table, the authors have taken into consideration previous documentation and their own teaching experience. The stages are purposely written in 'child speak' as 'I can' statements so that teachers can use these with the children for self-assessment. Teachers can find this table at the end of the chapter.

## PROGRESSION OVER TIME

Children demonstrate progress by:

- showing that they understand and produce more and increasingly complex language;
- reusing language in new contexts or topics;
- understanding better how language works;
- speaking with increasingly accurate pronunciation;
- dealing with unfamiliar/unexpected language;
- becoming more independent learners across all four skills; and
- increasing understanding of their own and other cultures.

In all subject areas assessment needs to be manageable for the busy primary teacher. There are some useful generic assessment-for-learning strategies, which can be used to assess children's understanding and progress within lessons.

Assessment for learning involves working in partnership with the children. One recognised way of doing this is to share the learning journey by explaining learning outcomes and success criteria. This can be done at the start of a topic as well as at the beginning of each lesson. As mentioned in the 'Mapping the way' chapter, sharing the 'big picture' at the start of a unit of work gives children a 'road map' which helps them to understand where they are going and the reason for the journey. This can motivate them to work with the teacher in order to achieve the learning outcomes (Smith and Call, 2001).

A visual display of the learning journey serves as a reminder and reference point to help the children make sense of the learning and understand how the big picture fits together. Such displays are often referred to as 'learning walls' and are regularly used to support teaching and learning in literacy and mathematics. The display initially outlines key steps and outcomes that will take place over the course of a period of time or unit of work. Regularly updated and evolving gradually as the learning progresses, it contains children's work, photographs, Post-it notes of children's thoughts and ideas and other evidence that captures the learning.

Having a display wall to show work in progress in the new language is beneficial. Children appreciate having the new vocabulary on display; seeing the written word helps them in lessons and embeds the language for future use. The display can also provide a written reminder for grammatical knowledge and children's 'top tips' for learning.

## LANGUAGE LEARNING STRATEGIES

Discussing different strategies for understanding, remembering and reproducing new language is important. By sharing their ideas and funny stories, children help each other in their learning. A boy once said that he would remember the French word for pencil case (*une trousse*) by thinking of his pencil case filled with different flags. When asked to explain how this image would help him recall the French word for pencil case, he explained that the flags made him think that the countries were having a *truce* rather than fighting. His association and visualisation made both the meaning and the pronunciation of the word memorable. Other children could also remember the word after hearing this story. Encouraging the children to share their ideas provides the teacher with an opportunity for informal assessment. Furthermore, the process of verbalising the learning or teaching others embeds it more securely. Children's learning strategies should be a regular focus for discussion within a lesson and may be added to the learning wall.

Although language learning strategies are not specifically mentioned in the key stage 2 languages programmes of study, it is invaluable to discuss with the children how they learn, what is easy/hard and what can help them learn. As in other curriculum areas, teachers aim to create independent learners and to encourage children to develop language learning strategies that are effective for them individually. This will help them to make progress, not only in the language being studied at primary level but also in any subsequent language study. In order for children to develop their personal learning strategies, they need to be exposed to a variety of techniques, in addition to having an opportunity to discuss and reflect on the effectiveness of those strategies. Some well recognised techniques are listed below:

### Strategies for memorisation

- adding a physical response to a word/phrase;
- playing games;
- making a word association and using rhyme;
- clapping the rhythm of a word/phrase;
- visualising the word; and
- writing new words.

### Strategies for understanding

- listening attentively;
- looking at the face of the speaker;
- asking for repetition or clarification;
- listening for key words; and
- using tone of voice as a clue.

### Strategies for pronunciation

- observing native speakers;
- speaking aloud;
- making recordings;
- practising language with a friend; and
- applying knowledge to unknown words.

### Strategies for reading and writing

- sorting and categorising known words/new words;
- investigating the characteristics of new language;
- applying prior grammatical knowledge to understand or create new language;
- using dictionaries;
- using context to determine some meaning;
- comparing with English;
- reading and memorising words; and
- finding opportunities to rewrite new words.

Children also need opportunities to:

- plan and prepare for language learning activities, analysing what they need in order to carry out a task (this helps them to use effective strategies); and
- recycle known language in a new context (a hierarchical skill, together with adapting language to fit a new context).

It is helpful to display a list of strategies in class as a visual reminder for both children and teacher. The list can be a useful checklist for the teacher when planning and for reference during discussions with the children.

## Classroom climate

It is important to build a climate of trust in the languages classroom, where children are prepared to try things without worrying about making mistakes. Celebrating mistakes that will help everyone learn can help to create this sort of working environment. Acknowledging them as 'useful' or 'helpful' mistakes that can really benefit everyone helps children to view mistakes as a positive learning step, rather than a negative one. It helps build resilience, which is a valuable quality for their development as successful learners.

Claxton (2002) considers resilience an importance aspect of children's learning, broadening the idea of perseverance to: a child engaging with learning, coping with distractions and being aware of what is happening around him or her.

## SELF- AND PEER ASSESSMENT

Children's reflection on their own learning and that of their peers is important in that it allows them to celebrate their achievements and identify next steps for learning. Additionally, it provides teachers with another source of evidence to inform their judgement about children's progress.

## Self-assessment

Using a series of 'I can' statements based on learning objectives is a useful form of self-assessment. Children enjoy ticking and colouring to show what they feel they have personally achieved. Inevitably, some children lack confidence and downgrade themselves and others overestimate their own ability but, on the whole, children are able to reflect honestly about what they think they can do. The Junior European Language Portfolio, which is available for schools either to download or purchase, is a child-friendly document that allows children to track and record their own progress and development as language learners. It includes the use of 'I can' statements. The document can be found by entering the title, followed by the word 'revised', into a search engine.

### Suggestions for self-assessment

The authors have created some examples of self-assessment charts, which could be used by children and stuck in exercise books. Children could be asked to indicate their own achievement at specific points in time, when the teacher feels they are ready.

The example below is a section from a year 3 self-assessment chart, which is intended to be used at different points of the year; there are several columns, which can be completed in different colours, or dated. The teacher can also use the sheet if s/he observes that an objective or learning goal has been achieved. Using a language stamp or signing in the teacher column as soon as this is 'spotted' provides the teacher with tangible evidence and the children with increased motivation. The chart below is created using the stage 1 objectives for speaking and listening from the skills progression table; a further sheet would be needed for reading and writing objectives.

☆   ☆   ☆   ☆   ☆   ☆   ☆   ☆   ☆   ☆   ☆

| | Speaking and listening Y3          Name: | | Me | My teacher |
|---|---|---|---|---|
| 1 | I try to listen carefully | | | |
| 2 | I can recognise sound and compare them with English | | | |
| 3 | I can show I understand simple words, phrases and some short sentences I hear | | | |
| 4 | I can understand some classroom instructions and praise words | | | |
| 5 | I can recognise sounds, rhymes and patterns when I listen | | | |
| 6 | I enjoy hearing simple stories | | | |
| 7 | I like joining in with songs and performing a | | | |
| 8 | I can | | | |

Two further self-assessment charts can be found at the end of the chapter. The first is for year 3 children, linked to a term's work about themselves ('language learning'). Children can colour the balloons when they feel they have achieved each objective. The second, on the topic of hobbies (*Les passetemps*) may suit a mixed year 5/6 class in which there is a wider spread of ability. The 'I can' statements in both charts are based on the stage 1 objectives in the skills progression table, but have been reworded in order to reference the specific language taught.

## Peer assessment

Children value the opinion of their peers and respond well to constructive advice and suggestions. However, they need to be trained as peer assessors in order to do this positively. One popular method of peer assessment is 'two stars and a wish', which involves the children in making two positive comments about their partner's learning and one comment giving a suggestion for improvement. This method is effective for peer assessment in the new language.

An example of this could be in the context of food tasting, where the children have learned to ask and answer questions about food likes and dislikes. The teacher might wish to assess the children's ability to answer and ask questions confidently. In order to do this, s/he could ask children to work in pairs, with small images of food or even real food samples, taking turns to ask and answer questions, for instance: *Tu aimes ça?* (Do you like that?) The reply might be as follows: *Oui/Non/Oui, j'aime ça/Non, je n'aime pas ça* (Yes/No/Yes, I like it/No, I don't like it).

When using peer assessment, as in any subject area, it is very important that the children are clear about the success criteria. These should be written for the children to refer to (either on the board or the sheet in front of them). This requires careful thought before asking them to complete the peer assessment task.

Here is an example of a possible 'two stars and a wish' task, based on fruit tasting. A version of this chart, with the assessment focus left blank, is available as a photocopiable master at the end of the chapter.

| Date: | | |
|---|---|---|
| Name: <br><br> Partner's name: | | |
| **Assessment focus** <br><br> **can ask the question** <br> **can answer the question** <br> **speaks clearly** <br> **sounds French** | **Partner** | **Me** |
| **Two stars and a wish** | **Partner's comments** | |
| ⭐ | | |
| ⭐ | | |
| 🪄 | | |
| **Two stars and a wish** | **My comments** | |
| ⭐ | | |
| ⭐ | | |
| 🪄 | | |

**Freeze-framing**

Freeze-framing the learning is another technique for helping children reflect on their own learning and providing helpful feedback for the teacher. This involves taking a photograph of children during a language learning activity and asking them to annotate the photograph to explain what they have learnt and how they learnt it. For example, the children might annotate a photograph of themselves tasting fruit and comment that they learnt to say in French whether they liked or disliked the fruit. The 'how' – which is important in order to develop their awareness of strategy – would be for them to recognise that practising language with a friend had helped them.

## LEARNER FEEDBACK

Getting feedback from children about their learning is vital and providing them with regular opportunities to do this is needed, either during or at the end of lessons. Mini-plenaries during the course of a lesson are often useful to check the progress of the learning, and to deal with any misconceptions that may have arisen.

Here are some useful questions that the teacher might consider asking as part of the learning process:

- Can you explain what we are learning?
- How are we learning . . . ? (song, story, game, repetition)
- Can anyone share any 'top tips' that could help us all?
- What have we learned so far?
- Is it easy/challenging/too hard?
- What could help us?
- What else do you want to know/be able to do?

Asking children to close their eyes and respond to questions with thumbs up or down is a quick and effective way of finding out how successful the learning outcomes have been. By asking children to close their eyes, they feel less conscious of others and are therefore more likely to give an honest answer. The teacher might assess progress against some questions asked, such as: Who is confident with the words learned today? Who feels they need more practice? Who thinks they can use the words in a sentence now? Some teachers like to ask the children to 'traffic light' their work using a colour code (red for 'I'm stuck', yellow for 'I'm getting there' and green for 'I really understand and am ready to move on'). Asking the children to write a learning comment (LC) in their books can be very helpful. It is useful to display a list of questions that they can choose to answer in giving feedback.

- Did you enjoy the lesson?
- What can you do now?
- Was the work easy or just right?
- Was anything too hard?
- Was there anything you didn't understand?
- What could make it better?
- What else would you like to know?

**TEACHER FEEDBACK**

Learners need to know what they have achieved. The teacher can begin a lesson by congratulating the children on a part of the learning that has gone well and explaining areas that s/he or the children have identified as requiring improvement. It might be that a particular sound needs to be worked on because the children had difficulty pronouncing it.

Written feedback in children's books should include praise words in the target language/stickers/stamps. See the chapter 'Allons-y! ¡Sí sí sí!' for ideas. In addition, it is seen as good practice to acknowledge where the learning objective has been met (literally highlighting the written objective) and any other positive comments. A different coloured highlighter can be used for examples of what needs to be improved. A symbol representing an area where improvement is needed (possibly a danger triangle coloured 'pink for think') or a next step (a staircase) can be added, as shown in the teachers' written comments below:

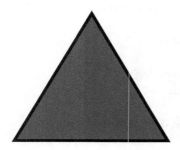

Attention! Articles (*un une*) – copy carefully.

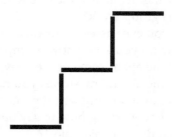

Can you make a new sentence by changing the noun?

## Questioning

This involves questions from teacher to children, children to teacher and children to other children. As previously mentioned in the 'Mapping the way' chapter, teachers should include a variety of questions at different levels to enable all learners to contribute and extend their thinking skills. This will not only help learners to make progress during lessons but inform the teacher of their progress.

Good questions from the children are an integral part of the learning process and inform assessment. Encouraging children to ask good questions and acknowledging the value of all questions establishes a positive classroom climate for learning. Furthermore, questions from the children show that they are engaged and motivated to learn. As an incentive and reward for asking good, relevant questions, teachers might consider having a celebratory tally chart. Claxton, who is a strong advocate of children asking good questions to advance learning, notes that some schools have a 'Wonder Wall', where both teachers and children can write their questions (Claxton, 2002: 27).

The value of children as co-teachers cannot be overestimated. Encouraging children to ask each other when they are 'stuck' can be very effective. Examples might be, one child asking 'the guardian of the phrase' for the correct target language, or allowing children to ask each other for learning strategies.

## PUPIL CONFERENCING

Schools usually allow subject leaders time during the academic year to look at planning and children's books, in order to cross-reference the two and assess the progress being made by the children. It is also valuable to spend time talking to some children from different classes across the key stage about their learning. They will be able to supply additional information about the learning, which will not always be obvious from their books. Below are some possible questions that the teacher could ask children about their language learning.

- How do you learn new words?
- How often do you have a French/Spanish lesson?
- Tell me about any displays in the classroom that help you learn.
- What things do you use to help you learn French/Spanish?
- Do people like learning French/Spanish in your class?
- How/when does your teacher tell you what you are going to learn?
- Tell me about a typical lesson. Do you work on your own sometimes? Is there pair/group work?
- Do you ever assess your own/your partner's work?
- How do you know how to improve?
- Tell me about some of the activities you have done.
- Tell me about any stories you have heard or read.
- Tell me about any writing you have done.
- Are you learning how to say new sounds? Which ones do you know?
- What do you enjoy most?
- What else could help you learn better?

## FURTHER ASSESSMENT OPPORTUNITIES

There are other ways of integrating simple formative assessment tasks, for each skill, into lessons. This should not become onerous but needs to be planned and manageable over the course of the year, with the teacher focusing on different skills at different times. Teachers must use their own judgement about when to include short, formative assessment tasks and ensure that sufficient time has been given to practise and consolidate the learning.

The suggested examples can be easily adapted to any language.

### Listening

The assessment of children's ability to understand a correct response to a question could be done through multiple choice answers. For example, they are asked *Comment tu t'appelles?* (What are you called?) and have to identify the correct answer:

A *J'ai un lapin*
(I have a rabbit).

B *J'ai onze ans*
(I am eleven years old).

C *Henri*
(Henry).

Another example in the context of ordering food might be: *Qu'est-ce que vous désirez?* (What would you like?)

A  *Je voudrais un café, s'il vous plaît*
    (I would like a coffee please).

B  *J'aime les fraises*
    (I like strawberries).

C  *Je joue au rugby*
    (I play rugby).

Progress in listening can be monitored by matching exercises. Ticking or numbering pictures or English text is ideal for showing comprehension of a short spoken passage presenting information.

For example, in the context of animals, the children could be asked to record the number of the animal they hear. This would be suitable for stage 1 (year 3) level assessment.

| | |
|---|---|
| cat | |
| dog | |
| cow | 1 |
| sheep | |
| horse | |
| pig | |

The teacher says, in Spanish: *una vaca* (a cow). The child writes 1 in the box beside the word (or picture) of a cow.

Listening tasks can be made more complex through getting the children to order a set of sentences. If the topic is visiting places in town, the children would be asked to listen carefully and put a number by each sentence they hear. This could be used to meet stage 2 objectives.

| | |
|---|---|
| I am going to the park | 3 |
| I am visiting the museum | 2 |
| I am going to the cinema | 4 |
| I am going to the city centre | 1 |
| I am visiting the castle | 5 |
| I am going to an Internet café | 6 |

As the children progress, they are expected to listen to a longer spoken passage for gist comprehension. For example, in the context of hobbies, the children might listen to a short spoken passage (read two or three times) and identify which sport each person likes to play, by ticking the correct box. In addition, to provide differentiation, children could record other information they hear about each person in a separate column.

*Example*:

> Listen to the information for each person and tick the box to show which sports s/he likes. You might also be able to give some extra information about each person.

This assessment would be appropriate for stages 3/4 (upper key stage 2).

> *Je m'appelle Alain et j'ai huit ans. J'aime jouer au basket. J'ai un petit lapin.*
>
> *Je m'appelle Pierre. J'ai un chien noir. J'adore le football.*
>
> *Je m'appelle Sophie. J'aime faire de la natation. J'adore la danse aussi. J'ai sept ans.*
>
> *Je m'appelle Sylvie. J'habite à Paris. Je déteste le rugby mais j'adore le football.*

|  | natation | rugby | football | basket-ball | danse | other information: e.g. age, pets |
|---|---|---|---|---|---|---|
| Alain |  |  |  |  |  |  |
| Pierre |  |  |  |  |  |  |
| Sophie |  |  |  |  |  |  |
| Sylvie |  |  |  |  |  |  |

## Speaking

This is a difficult area to assess because of the time factor and the inevitable shyness of some children. Furthermore, children tend not to see 'speaking' as real work. It is important therefore for them to understand the importance of participating in this skill area and to find ways and opportunities for different individuals to speak during lessons, in order for teachers to assess progress.

It might help if the teacher keeps a speaking chart and acknowledges children's contributions during lessons. This can be done by giving the children coloured stars to stick beside their name. Children are quite competitive and are motivated by this visible reward; this system also helps to raise the profile of speaking. Since it is impossible to assess all the children in each lesson, the chart could be used as a prompt for the teacher to target children who have gained fewer stars.

While as teachers we want to hear all the children speak, it is important to be sensitive to the needs of some shyer children. Allowing them time with a talk partner to practise new words, phrases, sentences and questions before expecting them to respond individually is beneficial. Alternatively, the teacher can listen to less confident children while they are engaged in paired or group activities – playing games or participating in role-plays.

What is important is that we involve all children – and not only those who readily put their hands up to answer. Many schools adopt the 'hands down' approach. This can be a useful method, for at least part of the time, in that it allows the teacher to target those who do not always volunteer an answer. Teachers might also feel that giving children the opportunity to discuss an answer with a partner before asking for a response is a useful strategy, in terms of providing peer support for less confident children.

## Differentiated questioning

Moving from closed to open questions has already been discussed in the 'Developing skills' chapter. This same approach can be used in conjunction with colour-coded straws (red, yellow, green) where each straw serves as a prompt to the teacher to ask different questions (challenging, open-ended or closed) to specific children. Drawing a red straw would lead to a closed question, such as: *¿Es un conejo?* (Is it a rabbit?) *Sí/No* (Yes/No). A yellow straw could be a slightly harder question, giving a choice of several answers; the child needs to identify and repeat the correct one. A green straw would indicate a more challenging question, for example the ability to recall the new vocabulary from memory – *¿Qué es?* (What is it?).

If working at sentence level, the question might be *¿Te gustan los conejos?* A red straw reply could be *Sí/No*. A yellow straw reply could be *Sí, me gustan los conejos* (Yes, I like rabbits). A green straw reply could be giving a reason such as *Sí, me gustan los conejos porque son divertidos* (Yes, I like rabbits because they are funny).

As previously stated, a natural linguistic progression is to move from learning some nouns, to using them within a sentence in order to respond to a question, and then being able to both answer and ask questions. Assessment of these skills could form a class display, which monitors the children's progress. For example, each child could have a named frog that can hop between lily pads once s/he is secure with each stage.

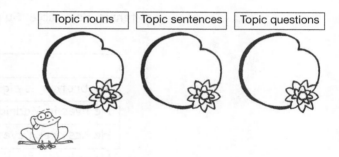

The key elements being assessed when a child is speaking are:

- being understood
- confidence
- fluency
- an attempt at accurate pronunciation.

## Reading

When testing reading comprehension skills, the easiest way is to ask the children to match a picture to a piece of written text. This could be matching a picture to a word, a phrase, a sentence or even a short paragraph.

For example, in the context of pets, at stage 1 (year 3), the teacher could assess the children's ability to read and understand statements about what pets they have, such as: *J'ai un chien* (I have a dog), by writing the letter for the picture that matches the written sentence. Here the children would write the letter A.

*J'ai un chien.*

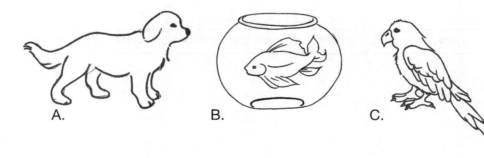

A.                              B.                              C.

This could be done at a higher level by giving the children a short description of a person, place or object and asking them to match it to the correct picture. For instance, in the context of physical description, the children could be given some descriptions of monsters which need to be matched to the correct pictures, focusing on the number of different body parts or their colours. It is worth remembering that there are many images readily available to teachers through their interactive whiteboard software and on the Internet.

Another way of assessing reading comprehension is to ask the children to read a short written passage and ask them to respond to a series of statements, indicating whether each one is True or False. The examples below would be appropriate for stage 3/4 assessment.

### *Example 1*

Read the short Spanish passage and circle to show if the statements are *verdadero* (true) or *falso* (false).

Mi hermano tiene diez años. Vive en Barcelona. Tiene el pelo rubio y corto. Tiene los ojos verde. Le gusta jugar al football pero odia el tennis. Es amable. Su animal preferito es el gato.

|  | V | F |
|---|---|---|
| My brother is eight years old. |  |  |
| He lives in Madrid. |  |  |
| He has green eyes. |  |  |
| He is kind. |  |  |
| His favourite animal is a dog. |  |  |

### *Example 2*

Read the short Spanish passage and complete the gaps with the correct words from the box underneath.

Mi hermano tiene _____ años. Vive en _____. Tiene el pelo negro y corto. Tiene los ojos _____. Le gusta jugar al _____ pero odia la _____. Es _____.
Su animal preferito es el _____.

| nueve   natación   basketball   verdes   energético   gato   Malaga |
|---|

## Example 3

Number the pictures according to the order in which they come in the text.

> Je suis allée au marché et j'ai acheté une banane. Plus tard, à la boulangerie, j'ai acheté un pain et des croissants. Finalement, au supermarché, j'ai acheté du fromage, des œufs et du jambon.

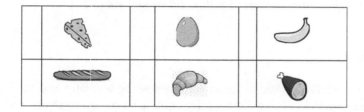

For differentiation, some children would like the challenge of looking for the clue as to who is shopping – a boy or a girl.

Reading for meaning can also be assessed through multi-choice questions. The game 'champion', mentioned in 'The magic of games' chapter, can provide a useful template for assessment in an engaging and interactive way.

## Reading aloud

This is more time-consuming since each pupil needs to be given the opportunity to read aloud individually. It is best to target a few children each lesson. This might be done during whole class teaching time by asking for volunteers to read from the board or those children who are more shy could be asked to read when the other children are working independently. It is helpful to have prepared some words/sentences on the topic for a few children to read aloud whenever an opportunity arises (at the start or end of a lesson). In this way, the teacher will be able to observe those children who have excellent pronunciation or any who might be struggling. The key elements being assessed when a child is reading aloud are:

- enjoyment
- confidence
- fluency
- accuracy of pronunciation
- attention to punctuation
- understanding of what is being read
- ensuring that the listener can hear and understand what is being read aloud.

## Writing

The first skill is for the children to be able to copy words carefully and accurately, paying attention to any necessary accents. Beyond this, with sufficient practice, children can be given opportunities to write words and phrases from memory. Recall of familiar words can be assessed by giving them mini-whiteboards and asking them to write as many words as they can remember for the topic. Children can also be asked to create a cloudburst or mind map of vocabulary they know/sentences they can write. The teacher could also give the children a list of words to write – mostly known words, but some unfamiliar words could be included, based upon the sounds they have been taught in phonics.

At this key stage, children will be expected to write with the use of models and writing frames for support. What is really being assessed here is the ability to follow the structure of a written text, copy carefully and adapt where necessary. The chapter on 'Developing skills' provides some suggestions for ways to support writing.

Once children have practised writing using familiar vocabulary and structures, they should be able to produce these increasingly for themselves so that they can write some sentences on a topic from memory by the end of key stage 2.

## CONCLUSION

In this chapter we have looked at reasons for assessing learning and the importance of formative assessment. We have discussed language learning strategies and the need for a positive classroom climate, before looking at different ways of assessing: peer and self-assessment; freeze-framing. The importance of both learner and teacher feedback has been noted and examples of further assessment opportunities have been shown.

**Table 13.1** Skills progression table

| National Curriculum key stage 2 programmes of study (NC KS2 PoS) | L = listening; S = speaking; R = reading; W = writing<br>Stage 1 (year 3); Stage 2 (year 4); Stage 3 (year 5); Stage 4 (year 6)<br>or first, second, third and fourth year of language learning | | | | | | | |
|---|---|---|---|---|---|---|---|---|
| | | Stage 1 | | Stage 2 | | Stage 3 | | Stage 4 |
| 1 Listen attentively to a spoken language and show understanding by joining in and responding | L1 | I try to listen carefully | L2 | I can concentrate when I listen | L3 | I can understand longer and more complex phrases and sentences | L4 | I can understand the main points when someone is speaking |
| | L1 | I can recognise sounds and compare them with English | L2 | I can recognise more sounds | | | | |
| | L1 | I can show I understand simple words, phrases and some short sentences I hear | L2 | I can show I understand simple sentences I hear | L3 | I can understand more classroom instructions | | |
| | L1 | I can understand some classroom instructions and praise words | | | | | | |
| 2 Explore the patterns and sounds of language through songs and rhymes, and link the spellings, sound and meaning of words | L1 | I can recognise sounds, rhymes and patterns when I listen | L2 | I can recognise more sounds, rhymes and patterns and can compare them with English | W3 | I can use my knowledge of sounds to help me remember how to spell some words | W4 | I can use my knowledge to help me remember and spell familiar words and begin to spell unfamiliar words |
| | R1 | I can read some sounds aloud | R2 | I am becoming more confident in reading new sounds aloud | | | | |
| | R1 | I can read and understand some words I have heard | | | | | | |
| 3 Engage in conversations, ask and answer questions, express opinions and respond to those of others; seek clarification and help | S1 | I can answer simple questions | S2 | I know different ways of giving an opinion | S3 | I can say why I like or dislike something | S4 | I can say I agree or disagree with other people and give my own opinion confidently |
| | S1 | I can ask some simple questions | S2 | I can answer more questions about myself | S3 | I can use several different ways to ask for something to be repeated (e.g. I can say: repeat, again, louder please) | | |
| | S1 | I can express a simple opinion | | | | | | |
| | S1 | I can show I don't understand through gesture, a word or short phrase | S2 | I can ask for something to be repeated when I don't understand | | | | |

**Table 13.1** continued

| National Curriculum key stage 2 programmes of study (NC KS2 PoS) | | Stage 1 | | Stage 2 | | Stage 3 | | Stage 4 |
|---|---|---|---|---|---|---|---|---|
| 4 Speak in sentences, using familiar vocabulary, phrases and basic language structures | S1 | I can repeat words, short phrases and simple sentences I hear | S2 | I can say some sentences from memory | S3 | I can make longer sentences | S4 | I am confident talking about myself and giving information on a topic |
| | S1 | I can use short sentences | | | S3 | I can adapt sentences by changing some words | | |
| 5 Develop accurate pronunciation and intonation so that others understand when they are reading aloud or using familiar words and phrases | S1 | I try to copy words carefully when I speak | S2 | I am becoming more confident in speaking accurately | S3 | I can say sentences I know with mostly accurate pronunciation | S4 | I can talk to others, using much more correct pronunciation and intonation |
| | S1 | I can ask a question by making my voice rise at the end of the sentence | R2 | I am remembering to use the sounds I know when I read aloud | R3 | I am more confident reading aloud with good pronunciation | R4 | I can now read words and phrases I know with accurate pronunciation |
| | R1 | I try to make the sounds I know when I read words and phrases aloud | | | | | | |
| 6 Present ideas and information orally to a range of audiences | S1 | I can tell a partner something about myself (e.g. my name, my age) | S2 | I can memorise a short spoken passage to present to others (e.g. simple life cycle of a plant) | S3 | I can remember a longer spoken passage (role-play e.g. shopping in a market) to present to others | S4 | I can present my ideas on a topic confidently to others (e.g. introduce and describe a family member), using some longer sentences |
| 7 Read carefully and show understanding of words, phrases and simple writing | R1 | I am beginning to read carefully and can show that I understand some words and phrases I've been taught | R2 | I am reading more carefully and can understand more words and phrases | R3 | I can read carefully and can show that I understand some of the main points in a short text | R4 | I read carefully and can show that I understand main points and some extra information in a short text |

L = listening; S = speaking; R = reading; W = writing
Stage 1 (year 3); Stage 2 (year 4); Stage 3 (year 5); Stage 4 (year 6)
or first, second, third and fourth year of language learning

| Objective | Level 1 | Level 2 | Level 3 | Level 4 |
|---|---|---|---|---|
| 8 Appreciate stories, songs, poems and rhymes in the language | **L1** I enjoy hearing simple stories<br>**L1** I like joining in with songs and stories by performing actions and mimes<br>**LS1** I can join in with some familiar words and repeated phrases in stories or songs | **LR2** I can compare simple stories with the same stories in English (well-loved tales)<br>**S2** I can say a short finger rhyme to others in my class | **L3** I can understand some main ideas in a story I hear<br>**S3** I can recite a longer poem to another class or in assembly | **L4** I can understand the main ideas and some extra information in a story I hear<br>**LR4** I can recognise why certain words in stories, songs or poems have been used for effect (e.g. alliteration, rhythm, rhyme, repetition) |
| 9 Broaden their vocabulary and develop their ability to understand new words that are introduced into familiar written material, including through using a dictionary | **R1** I can sometimes spot words that look a little like English<br>**R1** I can put words in dictionary order | **R2** I can often recognise words that look like English and also words we have learnt<br>**R2** I can find words in a word list/dictionary more quickly now | **R3** I can spot more words and am beginning to make sense of a paragraph/text<br>**R3** I can use a bilingual dictionary more confidently to find the meaning of words and check the gender of nouns | **R4** I can use several ways to work out the meaning of words I don't know in a text (e.g. from their position and the meaning of other words)<br>**R4** I can use a dictionary confidently to check the gender of nouns, as well as recognising nouns, verbs and adjectives |
| 10 Write phrases from memory and adapt these to create new sentences, to express ideas clearly | **W1** I can copy words carefully and write some words from memory | **W2** I can write words and some phrases from memory<br>**W2** I can complete sentences by adding missing words or phrases | **W3** I can write some sentences from memory<br>**W3** I am confident changing words to make new sentences | **W4** I can write a few sentences on a topic from memory, and possibly some longer sentences<br>**W4** I am confident changing words and phrases to create new sentences |
| 11 Describe people, places, things and actions orally and in writing | **S1** I can use some simple describing words (numbers, colours) in short sentences | **S2** I can say more short sentences about myself<br>**S2** I am beginning to say sentences to describe someone or something | **S3** I can talk about a place, thing or other people, using longer sentences (e.g. describing what a place is like or what someone likes doing), using a speaking frame at first | **S4** I am confident saying several sentences (including longer/more complex sentences) describing a person, place or thing |

**Table 13.1** continued

| National Curriculum key stage 2 programmes of study (NC KS2 PoS) | Stage 1 | Stage 2 | Stage 3 | Stage 4 |
|---|---|---|---|---|
| L = listening; S = speaking; R = reading; W = writing<br>Stage 1 (year 3); Stage 2 (year 4); Stage 3 (year 5); Stage 4 (year 6) or first, second, third and fourth year of language learning | | | | |
| 11 continued | W1 I can write some simple sentences about myself<br><br>W1 I can use a writing frame or word list to copy some simple describing words or phrases | W2 I can write more short sentences, with support, describing what I do (e.g. hobbies)<br><br>W2 I can write some short sentences, with support, to describe someone or something | W3 I can write some sentences describing other people, places or things, using connectives to form longer sentences, with the aid of a word bank or writing frame<br><br>W3 I can write some sentences from memory | W4 I can write a short passage including some longer or complex sentences to describe a person, place or thing, using a model or writing frame<br><br>W4 I can write sentences from memory |
| 12 Understand basic grammar appropriate to the language being studied including (where relevant): feminine, masculine, neuter forms and the conjugation of high frequency verbs; key features and patterns of the language; how to apply these, for instance, to build sentences, and how these differ from or are similar to English | | | | |
| | Stage 1 | Stage 2 | Stage 3 | Stage 4 |
| Gender | L1 R1 I can recognise the gender of a noun by listening/looking at the word that goes before it<br><br>S1 W1 I am beginning to use the right words for 'the/a' when I speak/write | L2 R2 I am better at remembering or checking which words are masculine and feminine<br><br>S2 W2 I can choose the words for 'the/a' more accurately when I speak/write them before a noun | S3 W3 I am mostly accurate when I use 'the/a' in a sentence when I speak or write | R4 I check carefully to make sure the plural words are correct when I write<br><br>L4 R4 I understand words for quantities of things in the language<br><br>S4 W4 I can use words which explain quantities of things in the language (some/a box/a packet) |
| Singular and plural | L1 R1 I can sometimes recognise when words are singular or plural | R2 I am beginning to read aloud, and write, some plural words<br><br>W2 I can compare the rules with English | | |
| Adjectives/other word classes | L1 R1 W1 I am beginning to understand that adjectives sometimes have different spellings and this can alter the sound | L2 R2 I understand that adjectives may change their position or their ending, compared with English | LS3 RW3 I can understand and create phrases with adjectives more confidently | S4 W4 I can use adjectives with the correct endings in sentences |

| | Stage 1 | | Stage 2 | | Stage 3 | | Stage 4 | |
|---|---|---|---|---|---|---|---|---|
| Adjectives/other word classes *continued* | W1 | I can copy simple adjectives carefully | W2 | I am beginning to use adjectives when I write a phrase or short sentence | W3 | My knowledge of word classes helps me to change part of a sentence | R4 | My knowledge of words classes helps me to understand what I read |
| | | | L2 R2 LS2 RW2 | I am more confident recognising word classes / I can understand and use some simple adverbs | LS3 RW3 | I can understand and use more adverbs | W4 | My understanding of sentence structure helps me write new sentences |
| Questions | L1 S1 | I can recognise when a question is being asked by listening to the end of the sentence going up and am beginning to use this myself | S2 | I know how to ask simple questions by making my voice go up at the end of the sentence | S3 | I can ask more questions/know more ways to ask a question | | |
| Negatives | L1 R1 | I can sometimes recognise negative sentences | S2 | I am beginning to make negative sentences with help | S3 W3 | I can make sentences negative and create new negative sentences | S4 W4 | I am beginning to use negative sentences more confidently |
| Connectives | LS1 RW1 | I can understand and am beginning to use 'and' in short sentences | LS2 RW2 | I can understand and use 'and'/ 'also' in sentences | LS3 RW3 | I can understand and use more connectives (but, because) | LS4 RW4 | I can understand and use connectives with compound/ complex sentences (because, so/ therefore, however) |
| Verbs | LS1 RW | I understand and can use some first person verbs | LS2 RW2 | I am beginning to understand and use some third person verbs to talk about someone/ something else (he/she/it) | LS3 RW3 | I can understand and use several verbs confidently in the first and third person form | LS4 RW4 | I am familiar with all parts of some really useful verbs |
| | LS1 RW1 | I understand and can use other simple sentence openers (It is / here is/are) | LS2 RW2 | I am more confident in understanding and using different sentence openers (e.g. there is/are) | LS3 RW3 | I understand and am beginning to use some past tense phrases (it was/were/there was/were) | LS4 RW4 | I can understand and use more past tense phrases |
| | | | | | | | | I went/bought/drank/ate/saw/ heard/played) |
| | | | | | | | LS4 RW4 | I can understand and use a future tense to say what I will do |

## CHART 13.1 *MOI* YEAR 3 SELF-ASSESSMENT EXAMPLE CHART

**CHART 13.2** *PASSETEMPS* **YEAR 5 AND 6 SELF-ASSESSMENT EXAMPLE CHART**

 Mes Passetemps

|  | Stage 2 | Stage 3 | Stage 4 |
|---|---|---|---|
| 1 | I can give simple opinions about hobbies – I like it/don't like it | I can say sentences about which hobbies I like/dislike e.g. I like swimming/I don't like cycling, and give reasons why I like/dislike them | I can express likes and dislikes confidently in a conversation and ask others for their opinions. |
| 2 | I can ask some simple questions to find out about what others like doing | I can ask others if they like different hobbies | I can confidently ask others about their hobbies |
| 3 | I can follow the story about hobbies and understand some familiar words and phrases | I can understand the main ideas in the story about hobbies | I can understand the main points in the story and some other information |
| 4 | I can use simple sentences to talk about my hobbies | I can use simple sentences to talk about my hobbies and what others do | I can say which hobbies I like and confidently give reasons for my opinions |
| 5 | I know the difference between 'le'/'la' and 'un'/'une' | I can use 'le'/'la' and 'un'/'une' quite accurately | I always use le/la/un/une accurately |
| 6 | I recognise plural nouns in a text | I recognise plural nouns and some irregular spellings of plural nouns | I am really confident in recognising and using plural nouns and can spell the words accurately |

## PM 13.1 TWO STARS AND A WISH PEER ASSESSMENT SHEET

| Date: | | |
|---|---|---|
| **Name:** | | |
| **Partner's name:** | | |
| **Assessment focus** | **Partner** | **Me** |
| | | |
| **Two stars and a wish** | **Partner's comments** | |
| ⭐ | | |
| ⭐ | | |
| 🪄 | | |
| **Two stars and a wish** | **My comments** | |
| ⭐ | | |
| ⭐ | | |
| 🪄 | | |

# 14 A world beyond the classroom

## RATIONALE

Intercultural understanding has always been an important part of primary education and was formerly one of three main strands in the KS2 Framework for Languages (DFES, 2005). Sharing and practising the new language outside the classroom gives children the opportunity to use language for a real purpose and provides valuable reinforcement for the learning. Apart from developing children's language skills, it increases motivation and, in the case of links abroad, gives opportunities for new friendships. It encourages openness to other people and cultures and develops an ability to empathise. In the words of the key stage 2 languages national curriculum (DfE, 2013): 'Learning a foreign language is a liberation from insularity and provides an opening to other cultures. A high-quality languages education should foster pupils' curiosity and deepen their understanding of the world.'

## AROUND THE SCHOOL

There are many opportunities for children to use their new language beyond timetabled lessons. Within the school itself, children can work with a parallel or similar age class, for example writing descriptions of themselves incognito and getting children in the other class to guess who they are. There are further opportunities to provide a selection of fiction and non-fiction foreign language texts in the school library, including some dictionaries. Language display boards in the communal areas could be used to celebrate children's work and show a link with a partner school abroad, while signage in the target language round the school keeps the language high-profile.

## LANGUAGE CLUBS

Lunchtime or after-school clubs provide scope for teaching other languages, in addition to the timetabled language. They often give children the chance to find out more about things of great interest to them, cultural and linguistic.

## PLAYGROUND GAMES

Playground games in the new language are an excellent way of reinforcing it through repetition and use. The teacher can also introduce playground games in turn from different countries round the world. Each class can keep a book of playground games, together with any objects they need to play them; this can be borrowed at playtime. It is a good idea to include some games that can be played indoors on a wet day. Below are some traditional playground games.

## Le Facteur – The postman

This is a popular French outdoor game. Children sit in a circle; one child (*le facteur*) walks round the outside of the circle while the others chant a song about waiting for a parcel to arrive:

> *Le facteur n'est pas passé.*
> (The postman has not come.)
>
> *Il ne passera jamais.*
> (He will never come.)
>
> *Une heure, deux heures,*
> (One o'clock, two o'clock,)
>
> *Trois heures, quatre heures,*
> (Three o'clock, four o'clock,)
>
> *Cinq heures, six heures,*
> (Five o'clock, six o'clock,)
>
> *Sept heures, huit heures,*
> (Seven o'clock, eight o'clock,)
>
> *Neuf heures, dix heures,*
> (Nine o'clock, ten o'clock,)
>
> *Onze heures, midi!*
> (Eleven o'clock, midday!)

After saying *midi*, the postman drops a package behind a child who then chases him/her round the circle and back to where s/he was sitting. The last child to reach the space then becomes the next postman.

## El Pañuelo – The handkerchief

In this traditional Spanish playground game, there are two teams in long lines, with a good space separating the two teams.

- Each child has a number in Spanish (1 uno, 2 dos, 3 tres, 4 cuatro, 5 cinco, 6 seis, 7 siete, 8 ocho, 9 nueve, 10 diez, and so on) and stands opposite someone with the same number in the other team.
- When the person holding *el pañuelo* calls out a number, the person on each side with that number runs into the middle to try to snatch the handkerchief and get back to their line.
- If they get back without the opposing person touching them they get a point for their team. If they are touched, no point is awarded.
- The first team to get to ten points wins.

## Un, deux, trois, soleil

- Everyone stands on a line, apart from one child who is 'on it' and stands at the opposite side of the playground with his/her back to everyone.
- The children try to move forward as the person 'on it' says *Un – deux – trois – soleil*.

(If facing a wall, this can be good to slow down the caller, since the wall has to be touched with both hands as s/he says *so–leil*.)

- S/he turns round and any child who is still moving is out.
- The first child to reach the person 'on it' and touch his/her back is the winner, and becomes the next caller.

## Katze und Maus – a German playground game

- The 'cat and mouse' game is played by larger groups, typically in the playground.
- One player is *die Katze* and the other is *die Maus*.
- The rest of the children form a circle and hold hands.
- The cat tries to catch (touch) the mouse.
- The mouse can run anywhere, including into or out of the circle.
- The circle helps the mouse by raising their arms to let the mouse through, or lowering their arms to try to block the mouse.

Many more playground games from countries worldwide can be found online.

## WHOLE SCHOOL EVENTS

### International event

Language activities for the whole school can be tried out during an international language day/week. These can focus on one or more countries, with teachers taking responsibility for organising different activities based on culture or language. A carousel allows children to move from teacher to teacher, extending their learning.

### Eurovision song contest

Activities based on worldwide musical events are popular and effective. A Eurovision song contest can be set up in the school, with each class learning a song from a different country. This can be held as an afternoon event, watched by the whole school and performed in front of a panel of judges. After a break, children return to their classrooms and vote for the winning song (3 points), the runner-up (2 points) and the third place song (1 point). Teachers vote separately. Points from all the classes are counted and added to the teachers' and judges' points. The winner is then announced.

### Sports themes

The World Cup and European Championships give good opportunities for using the new language in a geographical context, with numbers, colours and player profiles. An event that fits well with the European or World Cup Championships is a French breakfast, followed by a football tournament. In the author's school, teams across the year 6 group were allocated a country where French was spoken: that would be their identity as a football team. They researched different aspects of the country, learning about its customs and creating a piece of artwork associated with it, which was displayed round the walls at the breakfast; they also learned football terminology and practised this language during football coaching/skills lessons. The football tournament, played the same day as the French breakfast, ended with medals being awarded.

The Olympics give ample scope for language work around countries, flags, teams, sports, Olympic champions, dates and records broken. There are some published resources available to support learning new language linked to this theme. This includes French/German/Spanish topic packs by Brilliant Publications.

## INVOLVING PARENTS IN LANGUAGE WORK AT SCHOOL

Organising events for parents to attend in school allows the children's learning to be showcased and raises subject awareness. Below are some possible events and activities that schools could organise.

### French café

If the school curriculum is based on a topic approach, one topic could involve the whole school and be based on the country where the new language is spoken. Upper key stage 2 children in the author's school did a whole term topic on France, incorporating learning in Geography and Art. As part of the project, children researched aspects of the country at home – fashion, baking, a famous artist. Having learned how to talk about food and drink in language classes, they held a 4pm café. They had designed French menus and decorated the school hall with project work done at home and French music was playing in the background. Other children, teachers and parents were invited and were amazed by the variety of food on sale: crêpes, pains au chocolat, baguettes, croissants and cakes. The children had also contributed to a French-themed art gallery with work they had produced during art lessons and their framed paintings were sold.

### Languages event

Parents are invited after school to watch or participate in the following:

- children performing sketches and singing songs in the new language;
- recordings of different languages or a chart with different currencies could be prepared for parents and children to take part in a quiz with multi-choice answers;
- games of lotto in the new language are always popular with everyone.

### 'Bring a parent to school' day

This is also a good way of extending parents' knowledge of language methodology. It can be a stand-alone event or part of a language learning week where the parent participates with the child in a carousel of afternoon activities.

## PARENTS AND HOME LEARNING

Some parents have a certain amount of knowledge of the new language, which can be helpful for reinforcing it. Others who have little or no knowledge of the new language may be motivated to learn alongside the child. Where parents speak a language other than English at home, the new language can provide interest.

Ways in which children and parents can work together at home are to:

- make food from a recipe, brought from school, which has instructions in the target language;
- teach a parent/carer or younger brother/sister a song or a game they have learned at school – this can be great fun;
- work together on a research project about the new language or countries where it is spoken;
- visit a supermarket for children to look for worldwide food words, such as 'croissant', 'camembert', 'pizza';
- help to lay the table, naming cutlery items in the new language;
- explore cultural websites;
- enjoy dual language story books together;
- use applications for mobile devices designed for early language learning – possibly using one of the puppet applications to create plays together. This is discussed in the next chapter.

### Texting, using French/Spanish abbreviations

Many children are curious to know how a French or Spanish child might say 'see you later' or 'LOL' in a text message. Armed with their equivalents in French: *A+* and *MDR* (*mort de rire*), or Spanish, *hl – hasta luego*, they could practise sending a text in English (but including some French/Spanish abbreviations) to a family member or a friend in their class.

There are several websites which give texting abbreviations in other languages. It could be a task for the person receiving the text to work out what the abbreviations mean, for example, using frenchtogether.com for French texting-slang or doyou comprende.com for Spanish texting slang. See the chart below for some initial ideas.

| Bonjour | bjr | Hello |
|---|---|---|
| Bonsoir | bsr | Good Evening |
| Ok, d'accord | dac | OK |
| Dès que possible | DQP | ASAP |
| Mort de rire | MDR | LOL |
| Viens | V1 | Come |
| Il y a | ya | There is/there are |
| Bisous | biz | Kiss |

**French texting abbreviations**

| Hola | hla | Hello |
|---|---|---|
| No pasa nada | NPN | Nothing's happening |
| Está bien | Ta b | It's OK |
| | Jejeje/jijiji | LOL |
| Hasta luego | hl | See you later |
| | a2/bye | Bye |
| Perdon | xdon | Sorry |
| Besos | Bs | Kiss |

**Spanish texting abbreviations**

## Mobile-making project

As a further way of encouraging children to find out more about a country where the language they are learning about is spoken, a mobile competition could be set up as a home task. This might involve a member of the family: alternatively, two children could work together. Children would have a term (six weeks) to produce the mobile.

Here are some practical suggestions:

- The subject could be a region of a country where the language is spoken – or alternatively, things that represent the country.
- The mobile should be made from something light enough to be suspended (balsa wood/a coat hanger).
- They could be judged by someone other than the class teacher.
- Prizes are awarded for the best entries.

## SCHOOL LINKS ABROAD

The British Council is a reliable source of potential links for finding a partner school in another country (https://schoolsonline.britishcouncil.org/find-a-partner). For French, these might be with a French school, but also with a school in a French-speaking country (Morocco) or a former colony (Guadeloupe, Haiti). If the children are learning Spanish, there are many possibilities: a school in mainland Spain, the Canary Islands, Central or South America. Later in this chapter we will show how a school in Costa Rica developed a strong link with a school in South Gloucestershire. There are also e-twinning opportunities through the British Council.

Furthermore, it is possible to make contact with a French school on a short visit (forty hours or five days) abroad. This can be arranged through finding an email link for a primary school in the town to be visited and setting up a virtual link before the visit. During the visit, it may even be possible to arrange for the children to have lunch in the French school, or to meet the children at playtime. Obviously great care needs to be taken if sending photos electronically; it is essential that only children whose parents have given permission have photos sent and names should never be sent in the same mailing.

### A new slant on intercultural understanding

Understanding about the people and countries where the target language is spoken is essential for successful language learning and the following section about an exchange between two chimpanzees gives some helpful ideas.

### *Charlie and Chocolat*

As part of a link set up between primary schools in Rouen and English schools linked to the University of the West of England, the authors set up an unusual cultural exchange between two chimpanzees: Charlie, who was English, and Chocolat, who was French. At the start of the project, the chimpanzees wore T-shirts, signed by all the children in the class. Charlie accompanied a group of teachers going to France and was photographed at every point of the journey – checking in, taking his seat ready for take-off and arriving in France.

Charlie's journey
to France

Once in the French school, Charlie was handed over safely to a class teacher; he spent the next few months staying with different children each weekend and holiday and, of course, being photographed. Each French child wrote a diary for Charlie's adventures during his stay. Meanwhile, Chocolat returned home with the authors and was photographed on his journey to England (on boarding the plane, he visited the cockpit before taking his seat for departure). Apart from his photo at UK Border Control almost being confiscated, the journey was smooth!

Chocolat's journey to
England

A mixed age class of year 3/4 children in the English school hosted Chocolat and, as in France, each host child wrote about Chocolat's adventures with the family. This gave children practice in writing a recount text in the first person, from the monkey's viewpoint, and also writing for an audience. In writing in their own language as simply as possible, the aim was for their exchange class, albeit with some help, to develop their understanding of the other language.

The cultural impact of this project was significant, due to the insight into everyday family life, both inside and outside the home. The photographs accompanying the children's written text made the characters' diaries come to life and aided understanding. For example, Charlie went on a trip to Paris and visited a French zoo. Chocolat attended an

Extracts from Chocolat's diary

Extracts from Chocolat's diary – visiting London

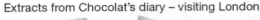

English birthday party, had a ride on a steam train, ate spaghetti bolognese in an English pub, found ancient objects with a metal detector, spent a weekend on a farm, visited Portugal for Easter, went on a trip to London, including a ride on the London Eye, and took part in the Race for Life, dressed as a fairy (this was mentioned on a local radio station).

The next section shows how a partnership between two classes can be established, using the example of a link with a Spanish-speaking school in Central America. This is described by the class teacher and languages coordinator in the English school, Katie D'Alton Goode.

### The Costa Rican link

This link, between my Church of England primary school in South Gloucestershire and the Escuela Central in Atenas, Costa Rica, was set up through a friend doing voluntary work in the school, where the English teacher was keen to establish a link project. It has been the most wonderful experience for us and goes from strength to strength. The variety of means of communication available has been invaluable – from snail mail to emails to considerable use of the Dropbox site for file-sharing (dropbox.com). As a general rule, we have tried to send something every two to three months.

It began with letters from a year 5 class in Atenas being brought back for the children in my year 6 class, complete with sparkles and souvenirs! The Costa Rican children spoke about their families and pets, what they liked at school, their hobbies and the music they loved. My children were delighted and curious to work out the meaning of the Spanish words. They felt a connection with the children, loving the fact that the letters were real! They proudly recognised some cognates and tried out the phrases that I repeated. They were fascinated to see the similarities between their lives and favourite things and that of children from another culture. The look on their faces was unforgettable. One girl exclaimed: 'That's just like me! I love Justin Bieber, too!'

My class reading the letters from the Costa Rican children

Shortly afterwards we organised an International Week and, inspired by the letters, each class in the school researched a different country. We learnt so much about Costa Rica, thanks to the information sent through from the other teacher and her year 5 children even made a video showing how to prepare a traditional dish, *gallo pinto*. We then had a go at cooking it ourselves – it was a huge hit!

Later in the year, all our classes prepared presentations about themselves for the Costa Rican school: a mixture of leaflets, PowerPoint presentations, handwritten letters and photos. We then sent them by post, accompanied by stickers, little presents such as key rings and postcards from our village shop.

At Christmas, videos were exchanged; my school sent a video of children singing at the church carol service. The school in Atenas sent Christmas wishes on their video with a slide show of each year 5 child holding up a Christmas card they had made. Following this, the teacher in Costa Rica extended the link to younger classes; a subsequent video from a year 3 class showed children singing a song about parts of the body.

We are currently preparing to send a video of a tour round our school and will certainly maintain the link with the children in Atenas.

### Top tips for class links abroad

- start small, with a limited number of projects per year;
- pre-plan an outline of a year's work with your partner school;
- think beyond purely topic-based themes, such as pets and hobbies;
- consider activities for whole class/groups/pairs, rather than just one-to-one;
- allow children to communicate in their own language and encourage them to write simply;
- make sure the partner school teacher asks the same of his/her class;

- exchange postcards/mini concertina books/annotated photos and drawings (children like receiving 'snail mail'!);
- avoid the temptation to say everything in the first letter – leave something for later.

Projects between linked schools give interest and a focus to learning. Here are some ideas:

- Each child creates a self-portrait, using three colours (eg my feet are blue because I've visited France; my tummy is green because I like Italian pasta).
- Learn about culturally specific items, for example, Bonfire Night, Shrove Tuesday; la Fête des Rois in France (6 January), Poisson d'avril (1 April), Bastille Day (14 July); el Día de los Reyes Magos (5/6 January), el Carnaval de Tenerife (February), la Tomatina de Valencia (26 August), el Día de los Muertos (31 October–2 November, Mexico).
- Exchange seasonal greetings cards.
- Send a short instructional text and video of children singing a song or playing a playground game for the other school to learn, perform and video.
- Set up a comparative recycling exercise.
- Design and maintain a school garden in each country.
- Swap information on environmental topics, such as local wildlife.
- Both schools hold an event on the same day, for example, picnic/mini-Olympics; send recipes and games in advance and share photos and video clips afterwards.
- Work done by the children can also be sent and sensitive feedback given by children in the partner school/class.
- Children read a story in their own language to each other. This is then sent to the partner school.
- Use storytelling techniques of mime and gesture, using a short text, for the partner school to see and understand.
- Share a favourite character (Paddington Bear, Astérix) and put a caption.
- Swap entries for a mini-Eurovision song contest where children make up a song in the new language to a familiar tune. They might do one verse in each language.


In conclusion, fostering intercultural understanding in the primary school is really important. The new language can be used as a vehicle for developing children's knowledge and appreciation of other cultures, with extra-curricular activities giving meaningful contexts for the learning – and more time for languages in the process. Such activities and events in turn raise the profile of languages in the school.

# 15 Technology tools

## RATIONALE

Technology can be used to motivate and support children's learning in a new language and is an important and time-saving resource for teachers. Furthermore, the creative use of technology in the primary languages classroom will also help to equip children with important skills for their future. It includes not only the use of computers and interactive whiteboard but also an array of other equipment: cameras, microphones, mobile technology, together with the many programs and applications that are now available.

In this chapter, we will look at the following areas:

- Internet;
- film;
- interactive whiteboard;
- programs and applications;
- cameras, video recorders, microphones; and
- assessment.

## INTERNET

The Internet can bring the world into the classroom by allowing teachers and children to explore the target language country through live webcams; this can provide interesting points for discussion. Virtual trips can be arranged around capital cities or famous museums. The Internet is excellent for children doing research, for example, finding out about festivals, food, travel and weather. Songs and stories can be heard being performed by native speakers; this helps teachers and children with vocabulary and pronunciation. Furthermore, it provides a wealth of free teaching resources and ideas, including authentic texts in the target language.

## FILM

### Culture

Using short film animations or purposely designed language film clips such as those on the Early Start DVDs (available in French and Spanish) is really useful in that the children can hear the language being spoken fluently. Allowing children to watch video clips of other children speaking the target language in different situations (greeting each other at school, playing on a beach or buying food in a market) demonstrates that the language they are learning is used by real people, for real purposes. Video clips can also lead to further discussion about cultural similarities and differences.

Many of the traditional songs are available on YouTube and the animation helps children understand them. Some also show lyrics, which has the added advantage of allowing children to follow a written text as they listen.

### Creative use of film

A short film can be shown, stopped at a certain point and children invited to predict what will happen next. They can be asked to draw or write in English beneath pictures or finish telling the story. Alternatively, the teacher and class can discuss what they think will happen before watching the rest of the film. The film could then be retold using key words and phrases that have been simplified to suit the age and ability of the children.

### Non-verbal clues

Film can also be used without sound to encourage children to 'read' the story through the use of pictures. It is also helpful to ask children to interpret the non-verbal communication clues when watching or listening to a film. Much communication happens through intonation, gesture and body language; children can be taught to look for these clues to aid communication and understanding.

### INTERACTIVE WHITEBOARD

At the time of writing, most schools use either Promethean or Smart boards. Both have their own software, with a variety of tools and features, which can be used to create teaching and learning language activities. They allow the teacher to: draw; use colour fonts; highlight; layer; erase; drag and drop; and hide and reveal. There is also a library of pictures and games and other useful tools, such as dice and timers – all of which make excellent language resources.

### Dragging

In developing oracy, the teacher can use pictures to practise speaking and listening; the children show their understanding by dragging, touching or drawing. In the example below, the children name the clothes as they drag them to dress the wolf.

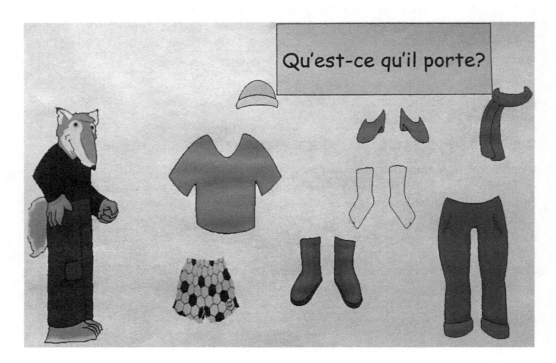

To develop literacy skills, the drag and match exercise can be used to match written text and pictures. The beginning and ending of a word can be dragged together to create the word. A child can also be asked to drag individual letters to spell a word. This activity can involve the whole class by making it a competition between children using mini-whiteboards to spell and hold up the word before the person dragging the letters at the board has finished arranging them.

 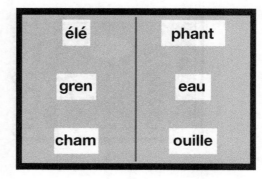

## Interactive dice

The interactive dice tool can be used to indicate the language children need to use. In the example below, the children practise a sentence beginning with the appropriate sentence starter, according to the number rolled on the dice.

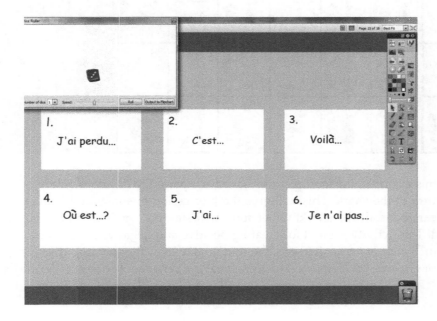

## Spotlight

This tool is particularly useful for practising or revising new vocabulary. Pictures can also be hidden behind shapes to motivate children to guess what is hidden. The use of an interactive dice adds an additional element of surprise.

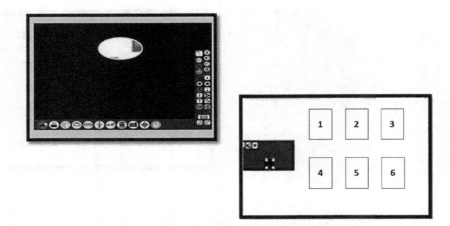

## Layering

The layering tool is also useful for practising words in a particular order or creating the illusion of words disappearing.

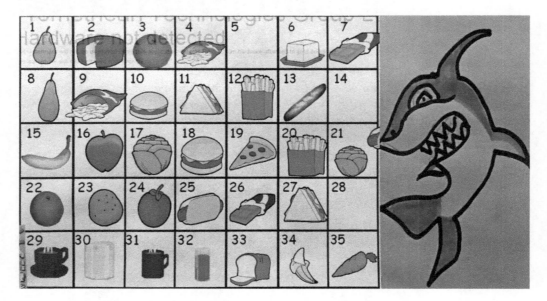

In this example, the food pictures have been placed to be either on top of or under the picture of the shark. This will give the impression of some food being eaten as it disappears beneath the shark. Other food will stay on top, looking as if it has been rejected. This activity is good for creating positive and negative statements: *Il mange la tomate* or *Il aime la tomate* (He eats the tomato/He likes the tomato); *Il ne mange pas la banane* or *Il n'aime pas la banane* (He doesn't eat the banana/He doesn't like the banana).

## Pens, highlighters and erasers

These are invaluable for sentence work and reading activities. In the example below, a white pen (to match the background screen colour) has been used to colour over the text. The pen can be rubbed out with the eraser tool to reveal the original sentences. In this example, children wait for the sentence to be revealed and, if correct, read it aloud.

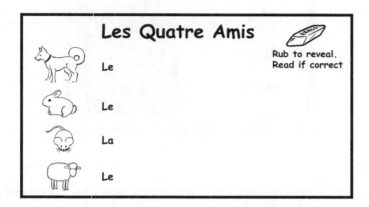

Coloured highlighters can be used to mark written texts and are useful for comparing word order and sentence structure in the new language and English.

## Coloured fonts and backgrounds

The ability to change font and colour background is useful for checking part of a word or phrase. In this activity, children move words from the middle column (coloured white) to the left (red for feminine) or right (blue for masculine). While in the middle column, the word (in these examples, possessive adjective or article) is hidden because it is written in a white font; once it is moved to a coloured background, it can be seen. This activity allows children to make their choice and check their answer. The child at the board can always 'ask the audience' (the rest of the class) to see if they agree, before making the final decision.

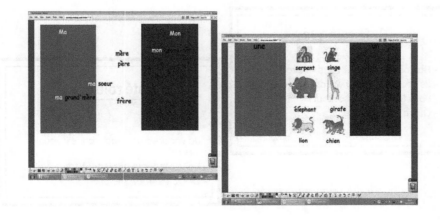

Children can also check the spelling of words using the different coloured fonts and backgrounds.

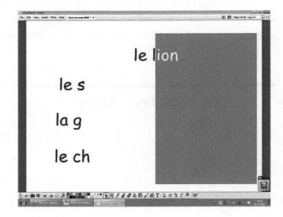

### The blind tool

This can be used to support the teaching of a dialogue, using the 'disappearing dialogue' technique discussed in the 'Developing skills' chapter. Whole lines can be masked on the whiteboard, by using the 'blind' tool. Pens chosen to match background colour can be used to mask individual words.

## OTHER USEFUL PROGRAMS AND APPLICATIONS

### PowerPoint

A dialogue can be projected on the whiteboard in a PowerPoint presentation. If taken out of slide-show mode, a shape can be placed at the top of the slide; this can be gradually expanded to cover the conversation, similar to the 'blind' tool. For the purposes of illustration below, an italic font has been used to highlight the dialogue. A good technique is to use different colours for each person speaking.

To delete words from the conversation in a gradual way, the teacher can create a series of slides in PowerPoint, from which an increasing number of words are removed. Kim's game (referred to in 'The magic of games') is also easily created by using this technique, shown on the next page.

As has already been mentioned, PowerPoint is a versatile tool for presenting and practising new vocabulary; it has the advantage that a sound effect or native speaker voice can be added. Flashcards that are created electronically can be printed for use in the classroom. This particularly benefits kinaesthetic learners, who enjoy handling the cards.

It is equally useful for developing literacy skills. Reading aloud can be practised through making written words fade in or appear from different directions. Highlighting and using colour for certain words is excellent. Photographs and pictures can be imported, or speech bubbles added, to make meaning clear.

For teachers wishing to teach another subject through the target language, creative PowerPoint presentations can help to convey meaning through the use of: animated photographs, pictures, labelled diagrams and sound. It is possible to use some of the whiteboard tools in conjunction with PowerPoint slides, such as the whiteboard pen and eraser. Children can also create their own PowerPoint stories or projects, which can be used to communicate with a partner school as an alternative to emails or e-cards.

## Word

Children can make their own labels, posters, texts in the new language while practising the basic skills of changing font, colour and size and adding images to the text.

## Electronic story book creators

Online tools are available that can be used by both teachers and children to create story books. This is highly motivational for children and the fact that they can print their book gives them a real sense of achievement and pride in their work, while making the learning memorable.

### Storybird (www.storybird.com)

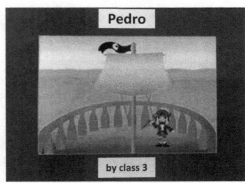

- Books are made by dragging and dropping animations from stock illustrations.
- Text can be added next to pictures.
- The book can be printed in A4 size – and used in the classroom for display/children can keep their work.
- Published copies can be ordered by parents or school and could be a good addition to the school library.

There are examples of e-books that have been created online: mfl-storybirds. wikispaces.com/French+Storybirds.

Storyjumper (www.storyjumper.com) is similar to Storybird but has the added advantage of allowing the users to import their own photographs and images.

### Puppet Pals

This application for the iPad is fun to use and enables children to create their own plays. There are limited characters and settings available free of charge; however, for a small charge, there is a 'director's pass' which enables access to a wider choice of characters and settings. Additionally, it allows the users to take/upload their own photographs of people and places, thereby creating more characters and settings of their own choice. This application allows children to rehearse, record, review and re-record their speech.

There are many more applications for mobile devices available for teaching and practising languages. One freely available for both Apple and Android devices is Duolingo, which covers many languages. This application is helpful in that it can provide additional practice for children learning another language, and for teachers who wish to improve their own linguistic skills. There are also links in the eResource to websites that teachers might use to develop their subject knowledge.

### Word cloud creators

These allow the user to create attractive word displays. Text can either be entered or imported for use, and greater prominence is given to words that are repeated. Presentation of the text, fonts and colours can all be changed. Creating word clouds provides an enjoyable way for children to present written work.

They can be designed by teachers for children to find and highlight:

- grapheme–phoneme links (words with *ch*/*on*/*oi* sound);
- masculine and feminine nouns, written without the article;
- different word classes in different colours; and
- topic-themed words.

They could also be used to:

- find and reconstruct sentences;
- look up unknown words as a warm-up activity.

Below are some useful word cloud creators:

- Wordle (www.wordle.net)
- Tagul (https://tagul.com)
- WordItOut (www.worditout.com).

## Podcasts

An auditory style of learning is important for many learners; therefore, opportunities for them to use any form of recording technology will be helpful in supporting their learning. Podcasts, which can be created through free programs, can be used by teachers as an instructional tool, or by children to create projects. They can be beneficial in the primary languages classroom to support the development of speaking and listening, encouraging active participation and giving children a real sense of purpose and audience. They can provide a way to celebrate children's work and share it with a wider audience, for example, through the school's own website. Podcasting can be used to record:

- an interview
- a short play
- an advertisement (for a new toy)
- a class performance of a poem/story/song.

## CAMERAS, VIDEO RECORDERS, MICROPHONES

### Cameras and video recorders

These allow teachers to capture the learning, which can then form the basis for further discussion and evaluation with the class. Children can also take their own photographs and make short videos/films for use in the primary language classroom. Photographs can be used to add a simple caption/speech bubble, or uploaded to create electronic presentations, story books or plays.

### Microphones

Handheld microphones or Talking Tins allow children to practise recording themselves speaking and performing in the new language. They can listen, re-record and improve their pronunciation. Alternatively, the teacher can record vocabulary as a model for the children. Talking Tins can be placed next to flashcards so that children can practise the new language independently.

## ASSESSMENT AND EVALUATION

Photographs and video evidence of what has been learnt are invaluable both for celebrating learning and also for assessment purposes. A speech bubble about the learning can easily be added to a photograph of the activity and placed on the learning wall or in a child's workbook. Some of the assessment tasks mentioned in the 'Assessment and progression' chapter are well suited to being displayed on the interactive whiteboard. A game such as 'champion', discussed in 'The magic of games' chapter, lends itself to being used as a form of interactive assessment.

In conclusion, this chapter has tried to demonstrate some of the technology tools that are invaluable for language teaching. We have also shown how other ideas, such as story book creators, iPad applications and podcasting, can be used to enhance primary children's learning.

# 16 A new stage: transition

## RATIONALE

It has long been important to ensure good transition in terms of language progression between primary schools teaching a language and secondary schools. With the teaching of a new language having become statutory at key stage 2 in September 2014 (primary national curriculum for languages [DfE, 2013]), all primary and secondary schools need to plan for careful transition between the key stages.

While this has sometimes appeared challenging to secondary schools, particularly those that have a large number of feeder primary schools, there are many ways in which transition can be eased and children have their prior learning acknowledged, and built on, rather than overlooked.

## LIAISON BETWEEN PRIMARY AND SECONDARY SCHOOLS

Where primary and secondary schools are closely linked, this has also led to a better understanding of the methodologies used at the other key stage. A true partnership between local secondary schools and their feeder primaries can be beneficial to all concerned.

It is important to pass on information about individual children's achievement in primary languages, and for this to be done in a way that busy teachers will find relevant, informative and manageable, as suggested by Bevis and Gregory (2005).

## TRANSFERRING INFORMATION TO THE SECONDARY SCHOOL

Some schools use the Junior European Languages Portfolio with its 'can do' statements; this is completed and passed on to the secondary school. Bevis and Gregory (2005) suggest that it is also useful to send:

- the primary scheme of work followed;
- information about topics so that the secondary school can either do different topics or a different slant on the same topic;
- key phrases that will be familiar to the children;
- a class list, showing how many years of prior learning different children have had;
- class links with other countries;
- children's achievements.

Bridging Units are a valuable way of ensuring progression between key stages and encouraging teachers to use shared methodologies. These units might be taught by the class teacher, by the secondary ML teacher, or in partnership. In the 'Mission Impossible' chapter, we have mentioned that this unit might form a Bridging Unit between primary and secondary; this could be introduced after SATs in the last term before transferring to secondary or, alternatively, at the start of year 7.

## LEARNING FROM EACH OTHER

Teachers benefit greatly from the opportunity to observe lessons in each other's schools; time rarely permits, but this should be the norm. Where primary teachers have the chance to visit a year 7 language class, they are surprised to see how much is covered in a lesson and with more target language use. Many secondary ML teachers recognise that they need to know more about primary methodology, classroom management strategies in the primary school and ways to assess, such as the 'two stars and a wish' approach.

Some schools organise a performance evening or celebratory event, where year 6 and 7 children come to perform sketches, poems and songs. This can be very useful for secondary modern language teachers to see what the incoming year 7s can achieve.

## THE BENEFITS OF KEY STAGE 2 LANGUAGE LEARNING

Teachers increasingly realise that those who have studied a new language at primary level are likely to have the following important attributes:

- confidence;
- enthusiasm about the new language;
- an openness to other cultures;
- a real interest in people from the country/countries where the new language is spoken;
- good phonic knowledge to aid the pronunciation of new words and sound–spelling links;
- an understanding of differences between English and the new language;
- literacy and language learning skills: strategies for decoding new language and remembering vocabulary; and
- a 'can do' approach to new texts.

It is important that secondary teachers celebrate children's achievements and help them progress in the language being taught in the secondary school. If this language is new to them, then they will bring useful language learning techniques to the task.

## STRATEGIES FOR MIXED EXPERIENCE LEARNING

Secondary schools deal with this in different ways:

- some start a new topic, with branching activities every third lesson; these provide support to enable new learners to catch up, while those with prior knowledge work on topic packs to reuse and extend their knowledge;
- alternatively, every third lesson is organised as a carousel, where children work at their own level;
- other schools put a new slant on a previously studied topic. For example, if some children know about rainforest animals, learning about zoo animals or pets will be new to them as well;
- buddying can be helpful; one child, who is new to the language, is helped by the other, who has some prior knowledge;
- those with prior knowledge can also be encouraged to take a lead as language monitors, asked to remember particular items of vocabulary for the class or to demonstrate good pronunciation.

## CONTINUITY IN YEAR 7

It is very important for pupils with KS2 experience of a language to feel that their experience is acknowledged. Where possible they need:

- familiar target language phrases in the classroom;
- some known songs and games, but progressing to new songs;
- a chance to use their honed language detective skills;
- an extension of the pair-work and group-work activities they are used to;
- some use of talk partners; and
- an opportunity to build on language strategies they know, such as mental hooks, mnemonics, chanting, rhythm, kinaesthetics (actions or air spelling).

Eva Lamb, in her Association for Language Learning Conference talk 'Managing transition creatively' (2010), spoke of the need for a paradigm shift in teachers' thinking. The teacher needs to provide opportunities for sharing and using the language; what is 'taught' needs to become using and expanding knowledge or used in a new context. Children learn from each other and presentation becomes discovery, sharing and investigation.

In conclusion, good communication between feeder primary schools and secondary schools is key. We have looked at some of the suggestions for primary schools transferring information to key stage 3, what children with prior experience of a language bring to the secondary classroom and how the needs of year 7 pupils, with prior experience of a language, can be met.

# 17 A helping hand: resources

## EVERYDAY RESOURCES

Many everyday resources found in the primary classroom can be used to help teach a language at key stage 2. Some have already been mentioned in previous chapters.

### Whiteboard and pens

- Drawing quick grids for number bingo;
- listening and choosing the correct answer (multiple choice A, B, C, D, E);
- practising early writing skills;
- guessing the secret word; and
- giving the children the freedom to practise writing known words/phrases/sentences.

### Dice activities

- Recalling numbers in the target language – dice (standard or multi-faced);
- rolling to practise the different operations of number (+ − × ÷). The number of dice rolled can be adapted to suit ability and purpose. Example: roll 3 dice and add the numbers together;
- linking (word/phrase/sentence) to the numbers on a dice, to be practised at random;
- using the above idea with a second dice (displaying emotions: happy, sad, angry, surprised), rolled simultaneously to indicate a mood or emotion in which the language should be spoken. Such dice can be purchased commercially but blank dice are inexpensive to buy; the teacher can adapt these by sticking pictures on the faces;
- rolling to select words or phrases to finish a sentence;
- practising all four skills through a relay game.

## Fans

- Practising number recall;
- showing understanding through a non-verbal response, where the number on the fan is used to identify an item of vocabulary – a picture or written text displayed on the interactive whiteboard;
- practising colours, using colour fans.

## Coloured cubes

- Building towers, or laying cubes out in order, in response to a spoken or written text, and practising word order by physically placing an object or flashcard followed by a coloured cube in front of them. This helps childeren construct a grammatically correct phrase/sentence.

## PUPPETS AND PROPS

Role-play is a fundamental part of learning to speak another language and getting into character makes it all the more purposeful. As already discussed, it is important to create opportunities for children to practise the new language in pairs or small groups in order to have a chance to speak individually. Puppets and props enhance this way of learning.

## Puppets

As mentioned in the 'Developing skills' chapter, a class puppet or mascot is an excellent idea. The mascot can be given an appropriate name in the target language – Pierre (French), Carlos (Spanish) – and is introduced as a native speaker with no English! The teacher can model new language through the voice of the puppet, demonstrate brief conversations, use the puppet to praise the children and pass the puppet round, enabling the children to practise new language. Some teachers prefer a puppet with a moving mouth. Behaviour management through the puppet can be effective when it is described as being very shy and only willing to appear if the children are quiet and well-behaved.

## Finger/hand puppets

Providing small finger or hand puppets is a good way to engage most children and particularly shy or less confident learners. Many children will speak through the identity of a puppet. Children love creating their own finger/hand puppets from small pieces of felt or fabric from the design and technology scrap box; a simple paper bag with a face drawn on it and some wool added for hair is also effective. IKEA stores are a good place to source small, felt finger puppets.

## Drama props

Dressing up and the use of props helps children enter another world and it is remarkable how make-believe can bring out a whole new person! Many props and dressing-up clothes are readily available in primary schools where there are key stage 1 classes.

Useful props include:

- one or more policeman's helmets. Year 6 children are just as keen to wear the hats as any budding detective in KS1! Children really love finding or solving a mystery;
- dressing up clothes to act out small plays;
- small cuddly toys, which are ideal for children to pass around in response to hearing a specific sound, word or phrase (again, in a story or song). Charity shops and car boot sales are also good places to find these;
- plastic fruit, vegetables or other foods.

## PE EQUIPMENT

- Coloured cones are good in that children can show colour recognition by running to the appropriate cone. More than one cone of the same colour should be used at the same time to prevent accidents! The colours can be combined with commands. For example: *Sautez vers le cone bleu!* (Jump to the blue cone).
- Hoops are useful for sorting or grouping words according to any criteria. The hoops can be placed in the middle of a circle and as the children draw words from a bag being passed round (similar to 'pass the parcel'), they must decide where to place them. For example, they could be used to sort: masculine and feminine words; practising articles with three hoops (one colour for masculine, another for feminine and a third for plurals); possessive adjectives; word classes; consonants and vowels.
- Parachute games.
- Beanbags or soft balls for brain breaks or throwing to children in turn to ask and answer questions.

### Talking dice (www.talkingdice.com)

This versatile resource is available in several languages. There are picture dice covering numerous topics as well as grammar dice (e.g. connectives, question words). The dice can be used for partner or small group activities and motivate children to engage in sentence building. Teachers' ideas have been incorporated into a book of activities using the dice.

## OTHER RESOURCES

- Surprise bag or box to play 'pass the parcel' or to create an air of mystery;
- fly swats (available from most hardware shops) are useful for ' Touch the board' in 'The magic of games' chapter;
- timers (egg timers/stopwatches/kitchen timers or electronic timers on the interactive whiteboard) to create an element of competition or suspense;
- Talking Tins for short recordings;
- microphones (for example, Easi-Speak) for intonation and pronunciation. These are also useful for children interviewing each other or acting as a roving journalist, sampling opinions around the class;

- digital still or video cameras to record performances (for example, a fashion show);
- computer programs and applications to reinforce learning;
- target language stamps and stickers;
- reward certificates.

## RESOURCES FOR FRENCH

### Traditional songs

Many traditional songs and *comptines* can be found on YouTube as short, animated films. Here are some examples:

| French songs |
| --- |
| Frère Jacques |
| Sur le pont d'Avignon |
| Savez-vous planter les choux? |
| Promenons-nous dans les bois |
| Dans la forêt lointaine |
| Il court, il court, le furet |
| Au clair de la lune |
| Pirouette, cacahuète |
| Jean Petit qui danse |

### Some suggested French story books : lower key stage 2

| Title | Author/ISBN | Content/topic/language |
| --- | --- | --- |
| Toutes les couleurs | Alex Sanders<br>2 211061559/022006 | Colours and sound words (e.g. splash) |
| A la mer | Raconte et Chante series<br><br>Short stories in both narrative and song form | Toys and colours |
| Les amis de la ferme | | Farm animals/names and greetings |
| Anniversaire à la ferme | | Animals/birthday/prepositions |
| Plic . . . plic . . . tombe la pluie | | Clothes and weather |
| Un pique-nique | | Food and simple opinions |
| Monsieur l'arbre et la petite fille | | Seasons |
| Maman | Anthony Brown<br>9782877674409 | Numbers and colours |
| Je m'habille et . . . je te croque! | Bénédicte Guettier<br>2211055974/10.2005 | Clothes/getting dressed |
| Loup y es-tu? | Sylvie Auzary-Luton<br>2211029647/05.2006 | Story based on the popular traditional song/clothes |
| Va-t'en Grand Monstre Vert! | Ed Emberley<br>2-87767-172-0/x1-06 | Body and colours (teaching adjectival position) |
| Roule galette | Natha Caputo,<br>Pierre Belvès<br>9782081601123 | A pie runs away through a forest |

*continued*

| Title | Author/ISBN | Content/topic/language |
|---|---|---|
| La chenille qui fait des trous | Eric Carle 9782871421740 | Days of the week/food/life cycles/ mini-beasts |
| Ours brun | Eric Carle 9782871421894 | Animals and colours/adjectival position |
| Aboie, Georges! | Jules Feiffer 9782211070355 | Animals and sounds. A mother tries to teach her pup to bark but he can only meow and oink. What has he been eating? |
| La chasse à l'ours | Michael Rosen and Helen Oxenbury French and English 978-1-85269-712-9 | Dual language text – visiting places and sound effects. Can also be simplified and adapted to practise repetitive phrases |
| La surprise de Handa | Eileen Browne 1852695099 | Dual language text – animals, fruits and descriptions |
| En marchant à travers la jungle | Debbie Harter 9781852698362 | Dual language text – animals, actions and habitats |

## Some suggested French story books: upper key stage 2

| Title | Author/ISBN | Content/topic/language |
|---|---|---|
| Le château du petit prince | Jean-Luc Englebert 9782211081696 | It is time for the prince to live in his own castle |
| C'est moi, le champion! | Philip Waechter 9782745922724 | About a boy who dreams of being a famous footballer |
| Dans Paris | Christophe Alline 9782278300075 | Sentence structure (there is/are) and prepositions |
| C'est moi le plus fort | Mario Ramos 9782211662684 | A wolf asks all those in the forest who is the strongest. All reply 'the wolf' except one! |
| Le loup sentimental | Geoffrey de Pennart 9782211052993 | The wolf leaves home with a list of all the things he can eat. He is sentimental and avoids eating goats, Red Riding Hood, the pigs. But what can he eat? |
| Une histoire sombre, très sombre | Ruth Brown 9782070561353 | Repetition to teach simple vocabulary |
| Au pays magique | Francois David and Eric Battut 9782848652597 | Descriptive vocabulary – a place where nothing is as it should be |
| Chez moi, c'est la guerre | Fatima Sharafeddine and Claude K. Dubois 9782871425847 | War theme – describes life for a child living in a country at war. Extend to discuss feelings |

## Other useful French books/resource packs

| Title | Author/ISBN | Content/topic/language |
|---|---|---|
| Take10 en Français | Chris Wakely and Helen Morrison<br>www.take10.co.uk<br>Dart Education<br>9781855229761 | Helps children practise their French, while taking part in short tasks of daily physical activity |
| Collins First Time French Dictionary | Collins<br>0-00-719650-4 | Useful for children and teachers. Covers core vocabulary and easy-to-use format |
| Chantez plus fort | Brilliant Publications<br>Rosemary Bevis, Martial Romanteau and Ros Hopwood<br>9781903853375 | Collection of twenty easy-to-learn songs, specifically to aid the teaching of French in the primary school |
| A&C Black Singing French | A&C Black<br>Helen MacGregor and Stephen Chadwick<br>0-7136-6898-9 | A collection of twenty-two photocopiable songs and chants for practising vocabulary and phrases when learning French |
| Le francais par le rythme et la musique de Monsieur X | Molliet Publishing<br>9780954982300 | Songs for practising French vocabulary and structures through music and rhythm |
| Physical French Phonics | Brilliant Publications<br>Sue Cave and Jean Haig | A resource to support the teaching of French phonics |
| Les Planètes Phoniques CD-ROM and DVD | www.trainingforlearning.co.uk<br>Wendy Adeniji | Helps children learn how to pronounce French correctly |
| French Theme Days: Olympics | La Jolie Ronde | Ideas for organising a whole school event round the Olympics |
| French on Display | Folens<br>Hilary Ansell<br>1-84191-446-0 | Displays and activities |
| Jeux de doigts | La Jolie Ronde | Finger rhymes and activities |

## Some suggested French films/DVDs

| Title | Publisher | Content |
|---|---|---|
| Salut (vol.1)<br>Où habites-tu? (vol.2) | Early Start<br>www.earlystart.co.uk | Short videos of French children |
| Mon Âne | www.little-linguist.co.uk | Animations of thirty traditional children's songs and rhymes |
| French Dance in the Primary Classroom<br>(Yannick Minvielle-Debat and Robin Shepherd) | www.little-linguist.co.uk | Five traditional French folk dances |
| La queue de la souris | Available on YouTube. Links are given in the eResource | A mouse outwits a lion |
| The Red Balloon (Le ballon rouge) | | No speech but culturally rich (1950s)<br>Show in short sections |
| Les Vacances de Monsieur Hulot | | A forerunner of Mr Bean – very French (1950s) |

## RESOURCES FOR SPANISH

### Traditional songs

Many traditional songs can be found on YouTube as short, animated films. Some examples:

| Spanish songs |
| --- |
| Los elefantes |
| A mi burro |
| De codín de codán |
| Cielito lindo |
| Mi barba tiene tres pelos |
| Al pavo, pavito, pavo |
| Juan Pequeño baila |
| Soy una taza* |

\* The YouTube clips for this song about a cup, a teapot and other kitchen items are particularly good.

The links to these are provided in the eResource.

### Some suggested Spanish story books: lower key stage 2

| Title | Author/ISBN | Content/topic/language |
| --- | --- | --- |
| ¡Hombre de color! | Jerome Ruiller 9788426133571 | Colours – a story retold over generations, which tackles the issue of racism sensitively |
| En la playa | Cuenta y Canta series Short stories in both narrative and song form | Toys and colours |
| Los amigos de la granja | | Farm animals – names and greetings |
| Un cumpleaños en la granja | | Animals/birthday/prepositions |
| ¡Mamá! | Mario Ramos 9788484701453 | Teaches numbers and colours |
| ¡ Fuera de Aquí Horrible Monstruo Verde! | Ed Emberley 9789707774636 | Body and colours (teaching adjectival position) |
| La gallina hambrienta | Richard Waring 978842613339 | A hungry fox is watching a hen get fatter waiting for his chance to pounce. There is a surprise ending |
| Y tú ¿Cómo te llamas? | Daniel Nesquens 9788466714020 | Humorous book introducing family |
| Caminando por la jungla | Debbie Harter | Animals and habitats |
| La oruga muy hambrienta | Eric Carle 978039923960 | Days of the week/food/life cycles/mini-beasts |
| Oso pardo oso pardo ¿Qué ves ahí? | Eric Carle 9780805069013 | Animals and colours/adjectival position |
| Soy más guapo | Nario Ramos 9788484704546 | A wolf puts his best suit on and believes he is very handsome. He takes a walk so that everyone can admire him! |

*continued*

| Title | Author/ISBN | Content/topic/language |
|---|---|---|
| Vamos a cazar un oso | Michael Rosen and Helen Oxenbury<br><br>French and English<br>9781852697129 | Dual language text – visiting places and sound effects.<br><br>Can also be simplified and adapted to practise repetitive phrases |
| La Sorpresa de Handa | Eileen Browne<br>1852695153 | Dual language text – animals, fruits and descriptions |

## Some suggested Spanish story books: upper key stage 2

| Title | Author/ISBN | Content/topic/language |
|---|---|---|
| ¡Cataplum! | Ramirez, Juan Carolos Chandro<br>9788484702351 | It is a wolf's birthday and the rabbits prepare a surprise! |
| David se mete en líos | David Shannon<br>10:8424186613 | A humorous look at a typical day in David's life. Good for boys. |
| El erizo | Gustavo Roldán Bonhomme<br>9788496473638 | A hungry hedgehog cannot reach an apple on a tree so gets help from some other animals! |
| ¡El lobo ha vuelto! | Geoffroy de Pennart<br>9788484701514 | Mr Rabbit finds out that the wolf is back in town. Every time there is a knock on the door, he is afraid that it is the wolf |
| ¡Soy el más fuerte! | Ramos Mario<br>9788484704003 | A wolf asks all those in the forest who is the strongest. All reply 'The wolf' except one! |
| ¿Si vivieras en . . . ? | Combel Editorial<br>97884982521050<br>www.little-linguist.co.uk | A story about the lives of children in different places round the world |

## Other useful Spanish books/resource packs

| Title | Author/ISBN | Content/topic/language |
|---|---|---|
| Take 10 en Español | Chris Wakely and Helen Morrison<br>www.take10.co.uk<br>Dart Education | Helps children practise their Spanish while taking part in short tasks of daily physical activity |
| Collins First Time Spanish Dictionary | Collins<br>9780007261116 | Useful for children and teachers. Covers core vocabulary and easy-to-use format |
| ¡Vamos a cantar! | Brilliant Publications<br>Colette Thomson and Len Brown<br>9781905780136 | Collection of twenty easy-to-learn songs, specifically to aid the teaching of Spanish in the primary school |
| A&C Black Singing Spanish | A&C Black<br>Helen MacGregor and Stephen Chadwick<br>10:0713688807 | A collection of twenty-two photocopiable songs and chants for practising Spanish vocabulary and phrases |

*continued*

| Title | Author/ISBN | Content/topic/language |
|---|---|---|
| Los Planetas Fonéticos CD-ROM and DVD | www.trainingforlearning. co.uk<br>Wendy Adeniji | Helps children learn how to pronounce Spanish correctly |
| Canciones infantiles españolas | Consejería de Educación, London | Traditional Spanish songs for young children |
| Spanish Theme Days: Olympics | La Jolie Ronde | Ideas for organising a whole school event round the Olympics |

## Some suggested Spanish films/DVDs

| Title | Publisher | Content |
|---|---|---|
| Tú y Yo (vol.1)<br>Mi ciudad y mi colegio (vol.2) | Early Start<br>www.earlystart.co.uk | Short videos of Spanish children |

Some useful websites for French and Spanish are available as an eResource, which will make it easier for teachers to cut and paste the URL links.

# Appendix

## English translations of the stories and songs

**MISSION IMPOSSIBLE SONG**

(Sung to the Oompa Loompa tune from *Charlie and the Chocolate Factory*)

Hello, hello, I am called . . .

If you listen to me, I've a puzzle for you!

Hello, hello, what are you called?

Pay attention and look at me!

Where are you going? I am going to Paris.

What are you going to do?

I am going to look for clues, see the monuments and eat a

croissant.

It's dangerous and I really . . . like . . . that!

I'm a French spy!

Hello, hello, I am called . . .

If you listen to me, I've a puzzle for you!

Hello, hello, what are you called?

Spy! Spy! French . . . spy!

**PEDRO THE PIRATE**

Once upon a time there was a pirate called Pedro.

On Monday he puts on trousers.

On Tuesday he puts on trousers and a shirt.

On Wednesday he puts on trousers, a shirt and some boots.

On Thursday he puts on trousers, a shirt, some boots and

a pirate hat.

On Friday he puts on trousers, a shirt, some boots, a pirate hat

and a scarf.

On Saturday he puts on trousers, a shirt, some boots, a pirate hat,

a scarf and an eye-patch.

On Sunday he is tired and he sleeps.

## TEDDY BEARS' PICNIC SONG

(Sung to the tune of 'The teddy bears' picnic')

We're going, we're going into the big woods.
We're going to have a big picnic.
We've got plenty of time for a picnic.
With our little teddy bears.
We're eating, we're eating honey and bread.
We're drinking, we're drinking lemonade.
Play, jump, dance quickly – we're having fun!

## THE LEGEND OF GYPTIS AND PROTIS

One day, some Greeks set off in a boat. Their captains were called Simos and Protis.

They arrived at the coast of the region that is now Provence.

The inhabitants of the region, the Segobrigians, welcomed the Greeks. The Greeks offered them Greek specialities – vines for producing wine and olive trees for the production of olive oil.

To thank them, Nannus, the King of the Segobrigians, invited the Greeks to a banquet.

Nannus's daughter, Princess Gyptis, had to offer a jug of water to her future husband. She chose to marry Protis.

King Nannus offered the Greeks some land. On this land they built a town which was called Marssila.

Today the town is called Marseille.

## NOISY WEATHER POEM

Open the doors!
Open the doors!
It's sunny
Let's go outside

Look at the sky!
Look at the sky!
There are clouds
Let's go indoors

Open the doors!
Open the doors!
It's sunny
Let's go outside

Look at the sky
Rain is falling
Oh no, not that!
Let's go inside

Look at the sky
Look at the sky
It's windy
Let's stay indoors

Look at the sky
Look at the sky
Close the doors
The wind is howling

Listen to the wind
Listen to the wind
Close the doors
The storm's coming

Look at the sky
Look at the sky
Listen to the thunder
The storm's coming

Listen to the thunder
Listen to the thunder
I'm afraid
The storm's coming

Listen to the rain
Listen to the wind
Listen to the thunder
The storm's coming . . . Boom!

I'm frightened
I'm frightened
Under the bed
The storm's coming

\*        \*        \*

The storm passes . . . it's calm
The storm passes . . . it's calm

## JEAN-LUC'S SURPRISE

Once upon a time there was a little boy called Jean-Luc.

One day, it is his Grandmother's birthday.
He decides to make a surprise for his Grandmother – a beautiful fruit salad.

He goes to the market . . .

Good morning, Sir. I'd like one banana, please.
Why <u>one</u> banana?
It's my Grandmother's birthday and I'm going to make a fruit salad.
Here's a banana. It's healthy.
Thank you. Goodbye.

Good morning, Madam. I'd like one orange, please.
Why <u>one</u> orange?
It's my Grandmother's birthday and I'm going to make a fruit salad.
Here's an orange. It's juicy.
Thank you. Goodbye.

Good morning, Sir. I'd like one pear, please.

Why <u>one</u> pear?

It's my Grandmother's birthday and I'm going to make a fruit salad.

Here's a pear. It's ripe.

Thank you. Goodbye.

Good morning, Madam. I'd like one peach, please.

Why <u>one</u> peach?

It's my Grandmother's birthday and I'm going to make a fruit salad.

Here's a peach. It's delicious.

Thank you. Goodbye.

Good morning, Sir. I'd like one mango, please.

Why <u>one</u> mango?

It's my Grandmother's birthday and I'm going to make a fruit salad.

Here's a mango. It's exotic.

Thank you. Goodbye.

Good morning, Madam. I'd like one pineapple, please.

Why <u>one</u> pineapple?

It's my Grandmother's birthday and I'm going to make a fruit salad.

Here's a pineapple. It's attractive.

Thank you. Goodbye.

Good morning, Sir. I'd like one kiwi, please.

Why <u>one</u> kiwi?

It's my Grandmother's birthday and I'm going to make a fruit salad.

Here's a kiwi. It's sweet.

Thank you. Goodbye.

At home, Jean-Luc prepares the fruit salad. What a beautiful fruit salad!

On the way to his Grandmother's, he slips on a banana skin!

The fruit salad falls on the ground.

Later at the hospital, his Grandmother arrives.

Hello, Jean-Luc.

Hello, Grandma.

I have a surprise for you, Jean-Luc. Here is a beautiful fruit salad.

A fruit salad! What a surprise!

## WE'RE GOING ON A PICNIC

Today it's fine weather.
We're going on a picnic.
We're going into the big woods.
Here is my new basket.
Come and prepare the picnic with me!

In my basket I put bread.
In my basket I put bread and butter.
In my basket I put bread, butter and honey.
In my basket I put bread, butter, honey and crisps.
In my basket I put bread, butter, honey, crisps and a knife.
In my basket I put bread, butter, honey, crisps, a knife and a radio.
Here's the picnic!

Who's coming with me?
Not Dad – he's watching television.
Not Mum – she's swimming.
Not my brother – he's listening to music.
Not my sister – she's doing gymnastics.

Ah, I know . . . Grandad . . . and my little teddy bear!
Off we go!

# References

Barbe, W. B., Swassing, R. and Milone, M. (1979) *Teaching through Modality Strengths: Concepts and Practices*, Columbus, OH: Zaner-Bloser

Barnes, J. (2011) *Cross-Curricular Learning 3–14*, London: Sage

Bevis, R. and Gregory, A. (2005) *Mind the Gap!* London: CiLT

Biggs, J. and Tang, C. (2011) *Teaching for Quality Learning at University*, Maidenhead: McGraw-Hill Education

Biriotti, L. (1999) *Grammar is Fun*, London: CiLT

Bloom, B. S. (ed.) (1956) *Taxonomy of Educational Objectives, Vol. 1: Cognitive Domain*, New York: McKay

Claxton, C. (2002) *Building Learning Power*, Bristol: TLO

Convery, A. and Coyle, D. (1999) *Differentiation and Individual Learners*, London: CiLT

DfE (2013) *National Curriculum in England: Languages Programmes of Study*

DfEs (2002) *The National Languages Strategy*

DfES (2004) *Access and Engagement in MFL for EAL Pupils*

DfES/CiLT (2004) *Piece by Piece: Implementing the National Languages Strategy*

DfES (2005) *Key Stage 2 Framework for Languages*

Dinçay, T. (2011) 'Advantages of learning a foreign language at an early age', available at www.todayszaman.com/op-ed_advantages-of-learning-a-foreign-language-at-an-early-age_263877.html (accessed 8 September 2015)

Fleming, N. D. and Mills, C. (1992) 'Not another inventory, rather a catalyst for reflection', in Professional and Organizational Development Network in Higher Education (ed.), *To Improve the Academy*, vol. 11, pp. 137–55

Gardner, H. (1993) *Frames of Mind: The Theory of Multiple Intelligences*, 2nd edn, London: Fontana

Golinkoff, R. M. and Hirsh-Pasek, K. (2000) *How Babies Talk: The Magic and Mystery of Language in the First Three Years of Life*, New York: Plume

Greaves, I. (2015) 'How to make creative writing even more creative!', in Association for Language Learning (ed.), *Languages Today*, vol. 21, pp. 22–3,

Hicks, D. (2005) *Le français par le rythme et la musique de Monsieur X*, Molliet Publishing

Hughes, S. (2007) 'Harry met Francis: the Field of the Cloth of Gold', *Primary History*, 47 (3): 30–1

King, K. and Gurian, M. (2006) 'With boys in mind: teaching to the minds of boys', *Educational Leadership*, 64 (1): 56–61

Lamb, E. (2010) 'Managing transition creatively', paper given to the Association of Language Learning (ALL) conference, Easter

OCR (Oxford, Cambridge and RSA) (2010) *Making and Marking Progress on the DCSF Ladder*, Cambridge: OCR

OUP (2014) *English Language Teaching Global Blog*, available at: http://oupeltglobal blog.com/tag/authentic-texts (accessed 16 September 2015)

QCA (Qualifications and Curriculum Authority) (2000) *Key Stage 2 Schemes of Work for Languages: French/Spanish/German*

Satchwell, P. and de Silva, J. (1995) *Catching Them Young*, Young Pathfinder 1, London: CiLT

Sharafeddine, F. and Dubois, C. K. (2008) *Chez moi, c'est la guerre*, Namur: Mijade

Smith, A. and Call, N. (2001) *The ALPS Resource Book*, Stafford: Network Educational Press

Wakely, C. and Morrison, H. (2004) *Take 10 en français*, Exeter: Dart Education

## FURTHER READING

Blythe, T. (ed.) (1997) *The Teaching for Understanding Guide*, New York: Jossey-Bass

Bruner, J. (1996) *The Culture of Education*, Cambridge, MA, and London: Harvard University Press

Carter, R. (1998) *Mapping the Mind*, London: Weidenfeld & Nicolson

Hannaford, P. (2012) *French/German/Spanish Olympics Topic Packs*, Dunstable: Brilliant Publications

# Index